BUSINESS SYSTEMS GROUP'S

NetWare
Programmer's
Guide

BUSINESS SYSTEMS GROUP'S

NetWare Programmer's Guide

····················

JOHN T. McCANN

Prentice Hall

Prentice Hall

New York   London   Toronto   Sydney   Tokyo   Singapore

First published in 1990 in North America by M&T Publishing, Inc., 501 Galveston Drive, Redwood City, CA 94063-4728, U.S.A., and co-published for sale outside North America by Prentice Hall International (UK) Limited, 66 Wood Lane End, Hemel Hempstead, Hertfordshire, HP2 4RG, England, a division of Simon & Schuster International Group.

British Library Cataloging-in-Publication Data and Library of Congress Cataloging-in-Publication Data are available from Prentice Hall International, (UK), Ltd

McCann, John T., 1966-
        The NetWare Programmer's Gudie/John McCann
        p. cm.

    ISBN 0-13-617283-0

93 92 91 90   4   3   2   1

Cover design: Lauren Smith Designs
Editor: Tova F. Fliegel

Dedicated to all those programmers out there that know hacking in its pure form, for the pleasure of it while not hurting anyone else.

Contents

FIGURES AND SAMPLE CODE

Chapter 7: VAPs

Chapter 8: NLMs

About Business Systems Group

Business Systems Group, Inc. is a national systems integration firm dedicated to providing insight into network technology. In keeping with this philosophy, we publish *The NetWare Advisor,* our monthly technical journal for LAN administrators and, along with M&T Books, have copublished our definitive reference manual, *The NetWare Supervisor's Guide*. Now we are happy to bring you our latest combined effort, *The NetWare Programmer's Guide*.

Business Systems Group, Inc. believes in network computing. And we believe in the power of "right-sized" as opposed to downsized applications for networks. For example, this book was created using network applications. the manuscript was written on a PC, then ASCII files E-mailed via CompuServe. They were then downloaded, translated (in some cases) to Microsoft Word on a PC, and transferred across a NetWare LAN to a Macintosh II. Finally the files were imported into QuarkXpress. A simple example, yet one that for the most part couldn't have been done ten years ago. Reflecting on where we've been helps us to realize how much more there is to come. By providing you with the knowledge in books like *The NetWare Programmer's Guide*, we hope to directly promote getting the job done in a better way.

Steven L. Guengerich
Director of Communications
Business Systems Group, Inc.
Houston, Texas

Acknowledgements:

I would like to thank the following people in helping me put together information necessary to completing this book:

Drew Major, Kyle Powell and Howard Davis of SuperSet
Steve Hochschild of Novell
Doug Woodward of Novell
Chip Webb of Novell
David Menendez and Jordon Olin of Business Systems Group
Eric Pulaski, of LAN Support Group
Vince Sondej of the *NetWare Technical Journal*

Preface

Since 1982, NetWare has played an increasingly prominent role not only in shaping the direction of the computer industry, but also in the way the world does business. Now more than ever, as networks are the accepted computing platform on which all applications must run, there is a need for more and better technical information for programming in the NetWare environment.

The NetWare Programmer's Guide is intended to help you, the experienced programmer and those interested in learning NetWare programming, become a better developer. If you want to get into programming for NetWare, this book will serve as a fine introduction. If you are already an experienced NetWare programmer, this book will show you new ways to program for NetWare, and offer insightful tips and techniques for achieving your ends.

How to Read this Book

The book is divided into three main parts, each of which contain multiple chapters. Part 1 covers 'Considerations for Programming in NetWare', including separate chapters on the Bindery and NetWare Queues.

Part 2 offers information on interprocess communications—specifically IPX/SPX and Named Pipes. It offers advice on choosing the right protocol.

Part 3, Server Applications, contains chapters with extensive information about VAPs and NLMs and how they communicate. There is also a chapter on converting VAPs to NLMs.

The Appendixes contain information on related topics, such as differences in determining rights between NetWare 286 and 386, complete programs which were too long to accommodate within the chapters, a helpful list of programming tools as well as some strategies for getting your programs to market.

If you have purchased the optional disk along with the book, you will find all of the source code there.

This book assumes that you are familiar with the C programming language and have access to one of the compilers supported by the NetWare C Interface for DOS. Familiarity with Pascal and Assembly are also helpful, although absolute knowledge of any of these languages is not necessary.

This book provides alternative methods for developing NetWare applications. For example, if a layered approach to building your special network function library does not work, this text shows you how to place calls to the NetWare API in your source code.

While using the C-interface is the starting place for most new NetWare programmers today, we have not limited this book to that realm. For the real world, there are as many programming styles and preferences as there are programmers, and what is best for one situation may not ring true universally. Thus, we have also included examples of programs written in Turbo Pascal and Assembly, which are chock full of clever and useful methods. In summary, we have attempted to provide you with a comprehensive guide to programming for NetWare in all its forms.

Why The NetWare Programmer's Guide is for You

If you are an experienced programmer who recognizes the established role that Novell's NetWare plays in the way companies do business, *The NetWare Programmer's Guide* is for you. It's clear examples will also help those of you who may be less experienced, but whose interest in NetWare is strong.

You benefit from the experience of one of networking's premier programmer's, John McCann. His work in installing more than 500 networks and in developing some of the industry's most well-recognized applications make this book the valuable resource it is. There is probably no one who can claim a more thorough knowledge of NetWare and, thus, no one more qualified to provide you with the tools and philosophy you need to improve your skills.

PART 1

Considerations for the NetWare Environment

The environments where computers are used dictate the basis for great change in programming. To be successful in a particular environment, you must adapt and improve upon your skills. With Local Area Networks (LANs) a corporate reality and with Novell's share of the market, I believe the NetWare environment is the single most important networking environment for programmers. This text is designed for experienced programmers who wish to expand their abilities from the stand-alone to the networked environment, or who wish to discover alternate network programming methods in NetWare. My goal in writing it is to provide an understanding of what the NetWare environment is and to explain how you can use it as a development platform.

I will discuss methods for adapting existing stand-alone applications to the NetWare environment. I will present new coding paradigms to show what you can do by programming in the NetWare environment. And I will pinpoint common errors and other obstacles to your success.

CHAPTER 1

Considerations for Programming in NetWare

Programmers creating network applications must first address the issues involved in network programming versus those involved in programming stand-alone operations. Probably the most common aspect of applications today is that they involve some form of database access. Every major LAN vendor today addresses the issue of multiuser database access, either through specific Application Program Interfaces (APIs), which provide access to predefined functions, or some other internal mechanism. But what about other issues of running your applications on a network? These issues might include:

- Allowing and controlling access to your application by multiple users
- Protecting information
- Printing via the network
- Communicating between your applications
- Lending aspects of client-server technology to your application

NetWare-Specific Functionality

If you are converting a stand-alone operation, evaluate the application's existing features in contrast to the new capabilities that NetWare provides through its APIs. An application developed for the NetWare environment can include specific functions, such as :

- Determining if NetWare is loaded
- Creating, accessing, and maintaining network user-specific information
- User-oriented security
- License/copyright protection
- Data sharing and security
- Interprocess/internodal communications
- Network printing capabilities

Multiuser File Access

In the area of primary concern–that of multiuser access, file access management is key for maintaining the integrity of the data contained in a network application. Programmers must consider the fact that multiple users may have access to a given file and developers must choose from among essentially three methods of maintaining data integrity:

- File locking
- Record locking
- Transaction tracking

The method selected for handling multiuser file access depends on how a program uses information at a basic level. If a file is the smallest logical unit of information, as with a word processing application, then file locking is appropriate. In most databases, the record is the lowest logical unit. Transaction tracking (files) helps keep tabs on changes that occur in several places at once or on a series of changes that take place as updates are made.

Sets

NetWare uses "sets" to allow your program to partially implement explicit transactions. You log one or more files/records into a set, and then either lock, release (unlock), or clear the files/records from the set. By using sets, NetWare allows the application to specify the characteristics of the lock(s) one by one before actually placing them. When you actually perform the lock, either all the members of the set must be lockable, or none will be locked. In this way, you are guaranteed that all of the data resources for a particular transaction are available before you proceed. And, you prevent a deadlock situation.

Transaction Tracking System

NetWare's Transaction Tracking System (TTS) records changes made to a record or set of records until they have been properly completed or aborted. That way, if the file server or workstation crashes in the middle of a transaction, TTS "backs out" any transactions that were in progress at the time of the crash. In the case of a file server crash, when the file server comes back up with TTS enabled, you are prompted about whether to roll back transactions.

TTS's action can be implicit or explicit as defined by the data file and application. In implicit mode, where the file is flagged "TTS," transactions begin when either a physical or logical record lock is put into place and end when all such locks are removed. Also, in implicit mode, the application need not be aware of TTS's operations. Thus, the application does not need to be specifically coded for TTS. Because some applications use a preset amount of record locks that are held for the duration of the application, the SETTS utility can be used to set the number of such locks.

In explicit mode, transactions are signaled by a specific command, "begin transaction," and ended with another specific command, "end transaction."(For more TTS information see Novell's *NetWare System Interface Technical Overview*, Chapter 14.)

If you do have files that are flagged as transactional, they should not be manipulated by your program with TTS function calls. If a file is flagged "TTS" and your application uses explicit TTS calls when working with that file, chances are TTS will not operate properly. On one hand you have implicit TTS tracking the file after so many record locks, and on the other hand you have the application doing explicit TTS tracking. It could work, but you are asking for trouble or, at best, unusual happenings if you use both implicit and explicit TTS with a single file. To avoid such trouble, have your application make a function call to determine if the file is flagged "TTS."

Directory Paths

The next design issue in programming for the NetWare environment is the handling of directories and file path names. One way to handle directories and file path names is to hard code those names in your program. However, this strategy is best avoided as it may limit the network managers' freedom in configuring networks. It not only can force the program to reside in a set directory, but it also forces the network manager to allow full security privileges for that directory to everyone who will be using the program. With NetWare, users with security privileges to a directory also inherit privileges to all of that directory's subdirectories. Hard coded directory names can also present a problem on networks that have different servers with identical volume names.

The application must still know the drive to which NetWare has mapped the current server and volume. An alternative is to have the application read an environmental variable that was set in system or user login script.

A third solution involves relying on the system administrator to establish search paths in user login scripts that are mapped to an application's data directory. If the application data directory is not in the user's local directory, NetWare checks the search paths as well. This approach is also imperfect as it increases the time it takes to search for files. See Appendix E for more on directory and file rights assignment.

Printer Sharing

Another design isssue is that of printer sharing. An application might allow for printer switching. Additionally the application might also be aware of network print queues. Due to the seamless implementation of printer redirection in the NetWare environment, an application need not be aware of NetWare print queues. Indeed, an application can print directly to any of the LPTx devices and have the output redirected to a NetWare print queue. This presumes that printer redirection (CAPTURE) has been initiated at that workstation before the application began execution. When an application uses NetWare queues, it runs through three basic steps:

- Print job definition; for instance, queue to use, form to use, etc.
- Begin the redirection
- End the redirection, that is, end of queueing, job is ready to print

For more information on print queues and NetWare queues in general, see Chapter 4.

Network Activity

Application development in a network environment requires a basic understanding of network activity. Most network environments that incorporate intelligent machines (such as PCs) can be represented by a pyramid of operation.

For DOS, the pyramid is:

APPLICATION

NETWORK SHELL (API Layer)

DOS

For OS/2 the pyramid is:

APPLICATION

OS/2

NETWORK SHELL (API Layer)

In the diagrams above, the Application is your application. The Network Shell is some sort of "in memory" (TSR in DOS, device driver in OS/2) redirector agent that seeks out network bound calls and provides a method of transporting them to another network device. The resident operating system (DOS or OS/2) would be in place with or without the network shell. The Application Programming Interface Layer (API), the resident O/S provides definition for network-bound requests. (A discussion of APIs follows on the next page.) These requests can be for network API services or can be direct communications between two or more nodes. These direct communications involve transport mechanisms (or protocols) such as IPX/SPX, NetBIOS, and Named Pipes. (I will discuss these transport protocols in Part 2.)

Note that the request filtering action is handled quite differently by DOS than it is by OS/2. With the DOS hierarchy, all "DOS" API calls (which could be for the local DOS machine or for another node, such as a file server, on the network) are first examined by the Network Shell. This shell will pass "local" DOS requests onto DOS itself while it will redirect network calls to whatever node the request is bound. Because the network shell is the first to examine the requests, it can process the network- bound requests more quickly than OS/2 can. The OS/2 method has the operating system examine all requests first before deciding if the request needs to be passed on to the network shell (called a requestor by Novell under OS/2). For network bound calls, this serves to slightly hamper performance, especially since OS/2 is not as quick as the shell (requestor) in making judgment calls on network-bound requests.

However, in either case, the network shell/requestor adds a layer of functionality to your local operating system. This extension of your local operating system allows it to interact with the network.

When communicating on the network, your application may communicate with at least two different types of *nodes*. Here a node is defined as a workstation, PC or any other intelligent device connected to the network. The two basic types of nodes are a *server* and a *peer-level node* (known as peer-to-peer communications). These different types of nodes may have one or more *resources*. A resource is defined as a facility or device attached to a node that is available for use by other nodes. For instance, printers, hard disks, modems, and the PC's CPU can all be resources.

APIs

In order to access the services provided by other nodes and their resources, developers use network application program interfaces (APIs). These network APIs, also known as function calls, can increase the functionality of your application, but also add complexity.

The code becomes more complex, because of network design-related issues that must be considered—for example, checking for network existence. Also, because APIs exist in the network, disparate nodes sometimes need to cooperate when performing tasks. For instance, printing a single page on a nonlocal printer may involve three different machines. The first machine is the originator, the one producing the page. The second machine queues up the printout, a temporary staging area. The third machine has the actual printer attached to it and provides for the production of the printout.

Further adding to the complexity of network-aware APIs is the increase in potential error situations. With each new API there is the chance that more errors will occur. You need to compensate for each kind of possible error.

Aside from errors based on incorrect syntax, you should expect the following possible error situations:

- Absence of the network shell (shell or requestor not loaded)
- Absence of a network (shell/requestor loaded but no servers or other nodes able to fulfill your application's needs)
- Absence/dysfunction of cooperating node(s) (due to NIC deaf/mute), or participating application is inactive
- Network media problems, including congestion, sluggish reactions; or physical faults, such as cable breaks, cable/media improperly installed
- Insufficient access rights
- Insufficient account balance
- Network failure

The NetWare C Interface for DOS

Novell provides a series of APIs that allow access to these capabilities from within your program. They include: The NetWare C Library for DOS; The OS/2 Programmer's Reference; NetWare System Calls; and The NetWare for the Macintosh Programmer's Reference. The NetWare C Interface is a library of functions developed by Novell to allow 'C' programmers access to NetWare capabilities from a DOS client workstation. The interface comes with libraries for the Watcom, Microsoft, Borland, and Lattice 'C' compilers. Although 'C' is the only high-level language supported, other programming language interfaces may be created using the Assembly language interface documentation. The NetWare interface products are available through Novell's Development Products Division at (800) RED-WORD, or (512) 346-8380.

NetWare, via its APIs, breaks groups of functions into related areas called services. The NetWare C Interface for DOS provides a set of 'C' language header files for accessing these services. There is one primary header file called nit.h, which includes the header files necessary for accessing all of the services that NetWare provides. Alternately, you may choose to use only the header files for the specific services in which you are interested.

The following table lists each of the header files and their associated services:

Header File	NetWare Service Provided
NITERROR.H	NetWare Error Codes
NXT.H	NetWare IPX and SPX services
NIT.H	Includes the following NetWare headers:
NWACCT.H	NetWare Accounting services
NWBINDRY.H	NetWare Bindery Services
NWCONN.H	NetWare Connection Services
NWCONSOL.H	NetWare Server Environment Services
NWDIR.H	NetWare Directory Services
NWFILE.H	NetWare File Services
NWLOCAL.H	NetWare Local Environment Services
NWMISC.H	Miscellaneous NetWare "Helpers"
NWMSG.H	NetWare Messaging Services
NWPRINT.H	NetWare Print Services
NWSYNC.H	NetWare Synchronization Services
NWTTS.H	NetWare Transaction Tracking Services
NWWRKENV.H	NetWare Workstation Services
NMPIPE.H*	Named Pipes DOS Extender

Figure 1-1. NetWare Header Files

Note that nmpipe.h is not technically part of the NetWare C Interface for DOS, but part of an optional product called the Named Pipes DOS Extender. The support for DOS workstations to access Named Pipes comes with the NetWare OS/2 Requestor v1.2. Named Pipes will be discussed in Chapter 6.

REPLY Buffer Length Too Short When Using NSCI

A common programming problem using APIs is that of using a REPLY buffer length that is too short. Many times a reply buffer that is too short (the length is indicated in lo-hi (word) order) will yield:

Network Error on Server FS1: Error receiving from network.
Abort, Retry?

However, it is very important to note that this error will appear on some, but not all, network types as the result of an insufficient reply buffer size. For instance, on IBM Token-Ring networks this error does not always occur when a reply buffer length is insufficient. But on ARCnet networks, this error is likely to pop up when the reply buffer is too small. This peculiarity occurs because of the subtle differences in the hardware drivers of the different network types.

One solution to this potential headache is to use an oversized reply buffer. For many calls, the oversized reply buffer just signifies to the shell that there is sufficient memory available for the receipt of the reply. But, depending on the NetWare version, some calls may return more and more information.

NetWare Shell Presence

In the NetWare environment, the NetWare shell is the common bond that allows access to the network. If you use NetWare APIs when the network shell is not present you will usually get incorrect results and sometimes lock your PC. Under DOS, testing for the presence of the network shell can be accomplished in many ways. There are two issues involved here. First, the application must know whether or not the NetWare DOS shell has been loaded in the workstation. Second, the application must know if the user has logged into the network so that it can take advantage of NetWare's user- and group-oriented functions.

If the NetWare shell is loaded, but the user has not logged in, there are still features of NetWare that your application can utilize. Specifically, the NetWare shell provides the interfaces necessary to perform peer-to-peer communications. These interfaces include NetWare's IPX (Internetwork Packet eXchange), SPX (Sequenced Packet eXchange), and Named Pipes (usually for communicating with OS/2-based server applications). All of these enable your application to "speak" to other workstations on the network without having to be logged in. Additionally, with the shell loaded, your application can perform dynamic attachments and logins to any file server on the internetwork. In other words, your application can log in to the network as a user when required.

Here is a simple series of calls in Assembly that determine if the NetWare shell is loaded.

```
mov   ax, 0C601h   ;AH gets C6h, AL gets 01h, C6 is NetWare's
                   ;Get or Set Lock Mode call
int   21h          ;set lock mode to 01h
mov   ax, 0C602h   ;AH gets C6h, AL gets 02
int   21h          ;get current lock mode
cmp   al,01h       ;is lock mode 01h?
jne   not_netware  ;if not equal, NetWare not loaded
```

There are many APIs that can be used to ascertain if a network is present. The following program is an example of how to determine if IPX/SPX and the NetWare shell are loaded, if a user is logged-in, and what the user name is for the current connection.

```
/*  ON_NET.C */

#include <stdio.h>
#include "nit.h"
#include "niterror.h"

#define OBJECT_NAME_LEN 48     /* Length of a NetWare object name */

void IsIPXSPXLoaded(int *IPXLoaded, int *SPXLoaded);
int IsShellLoaded(char *ServerName);
int IsUserLoggedIn(char *UserName);
void main(void);
```

The following function determines if IPX and SPX support is available. Because IPX and SPX can be loaded without the shell, your application can perform peer-to-peer communications. The reason that IPX and SPX are checked individually is that the NetWare shells available with NetWare 386 v3.1 allow IPX to be loaded without SPX in order to save memory for those users not needing SPX support.

```
/* IsIPXSPXLoaded
   Parameters:
   int *IPXLoaded—Pointer to an integer that is set to 1 if IPX is
   loaded and 0 if it is not
   int *SPXLoaded—Pointer to an integer that is set to 1 if SPX is
   loaded and 0 if it is not

   Returns: None
   */
void IsIPXSPXLoaded(int *IPXLoaded, int *SPXLoaded)
{
     int      Result;        /* Temporary result variable */
     BYTE     MajorSPXRev;   /* Major revision number of SPX support */
     BYTE     MinorSPXRev;   /* Minor revision number of SPX support */
     WORD     MaxConnects;   /* Max. number of SPX connections
     supported */
     WORD     AvailConnects;/* Number of SPX connections currently
                                                   available*/

     /* First initialize the input parameters to false */
     *IPXLoaded = 0;
     *SPXLoaded = 0;

     /* Now check to see if IPX is available by initializing the 'C'
     library's IPX interface routines.  This must be done before IPX
     API calls may be used. */

     Result = IPXInitialize();
     if (Result == SUCCESSFUL) {
       *IPXLoaded = 1;        /* IPX is loaded, now check for SPX */

       /* Check to see if SPX is available using the same method used
       to determine if IPX is available.  This function also returns
       information about the capacities of SPX support for this
       workstation. */

       Result = SPXInitialize (&MajorSPXRev,&MinorSPXRev,&MaxConnects ,
                             &AvailConnects);
       if (Result == SUCCESSFUL)
         *SPXLoaded = 1;
     }
     }
```

The next function, called "IsShellLoaded," determines if the NetWare shell is loaded by making a call to the shell. If the shell is loaded, the function then takes advantage of the initial connection that the shell makes with a file server to determine the name of the default file server.

```
/* IsShellLoaded

Parameters:    char *ServerName - Returns name of default file server

Returns:       1 if shell is loaded, 0 if not
*/
int IsShellLoaded(char *ServerName)
{

int            Result = 0;    /* Result of NetWare calls */
BYTE           MajorVersion;  /* NetWare shell major version number */
BYTE           MinorVersion;  /* NetWare shell minor version number */
BYTE           RevisionLevel; /* NetWare shell revision level */
WORD           DefaultConnID; /* Connection ID for default file server

/* Determine if the shell is loaded, Result should = 255 */
  Result =
          GetNetWareShellVersion(&MajorVersion,&MinorVersion,&Revisio
          nLevel);   if (Result == 255)
          { /* OK so far, shell is loaded */

/* Get the connection ID representing the "default" file server.  The
connection ID is an index to the table of file servers to which the
shell has attachments. The default file server was the first file
server to respond to the shell's request for file servers when it was
loaded, or the first file server explicitly attached or logged-into.
 */
DefaultConnID = GetDefaultConnectionID();

/* Now get the name of the file server with which the default
connection is established */

GetFileServerName(DefaultConnID,ServerName);
}
else
{
Result = 0; /* The shell is not loaded */
}
return(Result);
}
```

The next function checks to see if a workstation is logged into the network.

Based on the value returned by the shell for the default file server's current connection number, the bindery information pertaining to the current connection can be retrieved. The connection number is generated by the file server when a user attaches or performs a login to it. This is the "ID" that the file server uses to identify this workstation as unique from all others. The LoginTime that is returned is the day, date, and time that the user logged in to the default file server. If the result does not come back as 0, then the user is not logged in.

```
/* IsUserLoggedIn


Parameters: char *UserName - Name of user, if logged in

Returns: 1 if user is logged in, 0 if not
*/
int IsUserLoggedIn(char *UserName)
{

int    Result; /* Result of NetWare calls */
WORD ObjectType; /* Object type of current connection */
long  ObjectID; /* Object ID of current connection */
BYTE  LoginTime[7]; /* Time object logged into file server */
WORD  ConnectionNo; /* Connection number between shell and server */

/* Determine the Connection Number between this workstation and the
default server */
ConnectionNo = GetConnectionNumber();

/* Get object information from the shell for the current connection */
Result =
GetConnectionInformation(ConnectionNo,UserName,&ObjectType,&ObjectID,
LoginTime);
return(Result == SUCCESSFUL ? 1 : 0);
}
```

The following program checks to see if the NetWare shell is loaded, which is accomplished by first checking if the IPX/SPX layers were loaded. If at least IPX was loaded, then a check for the actual shell layer is performed. If the shell is loaded, you can determine whether a user has logged-in to the file server from this workstation.

```
/* ON_NET / main

*/
main()
{
char    ServerName[OBJECT_NAME_LEN]; /* Default file server name */
char    UserName[OBJECT_NAME_LEN]; /* User Name, if logged-in */
int     IPXLoaded = 0; /* 1 if IPX was loaded */
int     SPXLoaded = 0; /* 1 if SPX support is available */

/* First determine if the IPX layer was loaded */
IsIPXSPXLoaded(&IPXLoaded,&SPXLoaded);

/* If IPX was found, determine if the NetWare shell was loaded and get
the name of the default server */

if (IPXLoaded && IsShellLoaded(ServerName))
{
        printf("\nNetWare shell Is Loaded, Default Server: [%s]\n",
          ServerName);

/* Determine if a user is logged-in and, if so, return the UserName */

 if ((IsUserLoggedIn(UserName))
 {
     printf("User %s Is Logged Onto The Network.\n",UserName);
 }
 else
 {
     printf("This station is not currently logged in.\n");
 }
}
else
{
```

```
if (IPXLoaded)
{
    printf("\nThe NetWare Shell is not loaded.\n");
}
else
{
    printf("\nNetWare IPX support is not loaded yet.\n");
}
}
}
```

The following procedure, written in Turbo Pascal, presents another way to check for the existence of a NetWare network. It is also included in the example program USER_IS later in this chapter.

```
Procedure Will_It_Run;
Begin

    Regs.Ax:=$E300;

    cc.Native.wl:=$00;
    cc.Native.wh:=$01;
    cr.Native.wl:=$00;
    cr.Native.wh:=$ff;
    cc.Func      :=$46;
    cr.Mask      :=$00;
    cr.id.al     :=$00;
    cr.id.ah     :=$00;
    cr.id.bl     :=$00;
    cr.id.bh     :=$00;

    Regs.Es:=Seg(cr);
    Regs.Di:=Ofs(cr);

    Regs.Ds:=Seg(cc);
    Regs.Si:=Ofs(cc);

  MsDos(Regs);
```

```
   If (cr.id.al=$00) and
      (cr.id.ah=$00) and
      (cr.id.bl=$00) and
      (cr.id.bh=$00)
   then
   Begin
     TextColor(1);TextBackGround(3);ClrEol;
     Writeln(inc);
     ClrEol;
     Writeln('This utility requires Advanced NetWare to run.');
     TextColor(7);TextBackGround(0);ClrEol;
     Halt(4);
   End;

 Regs.Ax:=$E300;
 nr.Native.wl:=$00;
 nr.Native.wh:=$FF;

 nc.Native.wl:=$00;
 nc.Native.wh:=$05;

 Regs.Es:=Seg(nr);
 Regs.Di:=Ofs(nr);

 Regs.Ds:=Seg(nc);
 Regs.Si:=Ofs(nc);

 nc.func:=$36;
 nc.unique.ah:=cr.id.ah;
 nc.unique.al:=cr.id.al;
 nc.unique.bh:=cr.id.bh;
 nc.unique.bl:=cr.id.bl;

 MsDos(Regs);

 if hr.al <> 0 then
  Begin
    TextColor(1);TextBackGround(3);ClrEol;
    Writeln(inc);
    ClrEol;
    Writeln('This utility requires you to be logged into the network to run.');
    TextColor(7);TextBackGround(0);ClrEol;
    Halt(3);
  End;
End; { of Will_it_Run }
```

Using the NetWare Shell

The NetWare shell currently has the ability to allow a maximum of eight concurrent file server connections. Regular users define these connections through utilities such as ATTACH, LOGIN, and MAP. However you may wish to gain access to this "shell" information too. How this is done is no great secret, but knowing that this capability exists and knowing how to best use it should serve to unlock its potential for your applications. The following code examples show some of the things that can be accomplished.

Connecting With Other File Servers

The following are the steps to "attaching" to other file servers while maintaining any current attachments. Per the innate NetWare shell design no more than eight concurrent file server connections are simultaneously allowed. The example is in Assembly language. In pseudo code, here are the steps:

search server name table (or server mapping table), determine if you are currently connected to the desired file server

(next you could determine if any free server slots exist in the shell's memory—up to 8 are allowed. I do my search later, you could do it here)

get NET_ADDRESS of server which connection to is desired (use bindery call, Read Property Value to ascertain this)

get server mapping table, check for any available slots, remember maximum of 8 are allowed

if free slot found, set the slot in use byte to FF, and set up the NET_ADDRESS attach to that server

sort the NET_ADDRESSes, from the resulting ascending order, set up the server order numbers (slot numbers) (1-8)

get server name table address, add new server name to the table at the appropriate offset

if no free slots are found in the server mapping table, detach from server and remove connection (a single call does this) login as GUEST (or whoever) and that's it

Now an Assembly language example:

```
Are_we_connected proc

Had to connect    dw    0

 push    es
 ; Save whatever registers you need to, here I am saving ES

 mov     ax,0EF04h ;get server name table
 int     021h
 ; es:si now points at name table the name table is 8
 ; entries by 30h (48 decimal) characters each these represent the file
 ; server names, up to 47 char. name with a terminating null or 0
 ; for the assembly function cmpsb, we need es:di to point at our
 ; table, hence the following:
 mov     di,si ; set up es:di to point at server name table

 ; ds is still ds, so ds:si is ok (the other parameters cmpsb uses)
 mov     bx,8    ; 8 entries in table to search
                 ; remember, no more than 8 connections allowed at
                 ; once, per the shell's design
                 ; bx is used for the outer loop control

are_search:
   dec     bx       ; we dec one before searching
   cmp     bx,-1   ; does bx = -1?
   je      no_connection ; yes, which means we counted down through all
                         ; 8 connections and did not find one to the
                         ; server we wish to connect to
```

```
    mov     ax,030h                 ; mov 30h to ax
    mov     dx,bx                   ; set dx = bx (current name ptr)
    push    di                      ; save di
    call    mul_dance               ; get address of new pointer
    mov     cx,030h                 ; set cx = length byte, 30h
    mov     si,OFFSET w_servername  ; reset each time cuz repz bumps it
    repe    cmpsb                   ; strings equal?
    pop     di                      ; no flags affected by this pop,
                                    ; restore di
    jne     are_search              ; was the repe cmpsb successful?,
                                    ; i.e. did it fine a match?
                                    ; if not equal (jne) then search
                                    ; again otherwise, found!
    mov     HAD_TO_CONNECT,bl       ; we don't have to connect
    mov     ALREADY_CON,1           ; 0=not connected, 1=already
    jmp     are_done

no_connection:  ; no connection so we have to do one, weeee!

    mov     ALREADY_CON,0 ; 0=not connected, 1=already

    ; set up call for Read a Property Value
    ; get property value for NET_ADDRESS of named server(if there,
    ; if not found, HAD_TO_CONNECT -> FF which indicates no such server
    ; get EF 03 table (server mapping)
    ; look for an available slot, HAD_TO_CONNECT -> FE if no slots
    ; available add slot, fill in Slot in use, order#,
    ; full 12 byte NET_ADDRESS
    ; get EF 04 table (server name)
    ; fill in name at order# used *30h
    ; use F1 00, dl=order # to attach, if fail, set HAD_TO_CONNECT
    ; to fail code
    ; login as GUEST, set HAD_TO_CONNECT to F0 if login fails
    ; return (with HAD_TO_CONNECT to set to slot/order# used(1-8)

    push    ds ; save ds
    pop     es ; set up es correctly (pointing to whatever ds is)

    mov     si,OFFSET w_servername ; offset of variable with server name
    mov     di,si ; save this offset
    mov     cx,030h ; 30h is length of server name
```

```
are_determine_sname_len:
   cmp     byte ptr [si],0   ; find a null? (null terminates servername)
   je      are_got_sname_len ; yes, when we have length jump ahead
   inc     si                ; add one to si
   loop    are_determine_sname_len  ; loop till we figure out how long
                                     ; the server name is

are_got_sname_len:
   sub     si,di   ; subtract si-di, result is length of servername
                   ; in si
   mov     ax,011h ; length of request buffer w/o object name
   add     ax,si   ; length of request buffer w/object name(servername)

   mov     di,OFFSET w07_data ; a 1500 byte buffer that is used by many
                              ; functions, reused often
   mov     word ptr [di],ax   ; length of req, si still has length of
                              ; sname sets up length of request buffer
   inc     di
   inc     di                 ; adds two to di (two inc's)
   mov     word ptr [di],0003Dh ;set up func + 1st byte of obj type
                              ; function 3D (E3h sub 3Dh) is
                              ; Read Property Value
   inc     di
   inc     di
   mov     ax,si   ; set al = length of servername
   mov     ah,04h
   xchg    ah,al   ; exchange ah and al
   mov     word ptr [di],ax   ; setup 2nd byte of obj type+length of
                              ; sname
   inc     di
   inc     di
   mov     cx,si   ; length of servername, cx is used for looping
   mov     si,OFFSET w_servername ; offset of servername
   repz    movsb ;setup the sname in request buffer
   mov     word ptr [di],00B01h  ; setup segment# and prop name len
                              ; 0B is property name length
                              ; (NET_ADDRESS)  01 is the segment,
                              ; the first segment
   inc     di
   inc     di
   mov     cx,0Bh ;length of NET_ADDRESS
   mov     si,OFFSET NET_ADDRESS
   repz    movsb ;move property name over to request buffer
; that's it REQUEST BUFFER SETUP
```

```
     mov     di,OFFSET w07_data
     add     di,0200h ; push way up so reply buffer is out of our way
     mov     word ptr [di],00FFh ; setup reply buffer size, big,
                              ; big enough to handle our reply
                              ; from request

     mov     ah,0E3h
     mov     si,OFFSET w07_data
     mov     di,si
     add     di,0200h ; location of reply buffer, 200h beyond the offset
                      ; of the request buffer

     int     021h
     cmp     al,0       ; is al (return code) 0?
     je      are_got_net_address ; yes, it worked
     ; if we get here, must of failed, set HAD_TO_CONNECT to al(no, FF)
     mov     HAD_TO_CONNECT,0FFh ; error code
     jmp     are_done            ; leave now

are_got_net_address:
   ; now set up server mapping table
     mov     ax,0EF03h ;get server mapping table
     int     021h
   ; assume we got it because the shell always returns the
   ; segment:offset of this table as it is in the shell's internal
   ; memory and if we got this far we must be talking to a shell
   ; es:si points at table
   ; find first available entry


     xor     bx,bx  ; zeroes out bx quickly, same as "sub bx,bx"
are_find_slot2:
     cmp     bx,8     ; have we search all entries? (0 through 7)
     jge     slots_full ; yes, searched all and they are full
     mov     di,si              ; reset di to point at top of table
     mov     ax,020h            ; will multiply by 20h
     mov     dx,bx              ; set dx = bx (current ptr)
     inc     bx                 ; increase pointer by 1
     call    mul_dance          ; multiply ax*dx
     cmp     byte ptr es:[di],0 ; 0=free slot
     jne     are_find_slot2     ; this slot is not free
```

```
        ; slot found!           ; bx-1 will point at correct order number
        ; ds:si - > es:di
        mov    byte ptr es:[di],0FFh ; say we are using slot  FF=used
                                     ; this actually sets the memory in
                                     ; the shell directly
        inc    di                ; add one to di
        mov    byte ptr es:[di],bl  ; bl=order number/sequence #
        inc    di                ; add one to di
        mov    si,OFFSET w07_data
        add    si,0202h ; point at NET_ADDRESS value (the first 2 bytes
                        ; in the reply buffer are the length bytes, that's
                        ; why 202h not 200h
        mov    cx,0Ch   ; 12 bytes to move
        repz   movsb    ; move the bytes, repz is equivalent to repe


        ; NETADDRESS now set up in table (shell's internal table)
        mov    ax,0EF04h ; get address of server name tbl again
        int    021h
        mov    di,si          ;es:si pts at table
        mov    si,OFFSET w_servername
        dec    bx                    ; correct for 0 offset, bx - 1
                                     ; bx is still set from the search
                                     ; above in are_find_slot2
        mov    ax,030h               ; will multiply by 30h
        mov    dx,bx                 ; set dx = bx (current ptr)
        inc    bx                    ; set back to right sequence#
        call   mul_dance             ; multiply ax*dx
        mov    cx,030h               ; cx = length byte, 30h
        repz   movsb                 ; move new servername to shell's
                                     ; server name table

are_attach:
        mov    ax,0F100h             ; attach to server request
        mov    dl,bl                 ; setup which server to attach to
                                     ; this number is the sequence
                                     ; number in the shell's server
                                     ; mapping table, 1 through 8
        mov    HAD_TO_CONNECT,bl     ; setup to point at order number

        int    021h
        cmp    al,0                  ; did it work?
        je     are_login            ; yes, so proceed
```

```
        ; otherwise, fail
        mov     HAD_TO_CONNECT,al          ; set to fail code
        mov     ax,0EF03h                  ; get server mapping table
        int     021h
        ;es:si
        mov     ax,020h                    ; mul by 20h/32 bytes an entry
        mov     dx,bx                      ; set dx = bx (current ptr)
        dec     dx                         ; correct for offset
        xchg    ah,al
        xchg    dh,dl
        mul     dx                         ; multiply ax*dx answer in dx
        add     si,dx                      ; ->DI to offset we
                                           ; calc'd+original ofs

        mov     byte ptr es:[si],0         ; 0=free slot, free up slot we
                                           ; used unset the shell mapping slot
                                           ; saying that this slot is now free
                                           ; to be used for other connection
                                           ; attempts

        jmp     are_done                   ; leave

e3_14c  db      0Bh,0, 014h, 00, 01, 5, 'GUEST',0,0 ;0=password length, 0
e3_14r  db      0FFh,0

are_login:
        ; got this far means we can login now
        push    ds
        pop     es ; reset es to equal ds
        mov     ax,0F000h          ; set preferred server
        mov     dl,HAD_TO_CONNECT  ; point at newly attached server
        int     021h
        mov     ah,0E3h
        mov     si,OFFSET e3_14c   ; try to login as GUEST
        mov     di,OFFSET e3_14r
        int     021h
        cmp     al,0               ; could we login?
        je      are_up_lst;        ; yes, go on

        mov     ax,0F000h          ; set preferred server back to home server
        mov     dl,1               ; slot 1 is the home server, first we
                                   ; logged into
        int     021h
```

27

```
        mov     ax,0F101h           ; detach from server, destroy the
                                    ; connection too
        mov     dl,HAD_TO_CONNECT   ; point at newly attached server
        int     021h ; deattach     ; login failed, release connection NOW

        mov     HAD_TO_CONNECT,0F0h  ;login failed
        jmp     are_done

slots_full:
        mov     HAD_TO_CONNECT,0FEh  ;no slot available
        jmp     are_done

are_up_lst:
        ; at this point you need to sort the slot numbers of each
        ; server mapping entry (call to get table address is EF03, seen
        ; above), you sort the slot numbers based on the ascending
        ; number of each server's 12 byte NET_ADDRESS
        ; the slot number is also called the server order number, it is
        ; the byte which follows the slot in use byte found first in
        ; each (of the possible 8) 32 byte server mapping table

        ; this "slot number/order number" is used by the shell for certain
        ; file lock sequencing calls where locks are placed on files that
        ; are on different servers, it is a synchronization process that
        ; the shell uses
        ; It is possible to not set the slot numbers in sequence, but it
        ; is recommeded to so
        ;
        ; because of the sort routine's innate "messiness" I have not
        ; placed it here as you would spend more time figuring out the
        ; sort than realizing what it does
        ;
        ; if you are an assembly language programmer, chances are you have
        ; a sort routine which you can readily adapt to this need
        ;
        ; if you are programming in a higher level language you probably
        ; have a sort that you likewise use

        ; example:
        ; say you are connected to two servers with NET_ADDRESS's of:
        ;
        ; 00 00 00 01 00 00 00 00 00 A2
        ; 00 00 00 01 00 00 00 00 00 A3
        ;
```

```
; the 32 byte table (first 14 bytes) for each would be:
;
; FF 01 00 00 00 01 00 00 00 00 00 A2 ...
; FF 02 00 00 00 01 00 00 00 00 00 A3 ...
;
; if the first address was, instead, 00 00 00 05 00 00 00 00 00 A2
; then the table would be:
;
; FF 02 00 00 00 05 00 00 00 00 00 A2 ...
; FF 01 00 00 00 01 00 00 00 00 00 A3 ...
;
; etc.
; remember when doing the sort you are altering memory in the
; shell and that for each "sort" you DO NOT move any of the 32 byte
; "mapping" tables, you just change the slot number/order number
; value
; as an added tip, when I do my sorts, I make a copy of 8x32 (256
; byte) the shell server mapping table in my own ram space and
; proceed with the sort that way, further, for each unused slot
; (where slot in use is not = FF) I set the address field to all
; high values (i.e.FF FF FF FF FF FF FF FF FF FF, 12 bytes of FF)
; and since all FFs is high, all unused slots will appear last in
; the sort and since all FF's is an illegal NET_ADDRESS there is no
; problem with inadvertently using a viable address (which all FFs
; is not) and when updating actual shell memory I just ignore those
; with NET_ADDRESS of all FF's but, updating the shell with the slot
; numbers your sort comes up with will not hurt anything because the
; in use flag is not FF hence the shell will ignore their slot
; numbers anyway


are_done:
   pop es ; restore any values you saved, at the beginning I saved es
   ret    ; return to caller
Are_we_connected endp  ; endp = end of procedure
```

```
mul_dance proc

    xchg    ah,al           ; exchange ah and al
    xchg    dh,dl           ; exchange dh and dl
    mul     dx              ; multiplies ax*dx, answer in dx
    add     di,dx           ; point DI to offset we calc'd+
                            ; original offset
    ret                     ; return to caller

mul_dance endp
```

In Turbo Pascal, the following routine checks to see if the workstation is connected to a particular file server specified by name and shows how to see server name table:

```
Procedure SetServer;
Type
Convu = record
        Waste:String[1];
        Sname:String[78];
        end;
var
TempName: String[80];
TS      : Convu absolute TempName;
S,O,b   : Integer;
Go_On,
Found   : Boolean;
Begin

    Found:=False;
    Go_On:=False;

    Regs.Ax:=$F002;   {Get Effective Server}
    MsDOS(Regs);
    HomeServer:=Regs.Al; {save Home Server}
```

```
If (ParamCount > 1) then
Begin
    TempName:=ParamStr(2);
    { This procedure uses the 2nd command line parameter for the file
      server name identification... alternately, the third parameter
      is also checked }

    For a:=1 to length(TempName) do TempName[a]:=UpCase(TempName[a]);
    { above makes sure the name specified is all uppercase }

    For a:=length(TempName) to 79{max length} do TempName[a+1]:=^@;
    { above nulls the portion of TempName following the server name }

    If TempName[1]='S' then If TempName[2]='=' then Go_On:=True;
    { Further, this routine used S=<server name> for verification of
      the command line input, verifying it is the file server name that
      the user is defining }

    If (not Go_On) and (ParamCount>2) then
    Begin
     TempName:=ParamStr(3);

     { This procedure also checks the third command line parameter to
       see if it is the file server name }

     For a:=1 to length(TempName) do TempName[a]:=UpCase(TempName[a]);
     For a:=length(TempName) to 79{max length} do TempName[a+1]:=^@;
     If TempName[1]='S' then If TempName[2]='=' then Go_On:=True;


    End;



If Go_On then
Begin
 Regs.Ax:=$EF04; {Get Server Name Table address into ES:SI}
 MsDOS(Regs);

 TempName[2]:=chr( ord(TempName[0]) - 2);
 {set up length byte for TS.Sname}
 { note: in turbo pascal, byte 0 is a string's length, the -2 is used }
 {       because the first two bytes of the server name are S= }
 {Writeln('ServerName is [',TS.Sname,']');{ if you wanted to see it}
```

```
{Regs.ES and SI point at Name Table, search it}
S:=Regs.Es;
O:=Regs.Si;


a:=1; { a is used to search through the server name table, 1 is first
          server name }
While a<8 do
 Begin
 O:=Regs.Si;
 O:=O+((a-1)*48); { each entry is 48 bytes, each server name that is
                    has the potential to be 48 bytes }

  if Mem[S:O] <> 0 then { if null (0) then skip this entry, not used }
   Begin
    b:=1;
    While b<=length(TS.Sname){48} do
     begin
       If Mem[S:(O+b-1)]=ord(TS.Sname[b])
       then
        begin
         If (b=length(TS.Sname)) and (Mem[S:(O+b)]=0) then
         { did we fine the user entered server name? }
         begin
          Found:=True;
          b:=99; { breaks us out of the loop }
          NewHome:=a;
         end;
       end
      else
          b:=99; {get out}

    b:=b+1; {increment}
    end; { while b < 48, actually 48 is replaced with length of
          server name provided }

 End; { end of if not null }

a:=a+1; { a is used to go through the 8 server name entries, increase
         it to search the next entry in shell's table }

if Found then a:=99; { get out of loop }
End; {end of while a is 1..8}
```

```
End; {of if S= in paramstr}

If Go_On then
If not Found then
 begin
   TextBackGround(7);
   TextColor(Red);
   Write  ('Sorry, you are not attached to server ');
   Write  (TS.Sname);ClrEol;
   Writeln('.');
   Halt(1);
 end
Else
 begin
   Regs.Ax:=$F000;  {Set Preferred server to new home}
   Regs.Dl:=NewHome;
   MsDOS(Regs);
   { Writeln('Just set Pref Server to -> ',NewHome);{}
     regs.AX:=$DC00;
     MsDos(regs);
 end;


End; {end of if paramstr >1 }

End;  {end of SetServer}
```

USERIS: Three Different Ways

The following three program examples show you how to accomplish the same task three different ways. Given a command line argument, the programs will verify a user's login name on the current file server, for example:

USERIS JOHN

If JOHN is a valid LOGIN NAME on the current file server a DOS ERRORLEVEL of 0 is returned if not valid, a DOS ERRORLEVEL of 1 is returned if no command line argument is entered, 2 is returned. Note that this program makes use of the procedure WILL_IT_RUN discussed earlier in this chapter.

Immediately folllowing is the USERIS code in C which uses Novell's NetWare System Calls-DOS. Following this is the USERIS code in Turbo Pascal, and then the USERIS code written in C using Novell's C Libraries Interface for DOS.

USERIS Code in C

```
/*

John T. McCann, NOVUSER Wizard SysOp, 70007,3430
1/5/89
Written in Turbo C v2.0

This program will, given a command line argument, verify a user's login
name on the current file server, ex:

USERIS JOHN

if JOHN is a valid LOGIN NAME (for a user) on the current file server a
DOS ERRORLEVEL of 0 is returned

if not valid, a DOS ERRORLEVEL of 1 is returned

if no command line arguement is entered 2 is returned

if not logged into any file servers (but the shell is loaded) 3 is
returned

if the shell is not loaded 4 is returned
*/


#define inc         "UserIs, (c)1989 Wizard Stuff"
/* this program is provided as an example, feel free to
 * modify the code at will and distribute without
 * suppression, just don't include the (c) notice on code
 * you've modified,have fun and discover!
 */
```

```
#define Version       1.0

typedef union {
        struct {
                unsigned int Ax, Bx, Cx, Dx, Bp, Si, Di,
                             Ds, Es, FLAGS;
              } F;
        struct {
                unsigned char Al, Ah, Bl, Bh, Cl, Ch, Dl,
                              Dh;
              } H;
          } Registers;

typedef struct {
                unsigned char ah, al, bh, bl;
              }  Longs;

typedef struct {

                char          wh, wl;
              }  MyWord;

typedef struct {

                MyWord        Native;
                char          func;  /* $36 for get object name  */
                Longs         unique;/*  Unique ID for the object */
          }  e336cl;

typedef struct {

                MyWord        Native;
                Longs         id;      /*   same id as above   */
                MyWord        ObjTyp; /*   type of object      */
                char          name[47];
          }  e336rp;

typedef struct {
                MyWord        Native;
                char          Func;  /* $46 = get my bindery
                                            access level */

          }  chkcall;

typedef struct {
                MyWord        Native;
                char          Mask;
                Longs         id;
          }  chkrply;
```

```
typedef struct {
        MyWord    Native;
        char      Func;  /* 55 for Search for
                                Users  */
        Longs     last;  /* make it -1  */
        MyWord    ObjTyp; /*  Search for users
                                 0001  */
        char      ObjNml;  /*  1  */
        char      ObjNme[47];  /*  *, if search
                                      all is used  */
        } e33dcall;

typedef struct {
                MyWord      Native;
                Longs       Id;
                MyWord      ObjectType;
                char        PropName[47];
                   /* could add some space down here since I
                   tell it the reply buffer is 255 bytes long,
                   but that really isn't going to happen. */
        } e33drply;


#if defined(__TINY__) || defined(__SMALL__) || defined(__MEDIUM__)
#define Seg(ptr) _DS
#define Ofs(ptr) (unsigned)(ptr)
#else
#define Ofs(fp)      ((unsigned)(fp))
#define Seg(fp)      ((unsigned)((unsigned long)(fp) >> 16))
#endif

#define MsDos intr

#define length(s) strlen(s)
```

```
Registers      Regs;

chkcall        cc;
chkrply        cr;
e336cl         nc;
e336rp         nr;
e33dcall       pc;
e33drply       pr;
int            a;
char           Ruser[48];
char           accum[48];



void           UserI(argv)
char *argv[];
{
char           PS[80];  /*  just a string to hold the paramstr(1)
                            variable  */

  pc.last.ah = 0xff;    /*  set the last object seen to -1  */
  pc.last.al = 0xff;
  pc.last.bh = 0xff;
  pc.last.bl = 0xff;

  pr.Native.wl = 0x00;
  pr.Native.wh = 0xFF;/*  set up reply buffer size, note it really
                          isn't 255 bytes long, but neither is the possible
                          reply... */

  pc.Native.wl = 0x00;
  pc.Native.wh = 0x8 + length(argv[1]);   /*  set up length of request
                                              buffer  */


  pc.Func = 0x37;   /*  scan bindery objects  */

  pc.ObjTyp.wh = 0;
  pc.ObjTyp.wl = 1;   /*  01 = user object type  */

  pc.ObjNml = length(argv[1]);
```

```
    strcpy(PS, argv[1]);
    for (a = 0; a <= (pc.ObjNml % 48); a++)
     {
      if ( (PS[a]>96) && (PS[a]<123) )
      PS[a] = PS[a] - 32;    /* convert to Upper Case */
      pc.ObjNme[a] = PS[a];
     }

   Regs.F.Ax = 0xE300;

   Regs.F.Es = Seg(&pr);
   Regs.F.Di = Ofs(&pr);

   Regs.F.Ds = Seg(&pc);
   Regs.F.Si = Ofs(&pc);

   MsDos(33,&Regs);


   if (Regs.H.Al == 0) exit(0);else exit(1);

}
   /*  of Proc UserI  */



void           Will_It_Run()
{
int    subs;

    Regs.F.Ax = 0xE300;

    cc.Native.wl = 0x00;
    cc.Native.wh = 0x01;
    cr.Native.wl = 0x00;
    cr.Native.wh = 0xff;
    cc.Func = 0x46;
    cr.Mask = 0x00;
    cr.id.al = 0x00;
    cr.id.ah = 0x00;
    cr.id.bl = 0x00;
    cr.id.bh = 0x00;

    Regs.F.Es = Seg(&cr);
    Regs.F.Di = Ofs(&cr);
```

```
    Regs.F.Ds = Seg(&cc);
    Regs.F.Si = Ofs(&cc);
    MsDos(33,&Regs);

if ((cr.id.al == 0x00) && (cr.id.ah == 0x00) && (cr.id.bl == 0x00) &&
    (cr.id.bh == 0x00))
    {
        printf("%s\n",inc);
        printf("This utility requires Advanced Netware to run.\n");
        exit(4);
    }

  Regs.F.Ax = 0xE300;
  nr.Native.wl = 0x00;
  nr.Native.wh = 0xFF;

  nc.Native.wl = 0x00;
  nc.Native.wh = 0x05;

  Regs.F.Es = Seg(&nr);
  Regs.F.Di = Ofs(&nr);

  Regs.F.Ds = Seg(&nc);
  Regs.F.Si = Ofs(&nc);

  nc.func = 0x36;
  nc.unique.ah = cr.id.ah;
  nc.unique.al = cr.id.al;
  nc.unique.bh = cr.id.bh;
  nc.unique.bl = cr.id.bl;

  MsDos(33,&Regs);

  if (Regs.H.Al != 0)
   {
     printf("%s\n",inc);
     printf("This utility requires you to be logged into the network to
             run.\n");
     exit(3);
   }
```

```
    for (a = 0; a <= 47; a++)
        accum[a] = '\040';
    strcpy(Ruser, "Unknown User");
    subs = -1;

  if (Regs.H.Al == 0)
  {
        for (a = 0; a <= 47; a++)
          {
            if ((nr.name[a] > 0x20) && (nr.name[a] < 0x61))
            {
            subs++;
            accum[subs] = nr.name[a];
            }
          }   /* of for a... */

              strcpy(Ruser,accum);
  }

 if (cr.Mask != 0x33) /* optional */
 {
    printf("%s\n",inc);
    if (Regs.H.Al == 0)
     {
       printf("I'm sorry ");
       for (a = 0; a <= subs; a++)
       printf("%c",Ruser[a]);
     }
    printf(", you must have Supervisor Equivalence to run this
            utility.\n");
    exit(10);
 }

}
  /*  of Will_it_Run  */



main(argc,argv)
int argc;
char *argv[];
{
```

```
    if (length(argv[1]) < 1)
  {
    printf("%s\n",inc);
    printf("Usage: USERIS xxxxx where xxxxx is the username to check\n");
    printf("        existence of on the current file server\n");
    exit(2);
  }

 Will_It_Run();

 UserI(argv);

}
```

USERIS Code in Turbo Pascal.

```
Program USERIS;
{
by: John T. McCann, NOVUSER Wizard SysOp, 70007,3430 1/5/89

 Written in Turbo Pascal v5.0


 if not logged into any file servers (but the shell is loaded)
 3 is returned

 if the shell is not loaded 4 is returned
}

Uses Crt, Dos;

Const

   inc = 'UserIs, (c)1989 Wizard Stuff';
   Version = 1.0;

Type

HalfRegtype = record
                Al,Ah,Bl,Bh,Cl,Ch,Dl,Dh:byte
              end;
```

```
longs    = record
              ah,al,bh,bl:byte;
           end;

MyWord   = record
              wh,wl : byte;
           end;

e336cl   = record
              Native : MyWord;
              Func   : Byte;     { $36 for get object name }
              unique : Longs;    { Unique ID for the object }
           end;

e336rp   = record
              Native : MyWord;
              id     : longs;       { same id as above }
              ObjTyp : Myword;      { type of object    }
              Name   : array [1..48] of byte;
           end;

chkcall  = record
              Native: MyWord;
              Func  : Byte;   { $46 = get my bindery access level}
           end;

chkrply  = record
              Native: MyWord;
              Mask  : Byte;
              id    : Longs;
           end;

E33dcall = record
              Native: MyWord;
              Func  : Byte;   { 55 for Search for Users }
              Last  : Longs;  { make it -1 }
              ObjTyp: MyWord; { Search for users 0001 }
              ObjNml: Byte;   { 1 }
              ObjNme: array[1..48] of Byte; {*, if search all is used}
           end;
```

```
E33drply   = record
              Native    : MyWord;
              Id        : Longs;
              ObjectType: MyWord;
              PropName  : array [1..48] of Byte;
              { could add some space down here since I tell it the
                reply buffer is 255 bytes long, but, that really isn't
                going to happen...}
            end;

Var
Regs   :  Registers;
hr     :  HalfRegType absolute Regs;

cc     :  chkcall;
cr     :  chkrply;
nc     :  e336cl;
nr     :  e336rp;
pc     :  e33dcall;
pr     :  e33drply;
a      :  Integer;


Procedure UserI;
var
PS     :  String[80]; { just a string to hold the paramstr(1) variable }

Begin

with pc do
  begin
    last.ah:=$1f; { set the last object seen to -1 }
    last.al:=$ff;
    last.bh:=$ff;
    last.bl:=$ff;
  end;

  pr.Native.wl:=$00;
  pr.Native.wh:=$FF; { set up reply buffer size, note it really isn't
                       255 bytes long, but neither is the possible
                       reply...}

  pc.Native.wl:= $00;
  pc.Native.wh:= $8+length(paramstr(1)); { set up length of request
                                           buffer }
```

```
    pc.Func       := $37; { scan bindery objects }

    pc.ObjTyp.wh:= 0;
    pc.ObjTyp.wl:= 1; { 01 = user object type }

    pc.ObjNml     := length(paramstr(1));




  PS:=paramstr(1);
  for a:=1 to (pc.ObjNml mod 48) do
   begin
     if ord(PS[a]) in [97..122] then PS[a]:=chr(ord(PS[a])-32); {convert
                                                                 to
                                                                 Upper
                                                                 Case}
     pc.ObjNme[a]:=ord(PS[a]);
   end;


  Regs.Ax:=$E300;

  Regs.Es:=Seg(Pr);
  Regs.Di:=Ofs(Pr);

  Regs.Ds:=Seg(Pc);
  Regs.Si:=Ofs(Pc);

  MsDos(Regs);

  if hr.al=0 then halt(0) else halt(1);


End; { of Proc UserI }



Procedure Will_It_Run;
Begin

  TextColor(7);
```

```
Regs.Ax:=$E300;

cc.Native.wl:=$00;
cc.Native.wh:=$01;
cr.Native.wl:=$00;
cr.Native.wh:=$ff;
cc.Func      :=$46;
cr.Mask      :=$00;
cr.id.al     :=$00;
cr.id.ah     :=$00;
cr.id.bl     :=$00;
cr.id.bh     :=$00;

Regs.Es:=Seg(cr);
Regs.Di:=Ofs(cr);

Regs.Ds:=Seg(cc);
Regs.Si:=Ofs(cc);



MsDos(Regs);

  If (cr.id.al=$00) and
     (cr.id.ah=$00) and
     (cr.id.bl=$00) and
     (cr.id.bh=$00)
then
   Begin
      TextColor(1);TextBackGround(3);ClrEol;
      Writeln(inc);
      ClrEol;
      Writeln('This utility requires Advanced Netware to run.');
      TextColor(7);TextBackGround(0);ClrEol;
      Halt(4);
   End;

Regs.Ax:=$E300;
nr.Native.wl:=$00;
nr.Native.wh:=$FF;

nc.Native.wl:=$00;
nc.Native.wh:=$05;
```

```
    Regs.Es:=Seg(nr);
    Regs.Di:=Ofs(nr);

    Regs.Ds:=Seg(nc);
    Regs.Si:=Ofs(nc);

    nc.func:=$36;
    nc.unique.ah:=cr.id.ah;
    nc.unique.al:=cr.id.al;
    nc.unique.bh:=cr.id.bh;
    nc.unique.bl:=cr.id.bl;

    MsDos(Regs);

    if hr.al <> 0 then
     Begin
       TextColor(1);TextBackGround(3);ClrEol;
       Writeln(inc);
       ClrEol;
       Writeln('This utility requires you to be logged into the network to run.');
       TextColor(7);TextBackGround(0);ClrEol;
       Halt(3);
     End;

End; { of Will_it_Run }




Begin

If length(Paramstr(1)) <1 then
 begin
   TextColor(1);TextBackGround(3);ClrEol;
   writeln(inc);
   ClrEol;
   writeln('Usage: USERIS xxxxx  where xxxxx is the username to check');
   writeln('      existence of on the current file server');
   TextColor(7);TextBackGround(0);ClrEol;
   halt(2);
 end;
```

```
 Will_It_Run;

 UserI;

End.
```

USERIS in C Using Novell C Lib

```
/*
John T. McCann, NOVUSER Wizard SysOp, 70007,3430 1/5/89
Written in Turbo C v2.0
This program will, given a command line argument, verify a user's login
name on the current file server, ex:

USERIS JOHN

if JOHN is a valid LOGIN NAME (for a user) on the current file server a
DOS ERRORLEVEL of 0 is returned

if not valid, a DOS ERRORLEVEL of 1 is returned

if no command line argument is entered 2 is returned

if not logged into any file servers (but the shell is loaded) 3 is
returned

if the shell is not loaded 4 is returned
*/
#define inc "UserIs, (c)1989 Wizard Stuff"
/* this program is provided as an example, feel free to modify the
* code at will and distribute without suppression, just don't include
* the (c) notice on code you've modified, have fun and discover! */

#define Version 1.0

#include "stdlib.h"
#include "stdio.h"
#include "dir.h"
#include "errno.h"
#include "string.h"
#include "process.h"
#include "nwcalls.h"
#include "nwerror.h"
```

```
typedef char string48[48];
typedef unsigned char string128[128];

char Ruser[48];
char accum[48];

WORD CPS; /* Current Server Pointer */

/*
¤
¤¤¤¤¤¤¤¤¤¤¤¤¤¤¤¤¤¤¤¤¤¤¤¤¤¤¤¤¤¤¤¤¤¤¤¤¤¤¤¤¤¤¤¤¤¤¤¤¤¤¤¤¤¤¤¤¤¤¤¤¤¤¤¤¤¤¤¤¤¤¤¤¤¤¤¤¤¤
¤
*/
void      UserI(argv)
char *argv[];
{
string128 PS; /* just a string to hold the paramstr(1) variable */

DWORD scanID; /* scan'd object number */
WORD cc,gw1;
BYTE SobjF, SobjS,g1;
int a;

 scanID=-1;

 strcpy(PS, argv[1]);

 for (a=0;a<strlen(PS);a++)
  if ( (PS[a]>96) && (PS[a]<123) )
    PS[a] = PS[a] - 32;

 cc=NWScanObject(CPS,PS,OT_USER,&scanID,PS,&gw1,&g1,&SobjF,&SobjS);

 if (!cc)
   exit(0);
else
   exit(1);

}
 /* of Proc UserI */
/*
```

```
¤
¤¤¤¤¤¤¤¤¤¤¤¤¤¤¤¤¤¤¤¤¤¤¤¤¤¤¤¤¤¤¤¤¤¤¤¤¤¤¤¤¤¤¤¤¤¤¤¤¤¤¤¤¤¤¤¤¤¤¤¤¤¤¤¤¤¤¤¤
¤
*/

void        Will_It_Run()
{
WORD cc;
BYTE accessLevel;
DWORD myID;
string48 tName;
WORD tType;

    cc=NWGetDefaultConnectionID(&CPS); /* Get current server pointer */

    NWGetBinderyAccessLevel(CPS, &accessLevel, &myID);

    if  (!myID)
    {
     printf("%s\n",inc);
     printf("This utility requires Advanced Netware to run.\n");
     exit(4);
    }
    cc=NWGetObjectName(CPS, myID, tName, &tType);

/* In all reality you don't need to be logged in for this utility to
    work but, here's what one thing you could do if you need the user to
    be logged in to run the utility */

    if ((cc) || (!strlen(tName)))
    {
     printf("%s\n",inc);
     printf("This utility requires you to be logged into the network to run \n");
     exit(3);
    }
```

```
/* You can remove the check below if you don't care if the user is a
   Supervisor Equivalent or not */
   if (accessLevel != 0x33)
   {
    printf("%s\n",inc);
    printf("You must have Supervisor Equivalence to run this utility.\n",tName);
    exit(10);
   }

}
  /* of Will_it_Run */
/*
¤
¤¤¤¤¤¤¤¤¤¤¤¤¤¤¤¤¤¤¤¤¤¤¤¤¤¤¤¤¤¤¤¤¤¤¤¤¤¤¤¤¤¤¤¤¤¤¤¤¤¤¤¤¤¤¤¤¤¤¤¤¤¤¤¤¤¤¤¤¤¤¤¤¤¤¤¤¤¤
¤
*/

main(argc,argv)
int argc;
char *argv[];
{

if (argc); /* prevent compiler warning */

if (strlen(argv[1]) < 1)
 {
   printf("%s\n",inc);
   printf("Usage: USERIS xxxxx where xxxxx is the username to check\n");
   printf("       existence of on the current file server\n");
   exit(2);
 }

 Will_It_Run();

 UserI(argv);
}
```

CHAPTER 2

The Bindery

Ever wish you could save data in a secure area—an area that you as the developer would have control over, one that would always contain the data you needed? Certain information, while it could be saved to a disk file, is better off in more secure surroundings. Fortunately for developers, NetWare has built-in capabilities to protect critical data. Part of the NetWare operating system, the bindery plays a crucial role as a storehouse of system information. Primarily, developers use the NetWare Bindery Services to access various information, including security information, about users, groups, and file servers.

In a typical application, you might want to find out a few things about the current user. For example, from a cosmetic perspective, the user's full name would be handy. So is the ability to verify the user's password—an excellent way to make sure the user is really the user logged-in to a particular workstation. You can also determine whether this user is a member of the group of users associated with your application and, thus, whether they are allowed to run your application.

What Is The Bindery?

Conceptually, the bindery is a special purpose database used by the NetWare operating system to maintain information about objects or named entities (either physical or logical), known to a particular file server. There are many different types of objects stored in the bindery, each type having its own special function and descriptive properties. In turn, every property has a value or values. Some common object types with which you are probably already familiar are users, user groups, file servers, print servers, and print queues. Other object types also exist in the bindery, and third-party software developers often create new object types to meet their application requirements.

Applications can query the bindery to obtain information about its objects. Here, our primary concern is with which network facilities a user is allowed to access. By examining the bindery, we can inspect many characteristics of a user.

For example, the NetWare login procedure queries the bindery database to check user security profiles each time a user logs in to a NetWare file server.

The bindery is actually composed of files stored in the SYS:SYSTEM directory of every NetWare file server, with the attributes System and Hidden. These files are named NET$BIND.SYS and NET$BVAL.SYS for NetWare 286, and NET$OBJ.SYS, NET$PROP.SYS, and NET$VAL.SYS for NetWare 386. When the file server is booted, it opens these files and keeps them open and locked at all times. The bindery files may be closed temporarily for backup purposes.

The only access that DOS applications have to these bindery files is through the use of the NetWare Application Programmer's Interfaces (APIs), which are accessed through the NetWare Shell. Using these APIs, applications, such as SYSCON, can create, delete, and read/write bindery information. Similarly, third-party developers can use these APIs to create NetWare utilities that can access and manipulate the bindery database.

The Bindery, Technically Speaking

The bindery is composed of three types of data—objects, properties, and property values. An object is a named entity, such as a user, that is stored in the bindery. Every object has the following information associated with it:

Object ID— A four-byte hexadecimal number that uniquely identifies the object

Object Name—An ASCIIZ string, from 1 to 47 characters in length

Object Type— A two-byte hexadecimal number that identifies the object's type

Objects of different types may have the same name, but every Object ID must be unique. Typically this uniqueness is not a concern as the NetWare operating system creates the ID whenever an object is created. And there is no defined method for altering the object ID. Only one object ID is constant. That ID is 0x00000001, which is the user SUPERVISOR's ID. Object types from 0x0001 to 0x8000 have been reserved by Novell; object types from 0x8001 through 0xFFFE may be used by third-party developers. TYPE and ID of a bindery object are represented by unsigned bytes. The TYPE, or class, indicates the primary use of the object: 0001h is for users, 0002h for groups and 0004h for currently active file servers. Note NetWare's definitions of object types in Figure 2-1.

0000h	Unknown
0001h	User
0002h	Group
0003h	Print Server
0004h	File Server
0005h	Job Server
0006h	Gateway
0007h	Print Queue
0008h	Archive Queue
0009h	Archive Server
000Ah	Job Queue
000Bh	Administration
0026h	Remote Bridge Server
0047h	Advertising Print Server
up to 7FFFh	Reserved by Novell, used to define well-known types
8000h to FFFEh	Available for use of developers without restraint
FFFFh	Wild—can only be used for searches, not for creation

Figure 2-1. Object Types

The bindery resides in two files, NET$BIND.SYS and NET$BVAL.SYS, both are located in the SYS:SYSTEM directory. However, it's not where the files are stored but how they are accessed that makes them secure. (Note that in NetWare 386 there are three bindery files NET$OBJ.SYS, NET$PROP.SYS and NET$VAL.SYS.) Using the binderies itself is NET$OS (the NetWare Operating system). For instance, stored in the binderies are user definitions (including name, password, group membership), group definitions (name, members), and other file servers currently active on the network. Note that Trustee Assignments (directory rights) are *not* stored in the binderies, rather they are stored in DIRSTAMP.SYS (in the root directory of each volume), with NetWare 386, each subdirectory stores the directory and trustee assignments.

The ID is a random, unique number used to identify the bindery object. For each object TYPE there may be many objects (with unique IDs), but, for each object ID, there is only one object.

Each bindery object has a list of properties that describe and provide information about the object. For example, the property GROUPS_I'M_IN represents the groups in which an object is a member. Properties often reflect the real-world attributes of the object; for example, user objects have properties such as PASSWORD, LOGIN_CONTROL, GROUPS_I'M_IN and ACCOUNT_ BALANCE.

An object may have multiple properties, or no properties at all. Objects of the same type usually share a base set of properties, but each individual object may have properties unique to that object.

A property value (sometimes referred to as a property data set) is the actual data contained in a property, such as the password. All property values are stored internally as 128 byte blocks, referred to as segments, and a property value can have multiple segments (up to 255), or no segments.

Further, there are two types of property values—sets and items. A set property value is a list of other bindery objects, such as the GROUPS_I'M_IN property, which contains a list of the user groups to which a user belongs. Another example of a set property value is the SECURITY_EQUALS property that contains a list of objects to which a user is "security-equivalent." A set property value is interpreted as a collection of 0 to 32 object IDs (or members) per segment. Some property values of type set have been predefined by Novell, including those listed in Figure 2-2.

GROUP_MEMBERS	Members of a group
GROUPS_I'M_IN	Groups of which an object is a member
SECURITY_EQUALS	An object's security equivalences
Q_USERS	A print queue's users
Q_SERVERS	Print servers allowed to service a print queue
Q_OPERATORS	A print queue's operators
OPERATORS	File server console operators
MANAGERS	Workgroup managers (NetWare 386)
OBJ_SUPERVISORS	An object's managers (NetWare 386)

Figure 2-2. Set Property Values Defined by Novell

An item is a discrete quantity of information regarding an object. It can be as simple as an ASCII string—as in the IDENTIFICATION property, which contains the user's full name—or as complex as a data structure that contains fields of varying data types—as in the LOGIN_CONTROL property (see Figure 2.3), which contains a complex structure of user account restrictions.

Property: LOGIN_CONTROL		NetWare v2.1x	
Offset	Field	Size	Type
0	Accounting Expiration Date	3 bytes	byte
3	Account Disabled Flag	1 byte	byte
4	Password Expiration Date	3 bytes	byte
7	Grace Logins Remaining	1 byte	byte
8	Password Expiration Interval	2 bytes	word
10	Grace Login Reset Value	1 byte	byte
11	Minimum Password Length	1 byte	byte
12	Minimum Concurrent Connections	2 bytes	word
14	Allowed Login Time Bitmap	42 bytes	byte
56	Last Login Date and Time	6 bytes	byte
62	Restriction Flags	1 byte	byte
63	Unused	1 byte	byte
64	Maximum Disk Usage (in blocks)	4 bytes	long
68	Bad Login Count	2 bytes	word
70	Next Reset Time	4 bytes	long
74	Bad Login Address	12 bytes	byte

Figure 2-3. Property LOGIN_CONTROL fields

An item property value in general does not have a defined format. Rather, it must be interpreted by the program that accesses it. Some specific property values of type item, however, have structures that have been pre-defined by Novell, including those listed in Figure 2-4.

LOGIN_CONTROL	User account and time restrictions
IDENTIFICATION	Full name
NET_ADDRESS	A network address for a resource
NODE_CONTROL	Station restrictions
OLD_PASSWORDS	Password history for unique passwords
ACCT_LOCKOUT	Account lockout for intruder detection
ACCOUNT_BALANCE	Account balance
PASSWORD	Password
USER_DEFAULTS	New user default account and time restrictions
Q_DIRECTORY	A print queue's home directory
ACCOUNT_HOLD	Account hold
CONNECT_TIME	Connect time charge rates
REQUESTS_MADE	Service request charge rates
BLOCKS_READ	Block read charge rates
BLOCKS_WRITTEN	Blocks written charge rates
DISK_STORAGE	Disk space storage charge rates

Figure 2-4. Item Property Values Defined by Novell

Read/Write Security

Every object in the bindery has an object read/write security level, and every property has a property read/write security level. A combination of these security levels determines what degree of access an application has to read or write to an object or property. A user with SUPERVISOR equivalence has access to almost all information in the bindery; however, some information is accessible only to the operating system (such as the PASSWORD property with NetWare v2.1x and higher).

Dynamic versus Static

Every object and property in the bindery is characterized as either static or dynamic. Static objects and properties are permanent, while dynamic objects and properties exist only until the file server is downed (rebooted). Users and user groups as defined by SYSCON, are static objects; they will be in the bindery until they are manually deleted. File servers are dynamic objects; when a file server is downed, all objects of type "file server" (other than the file server being downed) are deleted from the bindery. Dynamic objects and properties are usually used for temporary information, such as advertising file servers.

Developers can have their programs configure the bindery to suit the individual needs of a particular application, user, group, or company. In light of the fundamental importance of the bindery to the NetWare operating system, it is surprising that the Novell utilities provide only limited access to the bindery data.

A Little More on the Bindery

Every NetWare server has a bindery. Accessing the bindery is the same regardless of the version of NetWare. Novell supplies a standard set of APIs which are exclusively used to converse with the bindery. Built into the APIs are levels of security ranging from access without being logged-in to access only using the NetWare kernel procedures. Levels falling in-between include access by any user (a Type 1 bindery object) logged-in, access by any object recognized (such as a print server, Type 7) to access by only those with security clearance of Supervisor. Due to this highly structured avenue of access, the bindery is quite resilient to illegal tampering. Data can be hidden (abstracted) through the use of more than 65,000 different object types as well as protected by invocation of different security levels imposed as needed. Thrown in at no extra charge is a complete set of error checking complemented by very specific errors to point out problems. These error codes are detailed in Appendix A.

Semaphore This! (An Application of the Bindery)

While the bindery can be used to track mundane information such as user definitions, there are other methods. Many applications written for NetWare, or with NetWare in mind, use semaphores to track usage. There are many downsides to the use of semaphores. For instance, they lack robustness—if a user who has locked onto a semaphore experiences an irregular shutdown (lockup) of the application, the semaphore isn't immediately released. Also, you can't directly track who is using a particular semaphore unless you assign

CONSOLE OPERATOR rights to all users of the application. Current versions (those prior to v2.1) of NetWare do not allow this. Obviously, this shortfall does not lend much to system security. Additionally, if a server comes down unexpectedly, it is impossible to determine which users were in applications that relied upon semaphores for tracking. Plus, using semaphores presents an extra load on the file server and its dynamic memory. There are ways to compensate for these weaknesses, but they aren't always optimal.

Instead of using the semaphore mechanism for tracking, use the bindery. Each time an application begins, the user's I.D. and logical station can be recorded in the bindery. You may include other information as your application dictates. And, when the application is done, the information can be removed. All this information is stored in a property of an object. The data is in a property because creating a new object requires Supervisor-level access, but writing/rewriting properties does not necessarily require those rights. In fact, the rights required to update a property's information are designated when the property is created.

At any time, a monitor application (or a monitoring feature of an application) can list out the other current users of an application. At this point, you may be wondering how the information will be deleted from the bindery if the user improperly exits the application. Fortunately, not only was the user's I.D. recorded, but so was the user's logical station. Use of Novell's Get Connection Information call (E3h sub 16h) will reveal if that user is still logged-in to the network.

Further, since it is possible that 15 minutes may elapse between the time of a lock up (where the machine freezes) and time that the server releases the connection (due to the file server's watchdog process), you can provide an alternative means of communication. This alternate means could also handle the unlikely situation that your application exits to the system without releasing the bindery information. Providing this alternate means of communication is IPX or SPX (ref: Internodal Communications section under IPX). Your application could maintain one open receive buffer as a means of application to application communication. And, based on the logical connection number stored in the bindery, a GetConnectionInformation call would yield the address to send an "are you alive" communication. This means of interprocess communication would further ensure that the current user information stored in the bindery is accurate.

To provide an "automatic" cleanup process, all the bindery information can be created as dynamic. Dynamic data is not permanently stored in the binderies, it is only present until it is specifically erased or the file server is rebooted. There is one drawback to the use of the dynamic property in that a Supervisor (or equivalent) user would have to create the initial bindery object because the process mandates Supervisor-level security.

A Little More About Properties

First a few words about properties. There are four types of properties, static item, dynamic item, static set, and dynamic set. The property type "item", whether static or dynamic represents a value that the bindery itself will not attempt to interpret. The difference between a static and dynamic item is its storage classification. Dynamic properties are transient, they are not stored permanently. Just like dynamic objects, dynamic properties only exist while the server is up. Once the server is rebooted, dynamic properties need to be reestablished. For instance, the list of servers seen when SLIST is performed are all dynamic objects. Interestingly, a static property can be added to a dynamic object, but, because the object is dynamic, the property disappears when the object is removed. Defining a property type as "set" indicates to the bindery that the values within are a list of (unique) object I.D.s (each is 4 bytes long). Lists of group members are stored in properties defined as of type "set". Whether a property is of type item or set it can have one or more segments. Each segment consists of a 128 byte "record". Beginning with 1 (not 0), each segment represents a field. And these segments can be read and written in any order.

Limitations of the Bindery: A Word of Warning

The bindery is stored as a flat file. There are no built-in measures to ensure speedy or coordinated access. Information stored in the bindery should be as succinct as possible and be worthy of storage in the bindery. If the bindery is cluttered with redundant or excessive data, overall network performance will suffer. A large bindery can slow many operations as the bindery is an often-used resource of NetWare.

When performing bindery updates, the programmer must decide upon the exclusion method. Use of an exclusion method would preserve the accuracy of data in the bindery and prevent such vagaries as partial updates and incomplete data. Exclusion methods can range from the use of a semaphore to a separate bindery object/property that is used to grant access by some predefined access agreement.

Finally, Hands-on

Now, let's step through creating an object, then adding a property. Then we will examine the means to manipulate that property.

```
{TURBO PASCAL v4.0}
Program Demo_Bindery;

Uses Dos;

Type

HalfRegType = record
                Al,Ah,Bl,Bh,Cl,Ch,Dl,Dh:byte
              end;  /* this is not truly necessary in Turbo Pascal */

MyWord      = record
                wh,wl : byte;
              end;
Longs       = record
                ah,al,bh,bl:byte;
              end;


PropCall    = record
                native  : MyWord;
                func    : Byte;        { func 0x3e }
                objtyp  : MyWord;
                objnamel : Byte;
                objname : array[1..512] of byte;
              end;
```

```
CreateCall = record
             native   : MyWord;
             func     : Byte;
             flags    : Byte;
             security : Byte;
             objtyp   : MyWord;
             objnamel : byte;
             objname  : array[1..48] of byte;
           end;

CreateRply = record
             native   : MyWord;
           end;

ReadPropertyc = record
                native : MyWord;
                func   : byte;
                objTyp : MyWord;
                objNmel: byte;
                objName: array[1..200] of byte;
              end;

ReadPropertyr = record
                native : MyWord;
                data   : array[1..128] of byte;
                more   : byte;
                flags  : byte;
              end;

{ now, some common variable definitions }
var
regs : Registers;  { innate to Turbo Pascal v4.0 and v5.0 }
hr   : HalfRegType absolute Regs;
sc   : CreateCall;
sr   : CreateRply;
pc   : PropCall;
rpc  : ReadPropertyc;
rpr  : ReadPropertyr;

a,b    : integer;
```

```
Procedure CheckSuccess;
Begin
{ this routine will look at the current value of hr.al {al} {part of AX
register) and determine proper message          }

If hr.al = 0 then        { if we can create the lock... }
Begin
   WriteLn('Operation successfully completed!');
End
ELSE { there was an error, print it out if a common one }
   Case hr.al of
   237: WriteLn('Property already exists');
   238: WriteLn('Object already exists');
   239: WriteLn('Object name contains illegal characters');
   240: WriteLn('Attempt to use wild cards in wrong place');
   245: WriteLn('No Object Creation or Change privileges');
   247: WriteLn('No Property Creation or Change privileges for object');
   248: WriteLn('No Write privileges for property');
   249: WriteLn('No Read privileges for property');
   251: WriteLn('No such Property');
   252: WriteLn('No such Object');
   253: WriteLn('Unknown bindery request');
   254: WriteLn('Bindery temporarily locked, try later');
   255: WriteLn('Unrecoverable/Unknown error');
   else WriteLn('Unknown error code: ',hr.al);
   end; {of case}


End; { of CheckSuccess }

Procedure CreateObject;

var
user : Longs;
Begin

   With sc do
```

```
Begin
     native.wh := $07;    { set up request packet size }
                          { note that this size will vary}
                          { with the length of the object}
                          { name                         }
     native.wl := $00;
  sr.native.wh := $FF;    { set up reply packet size    }
  sr.native.wl := $00;
          func := $32;    { create object    }
         flags := $01;    { dynamic          }
      security := $11;    { Write Security is most      }
                          { significant nybble of the   }
                          { security byte:              }
                          { 0=anyone, even if not       }
                          { logged in }
                          { 1=anyone logged in          }
                          { 2=any object or supervisor  }
                          { 3=only supervisors          }
                          { 4=bindery only              }
                          { Read Security is least      }
                          {significant nybble of the    }
                          {security byte:               }
                          { 0=anyone, even if not       }
                          { logged in }
                          { 1=anyone logged in          }
                          { 2=any object or supervisor  }
                          { 3=only supervisors          }
                          { 4=bindery only              }
 { thus security = 0x11 write/read by anyone logged in }
      objtyp.wh := $88;   { set up object type }
      objtyp.wl := $88;
      objnamel := 1;      { set up obj name length     }
                          { that follows               }
   objname[1] := 74;      { define a name "J", cute    }
                          { huh? 74=ASCII J            }
end;  { of with sc }

hr.ah := $E3;                 { 0xE3 is Novell's API code }
```

```
    With regs do
    Begin
          DS := seg(sc); { set up pointers to seg:ofs of }
                         { request packet                }
          SI := ofs(sc);
          ES := seg(sr); { set up pointers to seg:ofs of }
                         { reply packet                  }
          DI := ofs(sr);
    end;  { of regs }

    MsDos(regs);           { call DOS, try to create }

    CheckSuccess;

End;  { of CreateObject }

Procedure CreateProp;
Begin

{ note this only creates the property, no value has yet }
{ been established }

With pc do
Begin
     sr.native.wl := $00;
     sr.native.wh := $FF;

        native.wl := $00;
        native.wh :=  21+17; { 17 is length of the name, }
                             { the only variable         }
                             { in the length of the      }
                             { request packet            }
              Func := $39;   { add a property to an object }
          objtyp.wl := $88;
          objtyp.wh := $88;

        ObjNamel := 1;  { object name length }

      ObjName[1] := 74; { the name of "J" again }

    ObjName[1+1] := $00; { 00= Static Flag and an item }
                         { type object }
                         { 01= Dynamic Flag, the byte  }
                             { immediately }
```

```
                                 { 02= Static Flag an a set type }
                                     { object following the last      }
                                 { character of the name, hence  }
                                 { 1+1 for clarity only }
        ObjName[1+2]  := $11;{ Security, 11 = any logged in }
        ObjName[1+3]  := 14; { PropName Length                 }
        ObjName[1+4]  :=$49; { I }
        ObjName[1+5]  :=$44; { D }
        ObjName[1+6]  :=$45; { E }
        ObjName[1+7]  :=$4E; { N }
        ObjName[1+8]  :=$54; { T }
        ObjName[1+9]  :=$49; { I }
        ObjName[1+10]:=$46; { F }
        ObjName[1+11]:=$49; { I }
        ObjName[1+12]:=$43; { C }
        ObjName[1+13]:=$41; { A }
        ObjName[1+14]:=$54; { T }
        ObjName[1+15]:=$49; { I }
        ObjName[1+16]:=$4F; { O }
        ObjName[1+17]:=$4E; { N }

end; { of with pc }

with regs do
Begin
  AX:=$E300;

  ES:=Seg(sr);
  DI:=Ofs(sr);

  DS:=Seg(pc);
  SI:=Ofs(pc);

end; { of with regs }

  MsDos(regs);

  CheckSuccess;

End;   { of CreateProp }
```

```
Procedure WriteProp;
Begin

With pc do
Begin
    sr.native.wl := $00;
    sr.native.wh := $FF;
       native.wl := $00;
       native.wh :=  135+1+14; { fixed length + object }
                               { name + property name  }
                               { length }
             Func := $3E;{ Write a Property Value }
       objtyp.wl := $88;{ object type }
       objtyp.wh := $88;

         ObjNamel := 1;  { object name length }

       ObjName[1] := 74; { object name }

    ObjName[1+1] := 1;   { Segment Number }
    ObjName[1+2] := 0;   { More Flag, 0 = last segment, }
                         { any existing segments beyond }
                         {this one will be deleted       }

    ObjName[1+3] := 14; { PropName Length                }
    ObjName[1+4] :=$49; { I }
    ObjName[1+5] :=$44; { D }
    ObjName[1+6] :=$45; { E }
    ObjName[1+7] :=$4E; { N }
    ObjName[1+8] :=$54; { T }
    ObjName[1+9] :=$49; { I }
    ObjName[1+10]:=$46; { F }
    ObjName[1+11]:=$49; { I }
    ObjName[1+12]:=$43; { C }
    ObjName[1+13]:=$41; { A }
    ObjName[1+14]:=$54; { T }
    ObjName[1+15]:=$49; { I }
    ObjName[1+16]:=$4F; { O }
    ObjName[1+17]:=$4E; { N }

    For a:=1 to 128 do
       ObjName[1+17+a] := 0;  {Null it out, could fill }
                             { with any info }

  End; { of with sc }
```

```
With regs do Begin

  AX:=$E300;

  ES:=Seg(sr);
  DI:=Ofs(sr);

  DS:=Seg(pc);
  SI:=Ofs(pc);

End; { of with regs }

  MsDos(regs);

  CheckSuccess;

End;  { of WriteProp }


Procedure ReadProp;
Begin

with rpc do
Begin
        native.wh := 6+1+14; { 6=fixed, 1=object name, }
                                  { 14=property name }
        native.wl := $00;

        fillchar(rpr.data,sizeof(rpr.data),0);

    { ensure the reply buffer starts out as all nulls   }


    rpr.native.wh := 130;
    rpr.native.wl := $00;
             func := $3D; { Read a Property Value }
         objtyp.wl := $88;
         objtyp.wh := $88;
           objnmel := 1;
       objname[1] := 74;

     objname[1+1] := 1;  { Segment to read }
```

```
    ObjName[1+2]  := 14; { PropName Length                    }
    ObjName[1+3]  :=$49; { I }
    ObjName[1+4]  :=$44; { D }
    ObjName[1+5]  :=$45; { E }
    ObjName[1+6]  :=$4E; { N }
    ObjName[1+7]  :=$54; { T }
    ObjName[1+8]  :=$49; { I }
    ObjName[1+9]  :=$46; { F }
    ObjName[1+10]:=$49; { I }
    ObjName[1+11]:=$43; { C }
    ObjName[1+12]:=$41; { A }
    ObjName[1+13]:=$54; { T }
    ObjName[1+14]:=$49; { I }
    ObjName[1+15]:=$4F; { O }
    ObjName[1+16]:=$4E; { N }

End; { of with rpc }

With regs do
Begin
        AX    := $E300;
        DS    := Seg(rpc);
        SI    := Ofs(rpc);
        ES    := Seg(rpr);
        DI    := Ofs(rpr);
End;

MsDos(Regs);

CheckSuccess;

End;  { end of ReadProp }


Begin

CreateObject;
CreateProp;
WriteProp;
ReadProp;

End.
```

THE NETWARE PROGRAMMER'S GUIDE

Accessing the Bindery Using the C Interface

As our next example, let's look at two functions that you can use in your application's NetWare install program. We will assume that the user who will be running this program is logged in as the network Supervisor or equivalent. A Supervisor or equivalent level is required because NetWare permits only Supervisors to create, delete, or rename bindery objects.

The first function of this program, MakeGroup, will attempt to create a new group called MY_APP_USERS. The information in this group object can be written to only by a Supervisor, but may be read by any user who is logged in. If the group already exists, the function will simply return as if the create operation was performed successfully. The second function of this program, AddUser, will add a user to the new group's GROUP_MEMBERS set property. A set property is used to contain a set of user IDs.

This function, Makegroup, attempts to create the group denoted by the parameter GroupName. If the group already exists, the function exits normally. Otherwise, the security level for the group is set so that Supervisors may write to it, and users that are logged in may read it. The #define'd constants used in this example are in the file nwbindry.h.

```
/* MakeGroup

Parameters: char *GroupName - Name of group to create

Returns: 0 == Success, !0 == Fail/NetWare error code
*/
int MakeGroup(char *GroupName)
{
 int    Result;                 /* Result of function */
 int    Temp;                   /* Temporary result */
 long   ObjectID;               /* Object's bindery ID */
 char   ObjectName[48];         /* Object name */
 WORD   ObjectType;             /* Type of returned object */
 char   ObjectHasProperties;    /* 255 = Object has properties */
 char   ObjectFlag;             /* Is object permanent or temporary */
 char   ObjectSecurity;         /* Object's read/write attribute */

 /* Attempt to create a new object */
 Result = CreateBinderyObject(GroupName,
```

```
OT_USER_GROUP,                        /* Object is a group of users */
BF_STATIC,                            /* This is a permanent object */
BS_LOGGED_READ | BS_SUPER_WRITE);     /* Object security */
if (Result == SUCCESSFUL)             /* Object created OK */
                        {

 /* Now add 'GROUP_MEMBERS' property */

 Result = CreateProperty(GroupName,OT_USER_GROUP,

  "GROUP_MEMBERS",                    /* "Well-known" property name */
  BF_DYNAMIC | BF_SET,                /* Permanent set property */
  BS_LOGGED_READ | BS_SUPER_WRITE);   /* Security */
  if (Result != SUCCESSFUL)           /* CreateProperty failed */
                        {

  /* Remove the bindery object */

  Temp = DeleteBinderyObject(GroupName, OT_USER_GROUP);
  }
} else
        if (Result == OBJECT_ALREADY_EXISTS)    /* Ignore error */
 Result = 0;
 return(Result);
}
```

The function Adduser is responsible for adding members of UserName to GroupName. If the user is already a member of this group, the function will return with a result indicating success. Once added to the group, the group must then be added to the user's GROUPS_I'M_IN property and the SECURITY_EQUALS property.

```
/* AddUser

Parameters: char *GroupName - Group to which user will be added
            char *UserID - User name to add to group

Returns: 0 == Success, !0 == Fail/NetWare error code
*/
int AddUser(char *GroupName, char *UserName)
{
 int Result;      /* Holds function result */
```

```
/* Add user to the group */
Result = AddBinderyObjectToSet(GroupName,OT_USER_GROUP,
  "GROUP_MEMBERS",UserName,OT_USER);

if (Result == SUCCESSFUL) {      /* User was added to group */

 /* Add group ID to user's "GROUPS_I'M_IN" property */
 Result = AddBinderyObjectToSet(UserName,OT_USER,
  "GROUPS_I\'M_IN",GroupName,OT_USER_GROUP);

 if (Result == SUCCESSFUL) {     /* Group was added to user */

  /* Now make security equivalent to the group */
  Result = addBinderyObjectToSet(UserName,OT_USER,
         "SECURITY_EQUALS",GroupName,OT_USER_GROUP);

  if (Result != SUCCESSFUL) {    /* Group NOT added */

   /* Remove group from user and visa-versa */
   TempResult = DeleteBinderyObjectFromSet(UserName,
    OT_USER,"GROUPS_I\'M_IN",GroupName,OT_USER_GROUP);
   TempResult = DeleteBinderyObjectFromSet(GroupName,
    OT_USER_GROUP,"GROUP_MEMBERS",UserName,OT_USER);
  }
 }
 else
 {       /* Could not add group to user */

  /* Remove user from group */
  TempResult = DeleteBinderyObjectFromSet(GroupName,OT_USER_GROUP,
   "GROUP_MEMBERS",UserName,OT_USER);
 }
}if (Result == MEMBER_ALREADY_EXISTS)   /* Ignore error */
else
 Result = 0;
 return(Result);
}
```

In this next example, there are two functions that you can use within your application to verify if this user is allowed to perform a certain function. The first function, GetFullName, is used to return the user's full name, and the second function, IsMember, will determine if this user is a member of a specific group.

GetFullName scans the bindery for this user object's IDENTIFICATION property. If found, the value of this item property is returned.

```
/* GetFullName

Parameters: char *UserName - The login name of a user
 char *FullName - The full name of this user (Must hold up to 128
bytes)

Returns: 0 == Success, !0 == Failure
*/
int GetFullName(char *UserName, char *FullName)
{
 BYTE MoreSegments;      /* Indicates if more segments exist */
 BYTE PropertyFlags;     /* Contains property's attributes */

 return(ReadPropertyValue(UserName,OT_USER,"IDENTIFICATION",
   1,FullName,&MoreSegments,&PropertyFlags));
}
```

This function determines if the passed-in user name is a member of the group defined by the GroupName parameter.

```
/* IsMember

Parameters: char *GroupName - Name of the group to check
 char *UserName  - User name to check for

Returns: 1 = TRUE, 0 = FALSE
*/
int IsMember(char *GroupName, char *UserName)
{
 int Result;  /* Holds function result */

 /* Determine if the user is a member of this group */
 Result = IsBinderyObjectInSet(GroupName,OT_USER_GROUP,"GROUP_MEMBERS",
   UserName,OT_USER);
 return(Result == SUCCESSFUL ? 1 : 0);
}
```

The following procedure is in Turbo Pascal (v4.0 or v5.0). It represents the basics of dealing with bindery objects on a Novell network. The entire program that the following code is excerpted is in Appendix A.

```
(***************%%%%%%%%%%%%%%BUILD USER%%%%%%%%%%%%%%%%%%%%%%%*)
Procedure BldUser;
Begin
{  This Procedure is used to create a User, assign a password, copy a
   login script to the new user's mailbox directory and assign group
   membership to a specified group
}

{  The following is the format of the sc and sr structures used below
  SecretCall  = record
                Native    : Word;
                Func      : Byte;
                Flags     : Byte;
                security  : Byte;
                objtyp    : WORD;
                objnamel  : byte;
                objname   : array [1..48] of byte;
             end;

  SecretRply = record
                Native    : Word;
             end;

    Username to create,
    Password,
    WHOSE LOGIN SCRIPT to COPY,
    Group to belong to,
}

With Regs do begin
  With HR do begin
  With sc do begin

  sR.Native.Wl:=$00;
  sR.Native.WH:=$FF;

    Native.Wl:=  $00;
```

```
    Func :=        $32;
    Flags:=        $00;
    Security:=     $00;

    OBJTYP.WL:=$01; {USER type}
    OBJTYP.WH:=$00;

    ObjNamel:=    ord( e[1][0] );
    for a:=1 to ObjNamel do
      ObjName[a] :=     ord( e[1][a]); {CREATE NAME}

    Native.WH:=  6+objNamel;

    END; { OF WITH PC }

  AX:=$E300;

  ES:=Seg(sr);
  DI:=Ofs(sr);

  DS:=Seg(sc);
  SI:=Ofs(sc);
  MSDOS(REGS);
{  writeln('AFTER THE CREATE [',hr.al,']');{}
{was it ok?}
if hr.al<>0 then writeln('Unable to create user ',e[1])
else
BEGIN

  nr.Native.Wl:=$00;
  nr.Native.WH:=$FF;

  gc.Native.Wl:=  $00;
  gc.Native.WH:=  $FF;

  gc.Func :=       $35;

  gc.OBJTYP.WL:=$01; {USER type}
  gc.OBJTYP.WH:=$00;

  gc.Namel:=    ord( e[1][0] );
    for a:=1 to gc.Namel do
      gc.ObjName[a] :=     ord( e[1][a]); {CREATE NAME}
    AX:=$E300;
```

```
   ES:=Seg(nr);
   DI:=Ofs(nr);

   DS:=Seg(gc);
   SI:=Ofs(gc);
   MSDOS(REGS);
{   writeln('AFTER THE GET ID [',hr.al,']');{}
{was it ok?}
if hr.al = 0 then
begin
   Script; {make the mail sub dir}

  (* NOW, the USER TO COPY LOGIN SCRIPT *)

   gc.Namel:=    ord( e[3][0] );
     for a:=1 to gc.Namel do
       gc.ObjName[a] :=    ord( e[3][a]); {COPY NAME}

   AX:=$E300;

   ES:=Seg(nr);
   DI:=Ofs(nr);

   DS:=Seg(gc);
   SI:=Ofs(gc);
   MSDOS(REGS);
 {  writeln('AFTER THE GET COPY ID [',hr.al,']');{}
{was it ok?}
     if hr.al=0 then COPY_SCRIPT;

   AddPwd;

end;
end;
end;

END;

End;{BLDUSER}
```

CHAPTER 3

Btrieve

Two of the most common requirements for network-aware applications are that they prevent unauthorized access to data and that they protect the data from multiple simultaneous updates. Generally, the primary reason for both requirements is to prevent the accidental corruption of data. Specifically, the reason for the first requirement, which seems obvious enough, is to prevent access to sensitive data and to prevent users from mistakenly tapping into someone else's files in another directory with the same name. The reason for the second requirement is that if two users update the same record in a database at the same time, one user's revisions may overwrite another's. NetWare provides several different features to allow and coordinate access to data by multiple users, but the best one is Btrieve.

What is Btrieve?

Btrieve is a set of database management APIs that enable applications to create and manipulate information databases with a consistent, open interface. In lieu of writing database access mechanisms directly, an application makes calls to Btrieve's APIs. The Btrieve APIs then hand off the calls to the Btrieve engine which provides the actual file management services.

There are at least three distinct advantages to using Btrieve:

- Greater application independence
- Less network overhead
- Fewer database access issues

Your application will be free to run with different versions of Btrieve without modification. Remember that Btrieve operates in stand-alone and networked environments. That's right, there is no need to recompile any of your application for it to work with a different Btrieve environment. However, other issues may come into play, including how to handle different error codes for different Btrieve implementations. Because Btrieve uses the same, consistent

API interface, applications need only focus on their Btrieve API needs, regardless of which Btrieve version is used.

In the NetWare environment, the Btrieve VAP or NLM reduce network traffic because the Btrieve VAP/NLM does much of the processing at the file server(s) and does not send unnecessary data to the workstations. For instance, if a workstation does a query for all records where the name field is equal to "SMITH," the workstation will only receive records that fit this criteria. Without the Btrieve VAP/NLM the workstation would receive all database records and the local instance of Btrieve do the qualifying of data to be passed back to the application.

Just by implementing the Btrieve VAP/NLM your Btrieve application will most likely note an increase in performance. Also, at the local workstations, the Btrieve TSR is smaller with the VAP/NLM than the Btrieve TSR when it is used without the VAP/NLM.

Because Btrieve handles all aspects of database file management, the application will not be concerned with low-level file management issues. For instance, Btrieve handles such issues as maintenance, manipulation, synchronization and storage of the database file(s). Naturally this frees time for more focused application development.

See Chapter 8, NLMs, for an example of how to create a Btrieve file within an NLM. This creation of a file within an NLM is very similiar to that under DOS.

More on Btrieve

Very simply, Btrieve is a record manager. Btrieve manages the storage and retrieval of records in a database file so programmers don't have to; it acts like a buffer between an application program and the file on the physical disk. As programmers grow more experienced with Btrieve, developing personal libraries of code which can be re-used from project to project, they will find it almost as easy to do database work with a relatively "low-level" language, such as C, as with a "high-level" language, such as dBase III Plus.

Except for some early (circa 1983) "buggy" releases, Btrieve has always been an excellent multi-user record manager. Although Btrieve is fast, its real claim to fame is that it was the first fault tolerant record manager for DOS language compilers; that is, it was the first to offer transaction tracking and pre-imaging capabilities. In fact, Btrieve was doing "fault tolerant" database management and "transaction tracking" long before Novell made the terms popular.

Using Btrieve

The easiest method for protecting your application from the problem of simultaneous access is to use a database access method that provides this kind of functionality. Novell, through its Development Products Division, offers a series of products based around Btrieve. Btrieve is a balanced B-tree based access method with network versions that run in many environments. But, there are versions specifically created and optimized for NetWare. These optimized versions are called the Btrieve VAP (Value Added Process) for NetWare 286 v2.1x, and the Btrieve NLM (NetWare Loadable Module) for NetWare 386 v3.x. When loaded, these versions add the functionality of a high speed database server to your network. The main advantages that Btrieve provides are speed, and data integrity in the form of Transaction Tracking—a feature inherent in the NetWare 286 and 386 operating systems. From a programmer's perspective, using Btrieve makes multi-user file access a straightforward process, through a direct set of function calls to the Btrieve interface.

Using DOS 3.1 Functions

A second approach for coordinating data access is to add function calls in your application to the DOS 3.1 interface for file and record locking. This method, although easy, is much less flexible than using NetWare functions, which we will discuss subsequently. Basically, DOS network functions allow you to use the INT 21 interface to open a file in shared or exclusive mode, and then for read-only, write-only, or read/write access. Once open, if the file is in shared mode, any range of bytes within the file may be blocked from access by another application or user on the network. The main drawback of this method is that DOS won't allow any other application to read a locked byte range, even if you are in shared mode. This situation could make it very difficult to convert report and inquiry programs that might be allowed to print or display a record even if it is locked by another workstation.

Using NetWare Functions

A third approach for coordinating data access is to design your application to directly access NetWare's file, record, and transaction protection mechanisms. Although a little more involved than the DOS 3.1 functions, NetWare's function calls lend your application the ability to completely control the level of resource sharing between your users and the files they need to access. The NetWare functions provide synchronized access to data under the categories of file locks, physical record locks, and logical record locks. Logical records represent a name for a record, versus a physical record's file handle (a 2-byte identifier), position, and length.

There are two parts to data protection provided by NetWare. First, NetWare uses the concept of sets to allow your application to partially implement explicit (like TTS's explicit actions) transactions. With respect to sets, you log one or more files/records into a set, and then either lock, release (unlock), or clear the files/records from the set. By using sets, NetWare allows the application to individually specify the characteristics of the lock(s) before actually placing them. When you actually perform the lock, either all of the members of the set must be lockable, or none will be locked. In this way, you are guaranteed that all of the data resources for a particular "transaction" are available before proceeding.

The second part of data protection provided by NetWare is a mechanism called the Transaction Tracking System (TTS), which records your changes in a separate area until they have been completed or aborted. That way, if the file server or a user's workstation crashes in the middle of a transaction, TTS "backs out" any transactions that were in progress at the time of the crash. In the case of a file server crash, when the file server comes back up with TTS enabled, you will be prompted as to whether the transactions should be rolled back. In the case of a workstation crash, when you re-login, or when the workstation is automatically logged out via NetWare's Watchdog process, any incomplete transactions will be rolled back. Thus, TTS places the files in a known state and assures that any index blocks were not partially updated.

TTS may also be used implicitly by flagging a file as transactional. But it is very simple to add transactional calls to your program, and this method provides a more tailored approach to your application's data integrity requirements. If you do have files that are flagged as transactional, they should *not* be manipulated by your program with NetWare's TTS function calls. This caution is to prevent any conflict with transactions that NetWare might be performing without your knowledge.

In order to clarify the concept of sets and transactions, the following code will use the logical lock mechanisms and TTS of NetWare. The basic logic of this code fragment is to:

1) Log a set of record names
2) Start the transaction
3) Lock the set of logical records
4) Perform updates to the files
5) Monitor the transaction until complete

At this time the records will be automatically unlocked. One of the advantages of using NetWare's logical locking is that a file's data is always available to be read by your applications. So that, if required, a report or inquiry program can still access the data while it is locked pending a change.

```
/* Example of using NetWare Synchronization and TTS calls */

int Result;
long TransactionID;

/* Add names to this workstation's logical record set */
if (((Result = LogLogicalRecord("CUSTOMER HEADER",0,0)) == SUCCESSFUL)
&&
  ((Result = LogLogicalRecord("SMITH, JOHN M.",0,0)) == SUCCESSFUL) &&
  ((Result = LogLogicalRecord("ORDER ENTRY HEADER",0,0)) == SUCCESSFUL))
  {
```

```
/* Start the transaction */
if ((Result = TTSBeginTransaction()) == SUCCESSFUL)
{

/*  Explicitly lock the logical records, try for 18 clock ticks
    (approximately 1 second).  You may need to experiment with this
    value depending on the amount of concurrent access to this file.*/
if ((Result = LockLogicalRecordSet(18)) == SUCCESSFUL)
{

  /* do some file I/O here */

if (Result == 0)
{      /* File I/O worked */

/* End transaction, and wait for physical completion */
Result = TTSEndTransaction(&TransactionID);
while (TTSTransactionStatus(TransactionID) ==
  TRANSACTION_NOT_YET_WRITTEN)
  ;

}
else {      /* File I/O failed  */

TSSAbortTransaction();
ClearLogicalRecordSet();   /* Remove logical locks */
printf("\nI/O FAILED. ERROR CODE: %d\n",Result);
}

}
else
{      /* Could not begin transaction */

TSSAbortTransaction();
ClearLogicalRecordSet();    /* Remove logical record locks */
printf("\nCOULD NOT LOCK. ERROR CODE: %d\n",Result);
}

}
else
{      /* Could not begin transaction */

ClearLogicalRecordSet();    /* Remove logical record locks */
printf("\nCOULD NOT BEGIN TRANSACTION. ERROR CODE:
%d\n",Result);
```

```
    }

} else {          /* Error locking records */

ClearLogicalRecordSet();      /* Remove any that were successful */
printf("\nCOULD NOT LOG RECORDS. ERROR CODE: %d\n",Result);
}
```

Btrieve Features

In addition to fault tolerance and transaction tracking, other key features of Btrieve include flexible indexing, large capacity, and multi-user security.

Btrieve's flexible indexing capability allows it to have up to 24 different indexes, or keys, per file and 14 different data types for key values. Keys can be made up of virtually any combination of different fields, called segmented keys. Separate index files can optionally be created and dropped on the fly, called supplemental indexes.

Btrieve's large capacity allows for files up to 4 billion bytes. There is no other limit on the number of records, and files can span physical disk drives (only two). Variable length records and data compression are also supported.

Through Btrieve's multi-user security, single and multiple record locks are supported. In addition, a "conflict error" is supported which notifies the application if the record being updated has been changed by another user since it was last read. A file can be given an "Owner name," so that only applications or users who know the Owner name can access the file. In addition, dynamic encryption and decryption is available, at a performance cost, using the Owner name as the encryption key.

Many of these important features must be "turned on" by the application that creates them. Although Btrieve is a very robust record manager, it is up to the programmer to make use of its features. This need for programmer knowledge makes some Btrieve applications more resilient and secure than others. Regretfully, many are probably less resilient than they could be. For example, most applications do not explicitly take advantage of the transaction tracking capabilities of Btrieve. Also, few of the third-party Btrieve application programs which are currently available allow the user to fine tune the security options that Btrieve can provide (such as Magic PC by AKER/Magic PC).

How Does Btrieve Work?

Every Btrieve data file is self-contained; no other configuration or index files are required. Although some types of supplemental files are optionally available, such as supplemental index files, they are not frequently used.

Each file contains a "header page," called the File Control Header (FCH), which contains information about the file. The FCH is followed by "index pages" and "data pages." Index pages contain lists of key values and record addresses. The record address of a particular key is the physical address within the data pages where the record with that key value exists. These indexes are kept in the form of B-trees; separate B-trees exist for each key defined for the file. Using the B-tree data structure, any record in a file can be accessed almost instantly by any one of its keys.

Every Btrieve file is created with a fixed page size. The header page, all index pages, and all data pages within the file are of the same fixed length, from 512 to 4096 bytes. Depending on the size of each record and the number (and types) of keys that the file has, a programmer can determine the optimal page size required to maximize disk space utilization and access speed. A well-written Btrieve application will probably use several files with different page sizes.

Fault Tolerance

For every Btrieve file, a file with the same name but with an extension of .PRE is created. Btrieve uses these pre-image files as scratch files while it is in the middle of updating records. In case of a system fault or power failure, Btrieve can use the pre-image file to restore lost data. If your application program uses transaction tracking, an additional file with the default name of BTRIEVE.TRN will be created. With transaction tracking, not only can Btrieve restore lost data but it can also roll back incomplete transactions from data files which may be left in an inconsistent state. If a Btrieve file is opened in accelerated mode, pre-imaging is turned off.

For example, suppose a user accidentally reboots his or her PC or loses power in the middle of posting data from a Payroll file to a General Ledger file. What if a Payroll record has been sent over to the General Ledger but has not yet been removed from the Payroll file? How would the LAN administrator know? By specifying BEGIN and END TRANSACTION calls within a Btrieve application, transactions can be tracked and rolled back.

LANs using any version of SFT NetWare allow use of the Transaction Tracking System (TTS) at the file server, in which case a BTRIEVE.TRN file will be created on SYS:SYSTEM. Rather than the Btrieve record manager handling the overhead of transaction tracking, NetWare will do it. The specific Btrieve data file must be flagged "transactional" with the FLAG command to let the operating system know to use TTS on it. With TTS enabled in this way, pre-image (.PRE) files will not be created, since NetWare (not Btrieve) handles file integrity for transactional files.

The Btrieve Record Manager

The Btrieve record manager is the communications agent between an application and the file system, e.g., DOS or NetWare. There are three different kinds of the Btrieve record manager: The Btrieve VAP, which comes with NetWare, versions 2.1 and newer, Btrieve NLM for NetWare 3.x, and Btrieve for DOS 3.1 Networks, which is delivered with most Btrieve applications. These Btrieve options have gone through different versions, each with their own peculiarities. As you can imagine, the possibility of different versions and different kinds of Btrieve on the same file server can often result in complex troubleshooting situations.

A traditional DOS 3.1 Btrieve application works in the following way. The Btrieve record manager, called BTRIEVEN.EXE is loaded as a terminate-and-stay-resident program (TSR) in the workstation. This TSR can occupy 100KB of RAM or more, depending upon the parameters used when Btrieve is invoked.

The user application communicates with the Btrieve record manager. When accessing files on a local hard disk, DOS manages the data transfer between the record manager and the physical disk. However, when accessing files on a network file server, the NetWare shell (in the user's PC) and the NetWare operating system (in the file server) team up to manage the data transfer between the record manager and the physical disk.

In either case, Btrieve adds a level of functionality that makes the task of program I/O activities much simpler. A single logical request from the user application, such as inserting a new record, may result in many separate update operations that the record manager must make on the file. Not only does the actual record have to be inserted into a data page, but many index pages probably have to be updated to reflect the new B-tree structure.

Figure 3-1 shows how the Btrieve VAP works. A program called BREQUEST is loaded in the workstation, instead of the regular BTRIEVEN program. The Btrieve VAP/NLM, called BSERVER, must beloaded in the file server. Together, BREQUEST and BSERVER make up the Btrieve record manager. The workstation or "client" portion of the VAP can be much smaller than BTRIEVEN—usually about 35KB—since the VAP does much of the work.

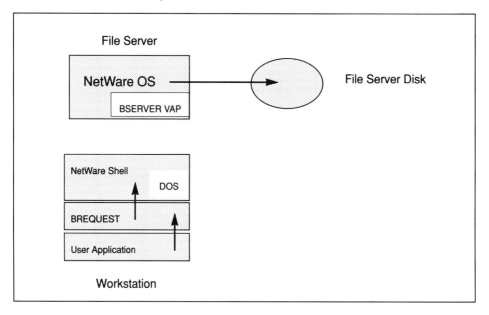

Figure 3-1. Schematic of an Application Using the Btrieve VAP

Just as with BTRIEVEN, one logical request may result in many separate operations, but BSERVER can handle those inside the file server. This approach reduces network traffic and creates the potential for faster response times on inserts and updates.

The NetWare Btrieve VAP/NLM and the Btrieve for DOS 3.1 Networks program can also work together. There are a couple words of caution, however, when using this mix-and-match approach. BREQUEST cannot access Btrieve files on NetWare version 2.0 file servers. Second, BREQUEST cannot access Btrieve files on file servers that do not have the Btrieve VAP/NLM active. Third, BTRIEVEN, but not BREQUEST, can access Btrieve files on local hard disks.

Based on these different options for using the Btrieve record manager, some additional tips for LAN-based Btrieve applications include the following:

1) Do not delete any .PRE or BTRIEVE.TRN files manually. You may compromise the integrity of your database by doing so.
2) Do not flag Btrieve data files "shareable." Btrieve data files should be FLAGged "Non-shareable Read/Write."
3) Do not flag Btrieve data files "transactional" on networks using the Btrieve record manager for DOS 3.1 Networks. BTRIEVEN will interpret the lock that NetWare's TTS puts on the file as an I/O error when other users try to access the file during a transaction.

Using the Btrieve VAP

With version 2.1, Novell began shipping the Btrieve VAP "in the box" as a value-added component of the operating system. In general, the VAP-based Btrieve does not provide much faster response to an interactive user than the regular BTRIEVEN. This response issue, of course, depends on data file indexes, file server and workstation speeds, and the location of the bottlenecks on a LAN. As NetWare file servers get faster, especially with the advent of NetWare 386, the file server-based Btrieve record manager will make a much more noticeable improvement on performance at the workstation.

Most of the problems with the Btrieve VAP have been resolved in the latest patches from Novell, but some rare errors still exist that can bring your server down.

There are some very good reasons for using the Btrieve VAP. First, the Btrieve for DOS 3.1 Networks program cannot maintain transaction integrity if your file server crashes, while SFT NetWare with TTS enabled can. Second, the Btrieve VAP has a much lower memory overhead at the workstation than the regular Btrieve record manager for DOS 3.1 Networks. Third, some software conflicts with BTRIEVEN, but not with BREQUEST. Fourth, when accessing Btrieve data files over a wide area network or low-speed transmission line, network overhead is cut nearly in half by using TTS on SFT NetWare servers since this method eliminates the need for pre-image files.

BROUTER

BROUTER is a Btrieve VAP which is required for other VAPs to communicate with BSERVER. BROUTER is to other VAPs what BREQUEST is to workstation-based application software.

Depending on these configuration parameters, Btrieve can take from 64KB up to 100KB or more of RAM. Btrieve will automatically use expanded memory, taking up only about 45KB of DOS RAM.

The /p parameter for setting page sizes can cause problems on networks running more than one Btrieve application. Suppose the batch file for one program loads Btrieve with a /p:2048, but does not remove Btrieve when it finishes. Another program may require /p:4096, but when it tries to load Btrieve it will get a "Program already loaded" system message, and the existing /p:2048 parameter will still be in effect. The application may proceed, thinking that it has invoked Btrieve itself, but when it tries to access a file with a page size greater than 2048 bytes, a page size error (error 24) is generated.

Some Btrieve applications are now designed to load Btrieve when they begin, and remove Btrieve when they quit. You may not even know which applications are using Btrieve. Most, however, load Btrieve in a batch file before the main program is called, but some do not remove Btrieve when they are done.

This can cause error messages, like the page size error just discussed, especially when multiple Btrieve applications are being run on the same file server.

In addition, running different versions of Btrieve can cause problems. However, do not delete the Btrieve programs that come with your application software. Instead, rename them using the DOS REN command, e.g., from BTRIEVEN.EXE to BTRIEVEN.OLD. To prevent running into conflicts between new versions of Btrieve and your old applications, you should retain the versions of Btrieve that come with the application software.

Sometimes, software vendors rename BTRIEVEN.EXE to BTRIEVE.EXE to make things appear simpler to network administrators. In any case, the load time message will tell you exactly what version you are running.

Other Btrieve Enhancement Products

In addition to the Btrieve programs, either the VAP or DOS networks version, Novell provides other programs that perform useful functions with Btrieve files. Two of these programs are the Btrieve Function Executor and Xtrieve.

The Btrieve Function Executor (B.EXE) is a program that comes on the Btrieve VAP diskettes with NetWare v2.1x and with NetWare 386. It is designed to help application developers debug and test Btrieve function calls.

Xtrieve is a Btrieve application from Novell that lets LAN administrators view, modify, and print data in Btrieve files. How a file is created affects what can be done with Xtrieve. For example, if a key for a file was not explicitly specified as modifiable when the file was created, you will not be able to change the key value with Xtrieve. If you try, you will get a duplicate key error message (error 5).

In terms of speed and data integrity, the Btrieve record manager is probably the best record manager available for use in Novell LAN environments.

Btrieve's Accelerated Mode and Inserting into Multiple Files

Accelerated Mode is called accelerated because pre-imaging is not done of Btrieve's data files. This behavior can serve to destroy your files' integrity. The purpose of opening a file in accelerated mode is to enhance performance on UPDATE, DELETE and INSERT operations. However, using accelerated mode to alternately insert data into multiple files can degrade performance. If you need to insert data into serveral files using accelerated mode, the preferred method is to finish inserting all records into one file, then start inserting into another file. Why? When a file is open in accelerated mode, Btrieve does not write file pages to the disk until the cache is full and the Least Recently Used algorithm selects a buffer to be overlaid. However, Btrieve's cache buffer contains data for only one file at a time. If you insert one record into another file, Btrieve needs to flush the cache buffers after inserting into each file, whether the buffers are full or not. This causes performance degradation and defeats the speed advantages of using accelerated mode.

Loading Btrieve Within Your Application

As discussed earlier, the Btrieve interface is a TSR. To use it, you must load the Btrieve interface into memory. This can be done before your application executes as well as during your application's execution.

When an application loads Btrieve from within, Btrieve will be loaded into an area of memory above the application. When the application exists and does not unload Btrieve, DOS releases the memory for the application. But, the memory freed cannot be used because DOS, by default, only uses contiguous memory that is found through the end of memory. And, because Btrieve is still in memory, and the application did not unload it, there is a hole in memory "under" Btrieve. Found "over" Btrieve in memory is the area of contiguous memory that DOS will use. Because of this hole in memory there is a loss of potential memory, specifically the amount of memory your application was using.

To remedy this hole in memory situation of loading Btrieve within an application and then exiting the application without unloading Btrieve, simply remember to unload Btrieve before your application exists. Provided by the

Btrieve interface is operation code 25. Executing operation 25 will cause Btrieve to free itself from memory.

Here are some explanations of under-described Btrieve statuses.

BTRIEVE STATUS 14

Usually Btrieve creates the pre-image file on the same logical drive as the file being pre-imaged. Except for Btrieve for Xenix and Btrieve for NetWare, all versions of Btrieve allow the redirecting of the pre-image file with the /I option. When the load time option /I is used, the logical drive to which you are redirecting the pre-image file needs to contain the same directory structure, including directory names as the logical drive where the actual Btrieve file resides. For instance, if the Btrieve file is found in the path J:\BTRIEVE and the /I option is specified as /I:K then drive K: must have the same path, that is, K:\BTRIEVE. If this is not true then Btrieve will return a status 14 when the preimage file is created or opened.

BTRIEVE STATUS 78

Introduced with Btrieve version 5.0 is status 78. The situation indicated by a status 78 is a deadlock. As found in Chapter 2 of the Btrieve manual, a deadlock occurs when two or more applications, likely running at different nodes, attempt to place a hold on the same set of records. If there were only one record being locked, then there cannot be a deadlock. But with more than one record where records are not locked by an all-or-nothing approach, it is possible to achieve a deadlock situation, as shown in Figure 3-2 on the following page.

1)   Thread A locks Data 1

2)   Thread A is put to sleep

3)   Thread B is awakened

4)   Thread B locks Data 2

5)   Thread B attempts to Lock Data 1, it cannot so it falls asleep

6)   Thread A is awakened

7)   Thread A attempts to lock Data 2, it cannot so it falls asleep

8)   Thread B is awakened

9)   Thread B attempts to lock Data 1, it cannot so it falls asleep

10) Repeat *ad infinitum* from Step 6

Figure 3-2. A Processing Deadlock

Here is why a status 78 can occur when only one node is accessing a file and why deadlock detection cannot be implemented with other versions of Btrieve.

Generally a deadlock situation in a network environment conjures thoughts of more than one node holding resources that other nodes are waiting for, and, in turn, those holding nodes are waiting for resources held by other nodes. In the NetWare environment an application can receive a status 78 even when only one node is in use. For instance, the following actions lead to a status 78:

OPEN a file
READ a record that you locked
BEGIN TRANSACTION
OPEN that same file

When an OPEN operation occurs inside the transaction, a file level lock is attempted on the file. But because the prior READ operation before the BEGIN TRANSACTION had a previous record level lock within the same file, that node will sit and wait for this record lock to be removed. However, since that node is the same that has the lock and is requesting a new lock, it will sit and wait forever—resulting in a status 78.

Because Btrieve version 5.0 has a centralized control system at the file server (NetWare only) that keeps track of who has a file open and who is waiting for what. With this centralized control, the Btrieve VAP or NLM "knows" all and is able to detect a deadlock. All previous versions such as Btrieve for DOS 3.1 Networks have no centralized control as Btrieve is loaded at each node. With the Btrieve VAP/NLM nodes load a Btrieve Requestor, they do not load the total Btrieve engine, just the interface. From there the Btrieve Requestor sends application requests to the file server for processing.

BTRIEVE STATUS 80

Returned during a Btrieve Update or Delete operation is the conflict status 80. The Btrieve manual states that it is caused by another station modifying the record since your station last read it. If you are using Btrieve for DOS 3.1 Network, it could also be caused by another station modifying another record that is on the same data page as your record.

Btrieve keeps a usage count on every page. Before an Update operation, it compares the usage count on its copy of the data page to the usage count on the disk copy. If the counts do not match, Btrieve knows that someone has changed the page, but cannot tell which record on the page has been changed. Thus Btrieve returns a status 80 to alert the application to reread the page.

Two common workarounds can prevent your application from rereading the record every time a status 80 is received. The first is to keep a dummy data buffer. Where the status 80 happens, the application rereads the record and compares the two buffers. If they match, then another Update operation is issued. If not, then a true status 80 is returned and the application is asked to reread the record.

The second workaround is to apply a record level lock, either a no wait or wait lock, on the Read operation. When the usage count on the page has been changed, Btrieve still executes the Update operation, because no one else can update a record that you have locked.

The fewer records per page, the lower the chance of a station 80 occuring. Thus, decreasing the page size can help circumvent status 80. But, remember that to maximize disk space utilitization, the optimal page size should have the least amount of unused space.

Finally, there are two possible reasons for a status 80. Either another station has updated your record or if you are using Btrieve for DOS 3.1 Networks, another station has updated another record on the same page. Your application can either reread the record and issue a second update, or apply a record level lock when you first read the record.

CHAPTER 4

Queue Considerations

NetWare's Queue Management System

Starting with NetWare v2.1, Novell introduced its Queue Management System, or, QMS. QMS is an evolutionary step in Novell's queue mechanism scheme. This same queue system has found its way into NetWare v3.x. As you discover the particulars of NetWare's QMS you will find it has a wide range of applications.

NetWare's QMS allows for queueing of data regardless of the data's type. This means data placed in a queue does not have to be destined for a printer (or plotter). Rather, due to the truly asynchronous interface of QMS, a server may be a printer server (just as with the previous queue system) but now, due to the queue methods of QMS, a server may be a batch-processing server or an archiving server or whatever. This is all possible because QMS makes available, for the first time in NetWare's history, a queueing system that allows user applications access from the front end (submittal of data) and from the back end (processing of that data). With the previous queue system, users could only submit data to the print queues and the server operating system performed all processing of the queue data.

The queue system's responsibility is to reliably gather data from clients (users of the queue system) and place it in the proper queue. The queue is a transitory place (residing at a NetWare server on disk) which stores client submissions (jobs) until they can be processed (serviced) by a queue server. Data is sent to a queue via one of many different mechanisms. You can submit queue jobs by redirecting one of the local LPT printer ports or by sending an entire file (NPRINTing). With QMS, up to three LPT ports can be set up to concurrently capture queue data. For instance, LPT1 could capture data bound for queue QUEUE_1, while LPT2 could capture data for QUEUE_89, and LPT3 for queue IMPORTANT_ONE. With older versions of NetWare not using QMS, only one

QUEUE_1, while LPT2 could capture data for QUEUE_89, and LPT3 for queue IMPORTANT_ONE. With older versions of NetWare not using QMS, only one LPT port could be "spooled" (i.e., captured) at a time. In any case, once in the queue, the client's data is termed a job. Each job, which has several attributes (see Figures 4-1 and 4-2), is processed, usually in the order received. Typically, once a job has been handled, the entry in the queue is deleted, indicating that the job is done.

In the case of NetWare, QMS is handled by NetWare file servers. All data for QMS is placed in queues. And with current versions of NetWare these queues are located on servers. That is, queues are currently not network-wide. The NetWare operating system provides the necessary APIs (Application Program Interfaces) to make QMS come alive. Because QMS is handled by a known agent, namely located at the file server operating system and, because QMS access APIs are guaranteed to be there, queue clients and queue servers will have a consistent operating environment.

With NetWare, information regarding queues is stored in the bindery. Each queue is recognized by its name and its bindery object type. The object type can be almost any bindery type available. Novell has defined a few specific types for queues (the bindery chapter lists them), but you can use your own object types for your queues. In the following figures (4-1, 4-2, and 4-3) you will find the layout of Novell's Queue Job Structure and the Queue Job Client Record area.

Changing Q_SERVER'S Rights to Q_USER's Rights

Though no example is included here, be aware that QMS allows a Q_SERVER to temporarily change its rights to that of the user who submitted the queue job. The C Library call to perform this is: ChangeToClientRights(). See the *NetWare C Library* manual for more information.

Q_USERS	Contains a list of users (or groups) authorized to use this queue, property type is set.
Q_OPERATORS	Contains a list of all users who are authorized to manipulate queue jobs, property type is set.
Q_SERVERS	Contains a list of servers that are authorized to process jobs from this queue, property type is set.
Q_DIRECTORY	Contains the directory path of the VOLUME:DIRECTORY on the server (where the queue is defined) where queue jobs are stored, property type is item.

Figure 4-1. Queue Properties

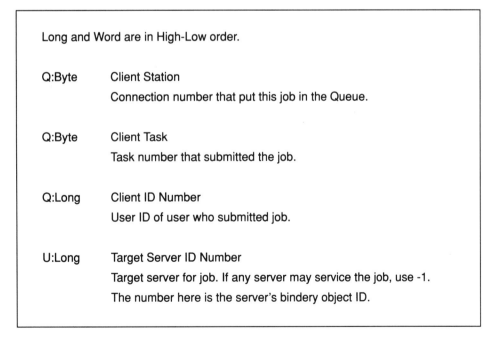

Long and Word are in High-Low order.

Q:Byte   Client Station
          Connection number that put this job in the Queue.

Q:Byte   Client Task
          Task number that submitted the job.

Q:Long   Client ID Number
          User ID of user who submitted job.

U:Long   Target Server ID Number
          Target server for job. If any server may service the job, use -1.
          The number here is the server's bindery object ID.

Figure 4-2. Queue Job Structure

97

U:Byte[6]   Target Execution Time

Time the Job should be executed. Year, Month, Day, Hour,

Minute, Second. All 0xFF means as soon as possible.

Q:Byte[6]   Job Entry Time

Time job was entered in queue. Same format as above.

Q:Word   Job Number

Job number for this print job.

U:Word   Job Type

This field will be used as the form number for print jobs.

M:Byte   Job Position

Position of this job in the queue.

U:Byte   Job Control Flags

80h: Set if job put on hold by operator.

40h: Set if put on hold by user.

20h: Set when you call CreateAQueueJob. Cleared when you

call CloseAndStartQueueJob.

10h: Set if job may be restarted in the event of a server failure.

08h: Set if job should be started if user has not done

CloseAndStartQueueJob and the users connection is terminated.

04h: Set if job to remain in queue if aborted.

Q:Byte[14]   Job File Name

File name created when CreateQueueJob was called.

Figure 4-2. Queue Job Structure (continued)

Q:Byte[6]   Job File Handle
              File handle for file, created when CreateQueueJob was called.

Q:Byte   Server Station
              Station number of server servicing the job. This is undefined unless
              the job is currently being serviced.

Q:Byte   Server Task
              Task number of queue server servicing the task.

Q:Long   Server ID Number
              Server ID of server servicing the task.

C:Byte[50]   Job Description Text
              Description of the job. This will usually be the name of the file
              being printed, but the user can change it.

C:Byte[132]   Client Record Area
              Special data that is only defined for print jobs.

Figure 4-2. Queue Job Structure (continued)

Definition of Client Record Area

This data applies only to print jobs. All of these fields must be set up by the client and may be changed by the client with QueueFunctionCalls.

Byte	Client Record Area version number. Current version is 0.
Byte	Tab Size. Number of spaces that tabs will be expanded to. Minimum is 0, maximum of 18.
Word	Number of copies.
Word	Control Flags.
0080h:	Set if banner should be printed.
0040h:	Set if text stream. If set, tabs are expanded and the lines per page and characters per line fields are ignored.
0008h:	Set if form feeds should be suppressed.
0004h:	Print job if interrupted during cature process.
Word	Maximum Lines per Page. Default 60.
Word	Maximum Characters per Line. Default 132.
Byte[16]	Null terminated form name.
Byte[6]	Reserved for future use, should be set to zero.

Figure 4-3. Definition of Client Record Area

Byte[13]   Banner Name Field

Text to be printed in the first box on the banner. This is usually the user name, but the user should be able to change it.

Byte[13]   Banner File Field

Text to be printed in second box on banner. This is currently used for the file name. But the user should be able to change it.

Byte[14]   Header File Name

File name printed in header of banner.

Byte[80]   Directory Path

Full path name of the file to be printed.

Figure 4-3. Definition of Client Record Area (continued)

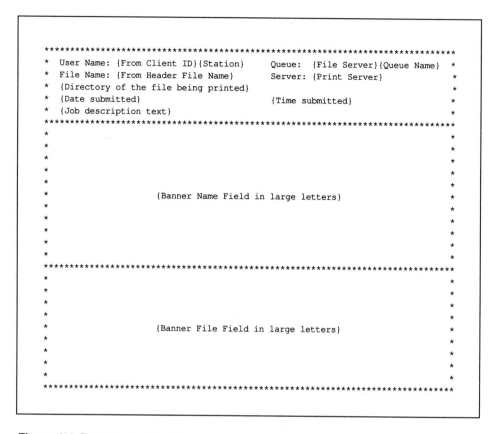

Figure 4-4. Format of a New Banner

When using NetWare utilities to define queues, their Q_DIRECTORY will always by SYS:SYSTEM\queueID. The directory "queueID" (that is, the bindery object I.D.) is a hexadecimal number, up to 8 characters long that uniquely identifies that queue. For instance, a queue directory might be: SYS:SYSTEM\20F00EF. For a trick regarding the alteration of PCONSOLE's use of SYS:SYSTEM, see the section "Changing Queue Directory's Location" later in this chapter.

If a user is not defined as a Q_USER, either directly or by membership in a NetWare group, they will not be allowed to submit jobs to that queue. Likewise, if a user is not defined as a Q_OPERATOR, directly or by group membership, they will not be allowed alter jobs in the queue. Q_SERVERS defines which "servers" are allowed to retrieve queue jobs for processing, and the removal of queue jobs once processed. Interestingly, these "servers" are not necessarily file servers. They may be other objects in the bindery, such as users or other bindery entities (probably created just to be queue servers). And, unlike pre-NetWare v2.1 queues, each QMS queue can be serviced by as many as 25 simultaneous queue servers. For instance, you could have 25 HP Laserjet's printing jobs from one queue. Similarly you could have up to 25 batch processing servers operating from one queue. Note in Figure 1 that a particular job can be routed to a particular job server if the client requesting queue submission is aware of this option (target Server ID Number).

Because QMS allows for practically any bindery object to be a queue server, applications of QMS are unlimited in respect to previous NetWare queue services. Due to this, it is important that the queue submittor (client) and the queue server be as independent as possible. If it were required for a queue server to be active during the submission of a queue job, QMS would not be a true queueing service. However, QMS is a true queueing service, one that defines a strict structure for job submission (by a queue user/client) and job servicing (by a queue server).

Because of this asynchronous definition, QMS allows any type of job to be submitted for processing by any type of queue server. For instance, you may notice that under pre-NetWare v2.1, when a file was NPRINTed, the file was the source of the queue server's (here, the file server's) processing. Now, under QMS, when a file is NPRINTed, it is transferred to that queue server's directory. This is because NetWare now abstracts itself from what is actually going into the queue; it makes no amends for highly NetWare-specific actions as it did with the pre-QMS system. Thus, with QMS, two copies of the NPRINTed file would exist immediately after the NPRINT operation, where before there was only one.

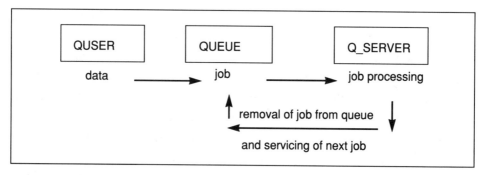

Figure 4-5. QMS

With QMS, NetWare has opened up its queueing system to all applications, not just those intrinsic to NetWare. Under this new system, users are given more freedom in the definition and setup of queue servers and a consistent interface by which access to those queues is possible.

Changing Q_DIRECTORY's Location

With NetWare, the PCONSOLE utility is often used to create queues. Unfortunately this utility always designates SYS:SYSTEM as the basis for a queue's "job directory". This directory is where queue jobs are stored. The full path of a queue directory might be: SYS:SYSTEM\E30033. However, it is possible to adapt PCONSOLE to use another volume (on the same server) for storage of queue directories and their associated jobs.The benefit to changing queue directory's location is that it eliminates the requirement that all print jobs go through SYS, thus freeing space on SYS:volume. Use a utility, such as Norton's Advanced Utilities, to search, for and edit the two "SYS:SYSTEM" strings within the PCONSOLE.EXE utility. To make it simple to search for the string, might copy PCONSOLE.EXE to a floppy disk and do your modification there. Afterwards, copy the changed PCONSOLE back up to the area from where you normally use it.

When modifying the "SYS:SYSTEM" string, be sure to make the new string match the old one in length, (that is, do not make the name longer or shorter than 10 characters, which is the length of SYS:SYSTEM). For example, you might use "VOL1:QUEUE". The new name that you use will become the basis for the full path of all queues defined with PCONSOLE. You should realize that, if your "other" volume should become unavailable, NetWare's queueing system will be unable to accept queue submissions from users. However, you might just pick another directory on your server, but still on the SYS:volume. Perhaps you would use "SYS:QUEUES".

This freedom of the location of queue directories is permitted because each queue has a Q_DIRECTORY property that details the directory path of that queue's jobs.

Because of the nature of the files in the queue directories, it is probably not pertinent to back them up. By placing them in their own directory tree, you allow for the easy exclusion of them from your normal backup routines. This is instead of having to type in the file exclude mask(s): * Q$*.SYS and Q$*.SRV.

With a little experimentation, you should be able to organize your queues in the most effective manner possible for your work situation.

NetWare's Queue System Prior to QMS

Previous to QMS, NetWare queues were strictly for printing at the file server. Novell only offered APIs for submitting print jobs to the print queues and a few routines to monitor and or update print queues' statuses.

For current shipping versions of NetWare, only ELS I v2.0a remains under the implementation of NetWare's old queue system (nonQMS).

NPRINTing with QMS

Pseudo code to NPRINT (short for Network PRINT) a file to a queue under NetWare's QMS system:

first, get QUEUE's ID by scanning the bindery for the Queue's Name or using the C Library call GetObjectID()

next, create a queue job (call where ah register=E3h, subfunction 68h) (CreateQueueJobAndFile())

next, open the file to NPRINT and open a file by the name of NETQ, the file NETQ is a special NetWare filename that will be used for copying the file to NPRINT to the queue; both opens are the file handle type open, not FCB, that is, DOS's open call where ah=3Dh

next, either copy the file with your own read and write calls or use the "ncopy" call (FileServerFileCopy()) in the C Library (call where AH=F3h); beware the "ncopy" call may not handle files that are on different file servers, in that case you will need to copy the file yourself

next, close the the queue job (call where ah=E3h, subfunction 69h) (CloseFileAndStartQueueJob())

End of NPRINT Pseudo code

The next feature of networked applications that we will examine deals with printing services. NetWare provides a very powerful interface to the Print Services facility through the 'C' language API set. Your application may turn remote printing on and off, as well as capture your application's printed output to a file for later printing or formatting. You are also given control over which printer, type of paper, tab interpretation, and other print job options to use.

The basic chain of events in tailoring printing in NetWare is as follows:

1. Modify the capture default appropriate for your printed output.
2. Start capturing data to the network printer.
3. Print your report.
4. Flush the capture so that the file server can start printing, or, cancel the capture to abort printing and restart the capture.
5. End the capture session.

Now, let's look at some examples of functions to perform those tasks.

```
/* SetPrinterDefaults

Description: This function is responsible for modifying some of the
default characteristics used by the capture facility of the NetWare
shell.  This function does not start the transfer, it simply sets the
capture environment.


Parameters:
 BYTE LPTNum - The local printer number (LPT1, etc.)
 BYTE TabSize - The width of each tab character in bytes
 char *Banner - Up to 13 characters; prints on first page
 int MaxLines - Maximum lines per page
 int MaxChars - Maximum number of characters per line
 char *FormName - Name of the form for this report
 BYTE NumCopies - Number of copies to print when done
Returns: 0 for Success, !0 for NetWare error code
*/
int SetPrinterDefaults(BYTE LPTNum, BYTE TabSize, char *Banner,
                       int MaxLines, int MaxChars, char *FormName,
                       BYTE NumCopies)


{
 CAPTURE_FLAGS CaptureFlags;      /* Initial capture info */
 SET_CAPTURE_FLAGS MyDefaults;    /* Updated capture info */
 int   Result;                    /* Function result */

 /* Get the current capture defaults */
 Result = GetDefaultCaptureFlags(&CaptureFlags);

 if (Result == 0) {       /* Everything OK so far */

  /* Make a copy and update specific fields */
  memcpy(&MyDefaults,&CaptureFlags,sizeof(MyDefaults));
  MyDefaults.localLPTDevice = LPTNum;
  if (TabSize) {
   MyDefaults.flags |= 0x40;  /* Turn on tab expansion */
   MyDefaults.tabSize = TabSize;
  }
  if (strlen(Banner)) {
   MyDefaults.flags |= 0x80;  /* Turn on the banner */
   strcpy(MyDefaults.bannerText,Banner);
  }
  if (MaxLines) {
   MyDefaults.maxLines = MaxLines;
```

```
  }
  if (MaxChars) {
   MyDefaults.maxChars = MaxChars;
  }
  if (strlen(FormName)) {
   strcpy(MyDefaults.formName,FormName);
  }
  if (NumCopies) {
   MyDefaults.numberOfCopies = NumCopies;
  }

  /* Now make the changes the new defaults */
  Result = SetDefaultCaptureFlags(&MyDefaults);
 }
 return(Result);
}
```

The remainder of this example is a review of the function calls to
flush and cancel a capture session. "Flushing" a capture session
effectively tells the file server that this print job is done and ready
to be printed on the file server's printer. It does not turn on the
capture that is in effect. "Ending" or "Cancelling," on the other hand,
will turn off an active capture.

To "Flush" a captured print job:

```
 Result = FlushLPTCapture();
```

To "End" a capture session and print any pending output:

```
 Result = EndLPTCapture();
```

To "Cancel" a capture and ignore any pending printed output:

```
 Result = CancelLPTCapture();
```

There are many more things that one can do to control NetWare printing
services. Those advanced functions are detailed in the API manual in
the section on "Queue Management Services."

The following two programs are examples of a Queue Server and a Queue Client. The Queue Server creates the queue and sets up the necessary rights for user SUPERVISOR to use the queue as a server and a client.

Because the Queue Server example creates the queue, it will need to be run first. The examples are in Turbo Pascal v4.0/v.5.0 using the NetWare System Calls Interface API calls. Also the examples are displayed in Watcom C using the NetWare C Library.

Program Queue_Server_Demo;

```
{ TURBO PASCAL
This is a Queue Server demo program. This utility will create Queue (if
it doesn't exist already) to be serviced. As part of creating the Queue
the user SUPERVISOR will be added as a Q_SERVER...doing this requires
the SUPERVISOR to be logged in at the station performing the Queue
functions. This is not the only way to do this, another user could be
used.


After the program creates the queue, it will add user Supervisor and
the Queue server status will be set. This status is just an FYI field
that can be used to indicate anything to the Queue's clients. Next the
Queue server will attempt to service a queue job if one exists.


For purposes of this demo the Queue Server will take the job and read
it as such:
  byte  0     = logical station number
  bytes 1..40 = message to send


Next the Queue server will finish servicing the queue job and attempt
to service another job. If the human Queue Server user stops the Queue
Server it will detach itself from the queue it is servicing. Note that
up to 25 Queue Servers can service a single queue simultaneously.
Note, however, that this utility does not do extensive error checking,
for instance, if a bad file handle is returned on the open NETQ
operation, this program will not recognize this. Remember, these
routines are to show you how to perform basic queue server operations,
not how to perform comprehensive error checking.
```

```
Uses Dos, Crt;


Type


 char60   = array[0..60] of byte;

 Long     = record
               a,b,c,d : byte;
            end;


 MyWord   = record
               wh,wl : byte
            end;


 e364c    = record
               native : MyWord;
               func   : byte; { will be 0x64, Create Queue }
               Qtype  : MyWord;
               QnameL : byte;
               Qname  : array[1..4] of byte; { can be up to 47 }
                                             { for purposes here I am }
                                             {using the fixed name "DEMO" }
               dirhnd : byte;
               pathL  : byte; { 1..118 }
               pathN  : array[1..20] of byte;
            end;

 e364r    = record
               native : MyWord;
               Qid    : Long;
            end;


 e335c    = record
               native : MyWord;
               func   : byte; { will be 0x35, Get an Object's Number }
               objtyp : MyWord;
               objnml : byte;
               objnme : array[1..4] of byte; {DEMO}
            end;
```

```
e335r    = record
              native : MyWord;
              Qid    : Long;
              objtyp : MyWord;
              objnme : array[1..48] of byte;
           end;


e341c    = record
              native : MyWord;
              func   : byte; {will be 0x41, Add a member to a property set }
              objtyp : MyWord;
              objnml : byte;
              objnme : array[1..4] of byte; {using name DEMO per above }
              propl  : byte;
              propn  : array[1..9] of byte; { Q_SERVERS }
              memtyp : MyWord;
              memnml : byte;
              memnme : array[1..10] of byte; { SUPERVISOR }
           end;

e341r    = record
              native : MyWord;
              junk   : byte;
           end;


e341Ec   = record
              native : MyWord;
              func   : byte; {will be 0x41, Add a member to a property set}
              objtyp : MyWord;
              objnml : byte;
              objnme : array[1..4] of byte; { using name DEMO per above }
              propl  : byte;
              propn  : array[1..7] of byte; { Q_USERS }
              memtyp : MyWord;
              memnml : byte;
              memnme : array[1..8] of byte; { EVERYONE }
           end;

e341Er   = record
             native  : MyWord;
              junk   : byte;
               end;
```

```
e36fc    = record
             native : MyWord;
             func   : byte; {will be 0x6F, Attach Queue Server to Queue}
             Qid    : Long;
           end;


e36fr    = record
             native : MyWord;
             junk   : byte;
           end;


e377c    = record
             native : MyWord;
             func   : byte; {will be 0x77, Set Queue Server Current Status}
             Qid    : Long;
             charge : array[1..4] of byte;
             status : string[59];
           end;


e377r    = record
             native : MyWord;
             junk   : byte;
           end;


e36bc    = record
             native : MyWord;
             func   : byte; { will be 0x6B, Get Queue Job List }
             Qid    : Long;
           end;


e36br    = record
             native : MyWord;
             jobcnt : MyWord;
             jobnum : array[1..250] of MyWord; { actual length is based
                                             { on jobcnt }
            maxjnm : MyWord;
           end;


e371c    = record
             native : MyWord;
             func   : byte; {will be 0x71, Service Queue Job and Open File}
             Qid    : Long;
```

```
              Target : MyWord; { will be 0xFFFF, all job types }
          end;

e371r    = record
              native : MyWord;
              cltnst : byte;
              clttnm : byte;
              cltID  : Long;
              tsID   : Long;
              texect : array[1..6] of byte;
              jobent : array[1..6] of byte;
              jobnum : MyWord;
              jobtyp : MyWord;
              jobpos : byte;
              jobcfl : byte;
              jobfln : array[1..14] of byte;
              jobflh : array[1..6] of byte;
              srvstn : byte;
              srvtsk : byte;
              srvID  : Long;
          end;


e372c    = record
              native : MyWord;
              func   : byte; {will be 0x72, Finish Servicing Queue Job and File}
              Qid    : Long;
              jobnum : MyWord;
              charge : Long;
          end;

e372r    = record
              native : MyWord;
              junk   : byte;
          end;


e370c    = record
              native : MyWord;
              func   : byte; {will be 0x70, Detach Queue Server from Queue}
              Qid    : Long;
          end;

e370r    = record
              native : MyWord;
```

```
            junk   : byte;
          end;


e104c     = record
            native : MyWord;
            func   : byte; { will be 0, Send a Broadcast Message }
            numstn : byte;
            stnlst : byte; { can be more than 1, here though, only 1 }
            meslen : byte;
            messge : array[1..60] of byte;
          end;

e104r     = record
            native : MyWord;
            numstn : byte;
            stnlst : byte; { can be more than 1, here though, only 1 }
          end;


e336c     = record
            native : MyWord;
            func   : byte; { will be 0x36, Get an Object's Name }
            objid  : Long;  ´
          end;


e336r     = record
            native : MyWord;
            Qid    : Long;
            objtyp : MyWord;
            objnme : array[1..48] of byte;
          end;


var

regs  : registers;
CQc   : e364c; { Create Queue }
CQr   : e364r;

GIc   : e335c; { Get an Object's ID }
GIr   : e335r;
```

```
a2gc  : e341c; { Add to (2) Group }
a2gr  : e341r;

aE2gc : e341Ec;{ Add to (2) Group }
aE2gr : e341Er;{ Add group EVERYONE to Q_USERS }


AQc   : e36fc; { Attach to Queue }
AQr   : e36fr;

SSc   : e377c; { Set queue Status }
SSr   : e377r;

GLc   : e36bc; { Get queue List }
GLr   : e36br;

SJc   : e371c; { Service queue Job }
SJr   : e371r;

FJc   : e372c; { Finish service of Job }
FJr   : e372r;

DQc   : e370c; { Detach from Queue }
DQr   : e370r;

SMc   : e104c; { Send Message }
SMr   : e104r;

GNc   : e336c; { Get Object Name }
GNr   : e336r;

theQ  : Long;  { holds our Queue ID }

Queuetype : MyWord; { holds our Queue type }

a     : integer;

{*-*-*-*-*-*-*-*-*-*-*-* Procedures below *-*-*-*-*-*-*-*-*-*-*-*-*}

Procedure DisplayError(code:byte; routine:byte);
Begin


  Write('Error from ');
  case routine of
```

```
 1: Write('CreateQueue');
 2: Write('AddSUPERVISOR');
 3: Write('AttachQueue');
 4: Write('SetStatus');
 5: Write('GetList');
 6: Write('ServiceJob');
 7: Write('FinishJob');
 8: Write('DetachQueue');
 9: Write('AddEVERYONE');
10:Write('MessageBy');
end; { end of case }


Write('-> ');
case code of
$96: Writeln('Server out of memory');
$99: Writeln('Directory Full');
$9B: Writeln('Bad Directory Handle');
$9C: Writeln('Invalid Path');
$D0: Writeln('Queue Error');
$D1: Writeln('No Queue');
$D2: Writeln('No Queue server');
$D3: Writeln('No Queue rights');
$D5: Writeln('No Queue job');
$D6: Writeln('No Job rights');
$D9: Writeln('Station not server');
$DA: Writeln('Queue halted');
$DB: Writeln('Max Queue Servers reached');
$E9: Writeln('Member already exists in property');
$ED: Writeln('Property already exists');
$EE: Writeln('Object already exists');
$EF: Writeln('Invalid name');
$F0: Writeln('Wildcard not allowed');
$F1: Writeln('Invalid bindery security');
$F5: Writeln('No object create privilege');
$F7: Writeln('No propery create privilege');
$FC: Writeln('No such object');
$FE: Writeln('Server bindery locked');
$FF: Writeln('Bindery failure');

else Writeln('<',code,'> - ? Unknown ?');
end; { end of case }


End; { end of DisplayError }
```

```
Procedure CreateQueue;
Begin


  with CQc do
  begin
   native.wh := 30;
   native.wl := 0;
   func       := $64;
   Qtype.wh  := QueueType.wh; { Arbitrary }
   Qtype.wl  := QueueType.wl;
   QnameL     := 4;
   Qname[1]  := 68; {D}
   Qname[2]  := 69; {E}
   Qname[3]  := 77; {M}
   Qname[4]  := 79; {O}
   dirhnd     := 0;   {0 means full pathname will be specified minus servername}
   pathL      := 10;
   pathN[1]   := 83; {S}
   pathN[2]   := 89; {Y}
   pathN[3]   := 83; {S}
   pathN[4]   := 58; {:}
   pathN[5]   := 83; {S}
   pathN[6]   := 89; {Y}
   pathN[7]   := 83; {S}
   pathN[8]   := 84; {T}
   pathN[9]   := 69; {E}
   pathN[10] := 77; {M}
  end;

  CQr.native.wh := 4;
  CQr.native.wl := 0;

  with regs do
  begin
   AX := $E300;
   DS := Seg(CQc);
   SI := Ofs(CQc);

   ES := Seg(CQr);
   DI := Ofs(CQr);
  end;
```

117

```
MsDos(regs);

if (regs.AL <> 0) and (regs.AL <> 238) then DisplayError(regs.AL, 1);

if (regs.AL = 0) then
begin
  theQ.a := CQr.Qid.a;
  theQ.b := CQr.Qid.b;
  theQ.c := CQr.Qid.c;
  theQ.d := CQr.Qid.d;
end;


if (regs.AL = 238) then {Queue already exists, get its id}
begin
 with GIc do
 begin
  native.wh := 8;
  native.wl := 0;
  func       := $35;
  objtyp.wh := QueueType.wh; {must match type defined in CreateQueue}
  objtyp.wl := QueueType.wl;
  objnml     := 4;
  objnme[1] := 68; {D}
  objnme[2] := 69; {E}
  objnme[3] := 77; {M}
  objnme[4] := 79; {O}
 end;

  GIr.native.wh := 54;
  GIr.native.wl := 0;

  with regs do
   begin
    AX := $E300;
    DS := Seg(GIc);
    SI := Ofs(GIc);

    ES := Seg(GIr);
    DI := Ofs(GIr);
   end;

MsDos(regs);

{ presumed it worked }
```

```
    theQ.a := GIr.Qid.a;
    theQ.b := GIr.Qid.b;
    theQ.c := GIr.Qid.c;
    theQ.d := GIr.Qid.d;

    end;


End; { end of CreateQueue }



Procedure AddSUPERVISOR;
Begin

  With a2gc do
  begin
    native.wh := 31;
    native.wl := 0;
    func       := $41;
    objtyp.wh := QueueType.wh; { same as Qtype in CreateQueue }
    objtyp.wl := QueueType.wl;
    objnml     := 4;
    objnme[1] := 68; {D}
    objnme[2] := 69; {E}
    objnme[3] := 77; {M}
    objnme[4] := 79; {O}
    propl      := 9;
    propn[1]   := 81; {Q}
    propn[2]   := 95; {_}
    propn[3]   := 83; {S}
    propn[4]   := 69; {E}
    propn[5]   := 82; {R}
    propn[6]   := 86; {V}
    propn[7]   := 69; {E}
    propn[8]   := 82; {R}
    propn[9]   := 83; {S}
    memtyp.wh := 0;
    memtyp.wl := 1; { regular USER type }
    memnml     := 10;
    memnme[1] := 83; {S}
    memnme[2] := 85; {U}
    memnme[3] := 80; {P}
```

```
    memnme[4]  := 69;  {E}
    memnme[5]  := 82;  {R}
    memnme[6]  := 86;  {V}
    memnme[7]  := 73;  {I}
    memnme[8]  := 83;  {S}
    memnme[9]  := 79;  {O}
    memnme[10]:= 82;  {R}
  end;

  a2gr.native.wh:=1;
  a2gr.native.wl:=0;

  with regs do
  begin
    AX := $E300;
    DS := Seg(a2gc);
    SI := Ofs(a2gc);

    ES := Seg(a2gr);
    DI := Ofs(a2gr);
  end;

  MsDos(regs);

  if (regs.AL <> 0) and (regs.AL <> 233) then DisplayError(regs.AL, 2);
  { 233 = Member already exists in property }

End; { end of AddSUPERVISOR }




Procedure AddEVERYONE;
Begin

  With aE2gc do
  begin
    native.wh := 28;
    native.wl := 0;
    func      := $41;
    objtyp.wh := QueueType.wh; { same as Qtype in CreateQueue }
    objtyp.wl := QueueType.wl;
    objnml    := 4;
    objnme[1] := 68;  {D}
    objnme[2] := 69;  {E}
```

```
    objnme[3]  := 77; {M}
    objnme[4]  := 79; {O}
    propl      := 7;
    propn[1]   := 81; {Q}
    propn[2]   := 95; {_}
    propn[3]   := 85; {U}
    propn[4]   := 83; {S}
    propn[5]   := 69; {E}
    propn[6]   := 82; {R}
    propn[7]   := 83; {S}
    memtyp.wh := 0;
    memtyp.wl := 2; { regular GROUP type }
    memnml     := 8;
    memnme[1] := 69; {E}
    memnme[2] := 86; {V}
    memnme[3] := 69; {E}
    memnme[4] := 82; {R}
    memnme[5] := 89; {Y}
    memnme[6] := 79; {O}
    memnme[7] := 78; {N}
    memnme[8] := 69; {E}
  end;

  aE2gr.native.wh:=1;
  aE2gr.native.wl:=0;

  with regs do
  begin
    AX := $E300;
    DS := Seg(aE2gc);
    SI := Ofs(aE2gc);

    ES := Seg(aE2gr);
    DI := Ofs(aE2gr);
  end;

  MsDos(regs);

  if (regs.AL <> 0) and (regs.AL <> 233) then DisplayError(regs.AL, 9);
  { 233 = Member already exists in property }

End; { end of AddEVERYONE }
```

```
Procedure AttachQueue;
Begin

  with AQc do
  begin
    native.wh := 5;
    native.wl := 0;
    func       := $6F;
    Qid.a      := theQ.a;
    Qid.b      := theQ.b;
    Qid.c      := theQ.c;
    Qid.d      := theQ.d;
  end;

  AQr.native.wh := 1;
  AQr.native.wl := 0;

  with regs do
  begin
    AX := $E300;
    DS := Seg(AQc);
    SI := Ofs(AQc);

    ES := Seg(AQr);
    DI := Ofs(AQr);
  end;

  MsDos(regs);

  if (regs.AL <> 0) then DisplayError(regs.AL, 3)
  else
  Writeln('Successfully Attached to Queue DEMO');

End; { end of AttachQueue }




Procedure SetStatus;
Begin

  with SSc do
  begin
    native.wh := 69;
    native.wl := 0;
```

```
  func       := $77;
  Qid.a      := theQ.a;
  Qid.b      := theQ.b;
  Qid.c      := theQ.c;
  Qid.d      := theQ.d;
  charge[1]  := 0;
  charge[2]  := 0;
  charge[3]  := 0;
  charge[4]  := 0;
  status     := 'This is a demo Queue Server';
end;

SSr.native.wh := 1;
SSr.native.wl := 0;

with regs do
begin
  AX := $E300;
  DS := Seg(SSc);
  SI := Ofs(SSc);

  ES := Seg(SSr);
  DI := Ofs(SSr);
end;

MsDos(regs);

if (regs.AL <> 0) then DisplayError(regs.AL, 4);

End; { end of SetStatus }


Procedure GetList;
Begin

  with GLc do
  begin
    native.wh := 5;
    native.wl := 0;
    func       := $6B;
    Qid.a      := theQ.a;
    Qid.b      := theQ.b;
    Qid.c      := theQ.c;
    Qid.d      := theQ.d;
  end;
```

```
    GLr.native.wh := $F8;
    GLr.native.wl := $01; {504 or 0x1F8}

    with regs do
    begin
      AX := $E300;
      DS := Seg(GLc);
      SI := Ofs(GLc);

      ES := Seg(GLr);
      DI := Ofs(GLr);
    end;

    MsDos(regs);

    if (regs.AL <> 0) then DisplayError(regs.AL, 5);


End; { end of GetList }


Procedure FinishJob(jobnumber:MyWord);FORWARD;
Procedure MessageBy(submit:Long);FORWARD;
Procedure SendMessage(request:char60; len:integer);FORWARD;


Procedure ServiceJob;
var
NETQ    : string[5];
request : char60;
a       : integer;
filehan : integer;
bytes2read : integer;
Begin

  with SJc do
  begin
    native.wh := 7;
    native.wl := 0;
    func      := $71;
    Qid.a     := theQ.a;
    Qid.b     := theQ.b;
    Qid.c     := theQ.c;
    Qid.d     := theQ.d;
```

```
   Target.wh := $FF;
   Target.wl := $FF;
end;


SJr.native.wh := 54;
SJr.native.wl := 0;


with regs do
begin
  AX := $E300;
  DS := Seg(SJc);
  SI := Ofs(SJc);

  ES := Seg(SJr);
  DI := Ofs(SJr);
end;


MsDos(regs);



if (regs.AL <> 213) then   { no queue job, this will occur when }
                           { someone opens a queue job but hasn't }
                           { closed it yet...}
Writeln;



if (regs.AL <> 213) then { repeated because I'd rather not indent }
                         { some more...!}
if (regs.AL <> 0) then DisplayError(regs.AL, 6)
else
begin

  with SJr do
  Writeln('Job Submitted by ID
  [',cltID.a,'][',cltID.b,'][',cltID.c,'][',cltID.d,']');

  MessageBy(SJr.cltID);


  regs.AX := $3D02;
  NETQ     := 'NETQ'^@;
  regs.DS := Seg(NETQ);
  regs.DX := Ofs(NETQ)+1;

  MsDos(regs);
```

```
      Writeln('File Handle from open NETQ = [',regs.AX,']');


      filehan := regs.AX;

      bytes2read := 57;
      regs.AX := $3F00;
      regs.BX := filehan;
      regs.CX := bytes2read;
      regs.DS := Seg(request);
      regs.DX := Ofs(request);

      MsDos(regs);

      {
        byte  0     = logical station number to send to
        bytes 1..56 = message to send
      }

      if (regs.AX > 1) then
       SendMessage(request,regs.AX)
       else
       Writeln('Job is of 0 length, nothing to process...');

      regs.AX := $3E00;
      regs.BX := filehan;

      MsDos(regs);

      FinishJob(SJr.jobnum);

    end;



End; { end of ServiceJob }




Procedure MessageBy;
var
a : integer;
Begin
```

```
with GNc do
begin
  native.wh := 5;
  native.wl := 0;
  func     := $36;
  objid.a  := submit.a;
  objid.b  := submit.b;
  objid.c  := submit.c;
  objid.d  := submit.d;
end;


GNr.native.wh := 54;
GNr.native.wl := 0;


with regs do
begin
  AX := $E300;
  DS := Seg(GNc);
  SI := Ofs(GNc);

  ES := Seg(GNr);
  DI := Ofs(GNr);
end;


MsDos(regs);

if (regs.AL <> 0) then DisplayError(regs.AL, 10)
else
begin
  Write('Processing job from: [');
  regs.AX := $0900;
  regs.DS := Seg(GNr.objnme);
  regs.DX := Ofs(GNr.objnme);

  for a:=1 to 48 do
   if (GNr.objnme[a]=0) then GNr.objnme[a] := ord('$');

  MsDos(regs);
  Writeln(']');
end;


End; { end of MessageBy }
```

```
Procedure SendMessage;
var
a : integer;
Begin

  if (len>57) then len:=57;

  with SMc do
  begin
    native.wh := 4+len-1;
    native.wl := 0;
    func       := 0;
    numstn     := 1;
    meslen     := len-1;
    stnlst     := request[0];
    a:=1;
    while (a<(len)) do
    begin
      if (request[a]<>0) then messge[a] := request[a]
      else
      begin
        meslen     := a-1;
        native.wh := 4+meslen;
      end;
      a:=a+1;
    end;
  end;

  SMr.native.wh := 2;
  SMr.native.wl := 0;

  with regs do
  begin
    AX := $E100;
    DS := Seg(SMc);
    SI := Ofs(SMc);

    ES := Seg(SMr);
    DI := Ofs(SMr);
  end;
```

```
  MsDos(regs);

  if (regs.AL <> 0) then Write('Unable to send message ')
  else
  Write('Message sent ');

  Writeln('to station [',request[0],']');

End; { end of SendMessage }




Procedure FinishJob;
Begin

  with FJc do
  begin
    native.wh := 11;
    native.wl := 0;
    func       := $72;
    Qid.a      := theQ.a;
    Qid.b      := theQ.b;
    Qid.c      := theQ.c;
    Qid.d      := theQ.d;
    jobnum.wh := jobnumber.wh;
    jobnum.wl := jobnumber.wl;
    charge.a  := 0;
    charge.b  := 0;
    charge.c  := 0;
    charge.d  := 0;
  end;

  FJr.native.wh := 1;
  FJr.native.wl := 0;

  with regs do
  begin
    AX := $E300;
    DS := Seg(FJc);
    SI := Ofs(FJc);

    ES := Seg(FJr);
    DI := Ofs(FJr);
  end;
```

```
  MsDos(regs);

  if (regs.AL <> 0) then DisplayError(regs.AL, 7);

End; { end of FinishJob }



Procedure DetachQueue;
Begin

  with DQc do
  begin
    native.wh := 5;
    native.wl := 0;
    func      := $70;
    Qid.a     := theQ.a;
    Qid.b     := theQ.b;
    Qid.c     := theQ.c;
    Qid.d     := theQ.d;
  end;

  DQr.native.wh := 1;
  DQr.native.wl := 0;

  with regs do
  begin
    AX := $E300;
    DS := Seg(DQc);
    SI := Ofs(DQc);

    ES := Seg(DQr);
    DI := Ofs(DQr);
  end;

  MsDos(regs);

  if (regs.AL <> 0) then DisplayError(regs.AL, 8)
  else
  Writeln('Successfully detached from Queue DEMO');

End; { end of DetachQueue }
```

```
Begin


      QueueType.wh := 3;
      QueueType.wl := 3;   { this is an arbitrary queue type... 0x0303 }

      clrscr;


      CreateQueue;

      Writeln('Qid is
      [',theQ.a,'][',theQ.b,'][',theQ.c,'][',theQ.d,']');

      AddSUPERVISOR;

      AddEVERYONE;


      AttachQueue;

      SetStatus;

      repeat

       GetList;

       Write('Number of jobs in queue [',GLr.jobcnt.wl,']');

       if (GLr.jobcnt.wl>0) then
       begin
         ServiceJob;
         if (regs.AL = 213) then for a:=1 to 40 do write(#8)
         else
         writeln('*end of job processing*');
       end
       else
         for a:=1 to 40 do write(#8);

      until keypressed;

      DetachQueue;


End.
```

Program Queue_Submitter_Demo;

```
{TURBO PASCAL
 This is a Queue Submitter demo program.

 This utility will accept input from a user, that input is a logical
 station number to send a message to, and then the message to send.

 The message to send can be up to 56 characters long, the "From:"
 portion produced by Novell's SEND utility is not defined here unless
 the user types it in...

 Also, the logical station number entered is not verified, the purpose
 here is to show how to submit a queue entry to our queue server...you
 can take it from here, go wild, have fun!


 Note that this utility does not do extensive error checking, for
 instance,if a bad file handle is returned on the open NETQ operation,
 this program will not recognize this..Remember these routines are to
 show how to perform queue submittal, not how to show comprehensive
 error checking...

 by: John T. McCann
     9/7/89

}


Uses Dos, Crt;


Type


  char60    = array[0..60] of byte;

  Long      = record
                 a,b,c,d : byte;
                 end;


  MyWord    = record
                 wh,wl : byte
                 end;
```

```
e335c    = record
             native : MyWord;
             func   : byte; { will be 0x35, Get an Object's Number }
             objtyp : MyWord;
             objnml : byte;
             objnme : array[1..4] of byte; {DEMO}
          end;

e335r    = record
             native : MyWord;
             Qid    : Long;
             objtyp : MyWord;
             objnme : array[1..48] of byte;
          end;



e368c    = record
             native : MyWord;
             func   : byte; {will be 0x68, Create Queue Job and File }
             Qid    : Long;
             cltnst : byte;
             clttnm : byte;
             cltID  : Long;
             tsID   : Long;
             texect : array[1..6] of byte;
             jobent : array[1..6] of byte;
             jobnum : MyWord;
             jobtyp : MyWord;
             jobpos : byte;
             jobcfl : byte;
             jobfln : array[1..14] of byte;
             jobflh : array[1..6] of byte;
             srvstn : byte;
             srvtsk : byte;
             srvID  : Long;
             txtjob : array[1..50] of byte;
             cra    : array[1..152] of byte; { Client Record Area }
          end;

e368r    = record
             native : MyWord;
             cltnst : byte;
             clttnm : byte;
```

```
                    cltID  : Long;
                    tsID   : Long;
                    texect : array[1..6] of byte;
                    jobent : array[1..6] of byte;
                    jobnum : MyWord;
                    jobtyp : MyWord;
                    jobpos : byte;
                    jobcfl : byte;
                    jobfln : array[1..14] of byte;
                    jobflh : array[1..6] of byte;
                    srvstn : byte;
                    srvtsk : byte;
                    srvID  : Long;
                  end;


e369c      = record
                  native : MyWord;
                  func   : byte; {will be 0x69, Close File and Start Queue Job}
                  Qid    : Long;
                  jobnum : MyWord;
                end;

e369r      = record
                  native : MyWord;
                  junk   : byte;
                end;



var

regs  : registers;

GIc   : e335c; { Get an Object's ID }
GIr   : e335r;

SQc   : e368c; { Start Queue job }
SQr   : e368r;

FQc   : e369c; { Finish Queue job }
FQr   : e369r;

theQ  : Long;  { holds our Queue ID }
```

```
Queuetype : MyWord; { holds our Queue type }

a     : integer;



{*-*-*-*-*-*-*-*-*-*-*-* Procedures below *-*-*-*-*-*-*-*-*-*-*-*-*}

Procedure DisplayError(code:byte; routine:byte);
Begin


  Write('Error from ');
  case routine of
  1: Write('StartJob');
  2: Write('QueueJob');
  3: Write('GetQid');
  end; { end of case }


  Write('-> ');
  case code of
  $96: Writeln('Server out of memory');
  $99: Writeln('Directory Full');
  $9B: Writeln('Bad Directory Handle');
  $9C: Writeln('Invalid Path');
  $D0: Writeln('Queue Error');
  $D1: Writeln('No Queue');
  $D2: Writeln('No Queue server');
  $D3: Writeln('No Queue rights');
  $D5: Writeln('No Queue job');
  $D6: Writeln('No Job rights');
  $D9: Writeln('Station not server');
  $DA: Writeln('Queue halted');
  $DB: Writeln('Max Queue Servers reached');
  $E9: Writeln('Member already exists in property');
  $ED: Writeln('Property already exists');
  $EE: Writeln('Object already exists');
  $EF: Writeln('Invalid name');
  $F0: Writeln('Wildcard not allowed');
  $F1: Writeln('Invalid bindery security');
  $F5: Writeln('No object create privilege');
  $F7: Writeln('No propery create privilege');
  $FB: Writeln('No such property');
```

135

```
$FC: Writeln('No such object');
$FE: Writeln('Server bindery locked');
$FF: Writeln('Bindery failure');

else Writeln('<',code,'> - ? Unknown ?');
end; { end of case }



End; { end of DisplayError }



Procedure StartJob;
Begin

 fillchar(SQc,sizeof(SQc),0);

 with SQc do
 begin
   native.wh := 5;
   native.wl := 1; { 261 or $0105 }
   func      := $68;
   Qid.a     := theQ.a;
   Qid.b     := theQ.b;
   Qid.c     := theQ.c;
   Qid.d     := theQ.d;
   tsID.a    := $FF;
   tsID.b    := $FF;
   tsID.c    := $FF;
   tsID.d    := $FF; { any server is the target server }
   texect[1] := $FF;
   texect[2] := $FF;
   texect[3] := $FF;
   texect[4] := $FF;
   texect[5] := $FF;
   texect[6] := $FF; { execution time is anytime, like now }
   jobtyp.wh := 0;
   jobtyp.wl := 0;   { job type 0 }
   jobcfl    := 0;   { job control flags, all cleared }
   {if you wish you may set up the text job area and the client record area}
   {in this example I leave them null}
   for a:=1 to 50 do txtjob[a] := 0;
   for a:=1 to 152 do cra[a]    := 0;
 end;
```

```
SQr.native.wh := 54;
SQr.native.wl := 0;

with regs do
begin
  AX := $E300;
  DS := Seg(SQc);
  SI := Ofs(SQc);

  ES := Seg(SQr);
  DI := Ofs(SQr);
end;

MsDos(regs);

if (regs.AL <> 0) then DisplayError(regs.AL, 1);

End; { end of StartJob }



Procedure QueueJob;
Begin

with FQc do
begin
  native.wh := 7;
  native.wl := 0;
  func      := $69;
  Qid.a     := theQ.a;
  Qid.b     := theQ.b;
  Qid.c     := theQ.c;
  Qid.d     := theQ.d;
  jobnum    := SQr.jobnum
end;

FQr.native.wh := 1;
FQr.native.wl := 0;

with regs do
begin
  AX := $E300;
  DS := Seg(FQc);
  SI := Ofs(FQc);
```

```
   ES := Seg(FQr);
   DI := Ofs(FQr);
end;

MsDos(regs);

if (regs.AL <> 0) then DisplayError(regs.AL, 2);

End; { end of QueueJob }




Procedure OpenWriteNETQ(request:char60; len:integer);
var
NETQ    : string[5];
filehan : integer;
Begin

    regs.AX := $3D02;
    NETQ     := 'NETQ'^@;
    regs.DS := Seg(NETQ);
    regs.DX := Ofs(NETQ)+1;

    MsDos(regs);

{    Writeln('File Handle from open NETQ = [',regs.AX,']');   }

    filehan := regs.AX;

    regs.AX := $4000;
    regs.BX := filehan;
    regs.CX := len;
    regs.DS := Seg(request);
    regs.DX := Ofs(request);

    MsDos(regs);

    {
      byte  0    = logical station number to send to
      bytes 1..56 = message to send
    }

    regs.AX := $3E00;
```

```
    regs.BX := filehan;

    MsDos(regs);


End; { end of OpenWriteNETQ }




Procedure GetQid;
Begin

 with GIc do
 begin
   native.wh := 8;
   native.wl := 0;
   func     := $35;
   objtyp.wh := QueueType.wh; {must match type defined in CreateQueue above}
   objtyp.wl := QueueType.wl;
   objnml    := 4;
   objnme[1] := 68; {D}
   objnme[2] := 69; {E}
   objnme[3] := 77; {M}
   objnme[4] := 79; {O}
 end;

 GIr.native.wh := 54;
 GIr.native.wl := 0;

 with regs do
 begin
   AX := $E300;
   DS := Seg(GIc);
   SI := Ofs(GIc);

   ES := Seg(GIr);
   DI := Ofs(GIr);
 end;

 MsDos(regs);

 if (regs.AL <> 0) then
 begin
   DisplayError(regs.AL, 3);
```

```
    Writeln('Unable to continue, cannot find queue DEMO',#7);
    Halt(2);
 end
 else
 begin
   theQ.a := GIr.Qid.a;
   theQ.b := GIr.Qid.b;
   theQ.c := GIr.Qid.c;
   theQ.d := GIr.Qid.d;
 end;


End; { end of GetQid }




Procedure GetMsg;
var
station : byte;
message : string[60];
request : char60;
Begin

{
 Please note that there is little input control here, incorrect input
 could cause a fatal error, but as this is not a program on how to
input I leave methods of input to you. .
}


Write('Please enter the station number to send a message to: ');
ReadLn(station);

WriteLn('Please enter your message, up to 56 characters:');
WriteLn('to abort just hit ENTER...');
ReadLn(message);

if (length(message)>0) then
begin
   request[0] := station;
   for a:=1 to length(message) do request[a] := ord(message[a]);

   OpenWriteNETQ(request, length(message)+1);
```

```
  end
  else
    Writeln('Message submittal aborted...');

End; { end of GetMsg }



Begin

    QueueType.wh := 3;
    QueueType.wl := 3;  { this is an arbitrary queue type... 0x0303 }

    clrscr;

    GetQid;

    StartJob;

    GetMsg;

    QueueJob;


End.
```

Now for C examples of the Turbo Pascal code just shown.

QSERVER_DEMO

```
/********************************************************************
 *
 * Program Name:   QSERVER.EXE
 *
 * Filename:       qs.c
 *
 * Version:        1.0
 *
 * Programmer:     John T. McCann
 *
```

```
 * Date:            October 4, 1990
 *
 */


/* START of include files */

#include <stdio.h>
#include <string.h>
#include <nxt.h>
#include <nit.h>
#include <nitq.h>
#include <nwmisc.h>
#include <signal.h>

/* END of include files */


/* START of defines, structures, and global variables */


#define Ofs(fp)        ((unsigned)(fp))
#define Seg(fp)        ((unsigned)((unsigned long)(fp) >> 16))


typedef union {
        struct {
                unsigned short Ax, Bx, Cx, Dx, Bp, Si, Di, Ds, Es,
                               FLAGS;
                } F;
        struct {
                unsigned char Al, Ah, Bl, Bh, Cl, Ch, Dl, Dh;
                } H;
            } Registers;
/* below is data structure used for IPX send/receive packets */
typedef struct
        {
        IPXHeader          Hdr;
        unsigned char      Data[546];
        } Packet ;


/* START of prototypes */

void DisplayError( int code, int routine);
```

```
void CreateQueueHere();
void AddSUPERVISOR();
void AddEVERYONE();
void AttachQueue();
void SetStatus();
void GetList();
void ServiceJob();
void MessageBy();
void SendMessage();
void DetachQueue();

/* Watcom prototypes for which I didn't have a .h file */
int  int86( int, Registers *, Registers *);
int  kbhit(void);

/* END of prototypes */


/* Global variables */

Registers Regs;
WORD      QueueType = 0x0303;
long      Qid;
WORD      jobCount, jobNumberList;
JobStruct job;
int       Qhandle;
char      request[100];
char      QName[16] = "DEMO1";

/* START of procedures */

/*
¤
¤¤¤¤¤¤¤¤¤¤¤¤¤¤¤¤¤¤¤¤¤¤¤¤¤¤¤¤¤¤¤¤¤¤¤¤¤¤¤¤¤¤¤¤¤¤¤¤¤¤¤¤¤¤¤¤¤¤¤¤¤¤¤¤¤¤¤¤¤¤¤¤¤¤¤¤¤¤¤¤
¤
*/
void DisplayError( int code, int routine)
{

  printf("Error from ");

  switch (routine)
  {
   case 1: printf("CreateQueue");break;
   case 2: printf("AddSUPERVISOR");break;
   case 3: printf("AttachQueue, Qid[%08lX]",Qid);break;
```

```
  case 4: printf("SetStatus");break;
  case 5: printf("GetList");break;
  case 6: printf("ServiceJob");break;
/*  case 7: printf("FinishJob"); procedure not needed...*/
  case 8: printf("DetachQueue, Qid[%08lX]",Qid);break;
  case 9: printf("AddEVERYONE");break;
  case 10:printf("MessageBy");break;

  default: printf("Unknown Procedure!");

 } /* end of switch */


 printf("-> ");

 switch (code)
 {
  case 150: printf("Server out of memory\n");break;
  case 153: printf("Directory Full\n");break;
  case 155: printf("Bad Directory Handle\n");break;
  case 156: printf("Invalid Path\n");break;
  case 208: printf("Queue Error\n");break;
  case 209: printf("No Queue\n");break;
  case 210: printf("No Queue server\n");break;
  case 211: printf("No Queue rights\n");break;
  case 213: printf("No Queue job\n");break;
  case 214: printf("No Job rights\n");break;
  case 217: printf("Station not server\n");break;
  case 218: printf("Queue halted\n");break;
  case 219: printf("Max Queue Servers reached\n");break;
  case 233: printf("Member already exists in property\n");break;
  case 237: printf("Property already exists\n");break;
  case 238: printf("Object already exists\n");break;
  case 239: printf("Invalid name\n");break;
  case 240: printf("Wildcard not allowed\n");break;
  case 241: printf("Invalid bindery security\n");break;
  case 245: printf("No object create privilege\n");break;
  case 247: printf("No propery create privilege\n");break;
  case 251: printf("No such property\n");break;
  case 252: printf("No such object\n");break;
  case 254: printf("Server bindery locked\n");break;
  case 255: printf("Bindery failure\n");break;

  default: printf("failure code <%x> is unknown\n",code);

 } /* end of switch */
```

```
} /* end of DisplayError() */
/*
¤
¤¤¤¤¤¤¤¤¤¤¤¤¤¤¤¤¤¤¤¤¤¤¤¤¤¤¤¤¤¤¤¤¤¤¤¤¤¤¤¤¤¤¤¤¤¤¤¤¤¤¤¤¤¤¤¤¤¤¤¤¤¤¤¤¤¤¤¤¤¤
¤
*/
void CreateQueueHere()
{
 int cc;

 cc=CreateQueue(QName, QueueType, (char) 0, "SYS:SYSTEM", &Qid);

 if ((cc) && (cc!=238))
   {
    DisplayError(cc, 1);
   }
   else
   {
    cc=GetBinderyObjectID(QName, QueueType, &Qid);

    if (cc) DisplayError(cc,1);
   }

} /* end of CreateQueue() */
/*
¤
¤¤¤¤¤¤¤¤¤¤¤¤¤¤¤¤¤¤¤¤¤¤¤¤¤¤¤¤¤¤¤¤¤¤¤¤¤¤¤¤¤¤¤¤¤¤¤¤¤¤¤¤¤¤¤¤¤¤¤¤¤¤¤¤¤¤¤¤¤¤
¤
*/
void AddSUPERVISOR()
{
 int cc;

 cc=AddBinderyObjectToSet(QName, QueueType, "Q_USERS", "SUPERVISOR",
       OT_USER);

 if ((cc) && (cc!=233)) DisplayError(cc,2);

} /* end of AddSUPERVISOR */
/*
¤
¤¤¤¤¤¤¤¤¤¤¤¤¤¤¤¤¤¤¤¤¤¤¤¤¤¤¤¤¤¤¤¤¤¤¤¤¤¤¤¤¤¤¤¤¤¤¤¤¤¤¤¤¤¤¤¤¤¤¤¤¤¤¤¤¤¤¤¤¤¤
¤
*/
```

```
void AddEVERYONE()
{
 int cc;

 cc=AddBinderyObjectToSet(QName, QueueType, "Q_USERS", "EVERYONE",
        OT_USER_GROUP);

 if ((cc) && (cc!=233)) DisplayError(cc,9);


 /* you might make sure members of the group EVERYONE can be q_servers,
    in your code you might wish to make the users privileged to be
    Q_SERVERS */

 cc=AddBinderyObjectToSet(QName, QueueType, "Q_SERVERS", "EVERYONE",
        OT_USER_GROUP);

 if ((cc) && (cc!=233)) DisplayError(cc,9);


} /* end of AddEVERYONE() */
/*
¤
¤¤¤¤¤¤¤¤¤¤¤¤¤¤¤¤¤¤¤¤¤¤¤¤¤¤¤¤¤¤¤¤¤¤¤¤¤¤¤¤¤¤¤¤¤¤¤¤¤¤¤¤¤¤¤¤¤¤¤¤¤¤¤¤¤¤¤¤¤¤¤¤¤¤¤¤¤¤
¤
*/
void AttachQueue()
{
 int cc;

 cc=AttachQueueServerToQueue(Qid);

 if (cc)
 {
  DisplayError(cc, 3);
 }
 else
 {
  printf("Successfully Attached to Queue %s",QName);
 }

} /* end of AttachQueue() */
/*
¤
¤¤¤¤¤¤¤¤¤¤¤¤¤¤¤¤¤¤¤¤¤¤¤¤¤¤¤¤¤¤¤¤¤¤¤¤¤¤¤¤¤¤¤¤¤¤¤¤¤¤¤¤¤¤¤¤¤¤¤¤¤¤¤¤¤¤¤¤¤¤¤¤¤¤¤¤¤¤
¤
```

```
*/
void SetStatus()
{
 int cc;

 cc=SetQueueServerCurrentStatus(Qid, "This is a demo Queue Server");

 if (cc) DisplayError(cc, 4);

} /* end of SetStatus() */
/*
¤
¤¤¤¤¤¤¤¤¤¤¤¤¤¤¤¤¤¤¤¤¤¤¤¤¤¤¤¤¤¤¤¤¤¤¤¤¤¤¤¤¤¤¤¤¤¤¤¤¤¤¤¤¤¤¤¤¤¤¤¤¤¤¤¤¤¤¤¤¤¤¤¤¤¤¤
¤
*/
void GetList()
{
 int cc;

 cc=GetQueueJobList(Qid, jobCount, jobNumberList, 250);

 if (cc) DisplayError(cc, 5);


 /* If this procedure is called and the call to GetQueueJobList
    returns a null pointer because there are no jobs you may get
    a NULL POINTER error after this program exits, this really
    isn't a big problem since this program won't try to access
    the null pointer if the jobCount is 0
 */

} /* end of GetList() */
/*
¤
¤¤¤¤¤¤¤¤¤¤¤¤¤¤¤¤¤¤¤¤¤¤¤¤¤¤¤¤¤¤¤¤¤¤¤¤¤¤¤¤¤¤¤¤¤¤¤¤¤¤¤¤¤¤¤¤¤¤¤¤¤¤¤¤¤¤¤¤¤¤¤¤¤¤¤
¤
*/
void ServiceJob()
{
 int cc;

 cc=ServiceQueueJobAndOpenFile(Qid, 0xFFFF, &job, &Qhandle);

 if (cc!=213) printf("\n");

 if ((cc) && (cc!=213))
```

147

```
 {
  DisplayError(cc, 6);
 }
 else
 {
  printf("Job submitted by ID %08lx", job.clientIDNumber);

  MessageBy(job.clientIDNumber);

  Regs.F.Ax = 0x3F00;
  Regs.F.Bx = Qhandle;
  Regs.F.Cx = 57;
  Regs.F.Ds = Seg(request);
  Regs.F.Dx = Ofs(request);

  int86(0x21, &Regs, &Regs);

  /*
    byte  0      = logical station number to send to
    bytes 1..56  = message to send
  */

  if (Regs.F.Ax>1)
  {
   SendMessage(request, Regs.F.Ax);
  }
  else
  {
   printf("Job is 0 length, nothing to process...\n");
  }

  FinishServicingQueueJobAndFile(Qid, job.jobNumber, (long) 1,
           Qhandle);
 }

} /* end of ServerJob() */
/*
¤
¤¤¤¤¤¤¤¤¤¤¤¤¤¤¤¤¤¤¤¤¤¤¤¤¤¤¤¤¤¤¤¤¤¤¤¤¤¤¤¤¤¤¤¤¤¤¤¤¤¤¤¤¤¤¤¤¤¤¤¤¤¤¤¤¤¤¤¤¤¤¤¤¤¤¤¤¤¤¤¤
¤
*/
void MessageBy()
{
 int cc;
 char Name[50];
```

```
cc=GetBinderyObjectName(job.clientIDNumber, Name, OT_USER);

if (cc)
{
 DisplayError(cc, 10);
}
else
{
 printf("Processing job from: [%s]", Name);
}

} /* end of MessageBy() */
/*
¤
¤¤¤¤¤¤¤¤¤¤¤¤¤¤¤¤¤¤¤¤¤¤¤¤¤¤¤¤¤¤¤¤¤¤¤¤¤¤¤¤¤¤¤¤¤¤¤¤¤¤¤¤¤¤¤¤¤¤¤¤¤¤¤¤¤¤¤¤¤¤¤¤¤¤¤¤¤¤¤¤¤¤
¤
*/
void SendMessage()
{
 int cc;
 WORD stn;
 BYTE results[2];

 stn=0;
 memcpy(&stn,&request[0],1); /* get stn number to send to */

 memcpy(request, request[1], 58);
 request[58]=0; /* make sure string is not longer than 57 characters */

 cc=SendPersonalMessage(request, stn, results, 1);

 if (cc)
 {
  printf("Unable to send message ");
 }
 else
 {
  printf("Message sent ");
 }

 printf("to station [%d]\n",stn);

} /* end of SendMessage() */
/*
¤
¤¤¤¤¤¤¤¤¤¤¤¤¤¤¤¤¤¤¤¤¤¤¤¤¤¤¤¤¤¤¤¤¤¤¤¤¤¤¤¤¤¤¤¤¤¤¤¤¤¤¤¤¤¤¤¤¤¤¤¤¤¤¤¤¤¤¤¤¤¤¤¤¤¤¤¤¤¤¤¤¤¤
```

```
¤
*/
void DetachQueue()
{
 int cc;

 cc=DetachQueueServerFromQueue(Qid);

 if (cc)
 {
  DisplayError(cc, 8);
 }
 else
 {
  printf("\nSuccessfully Detached from Queue %s",QName);
 }

} /* end of DetachQueue() */
/*
¤
¤¤¤¤¤¤¤¤¤¤¤¤¤¤¤¤¤¤¤¤¤¤¤¤¤¤¤¤¤¤¤¤¤¤¤¤¤¤¤¤¤¤¤¤¤¤¤¤¤¤¤¤¤¤¤¤¤¤¤¤¤¤¤¤¤¤¤¤¤¤
¤
*/
main()
{

 CreateQueueHere();

 printf("Queue ID is [%08lX]\n", Qid);

 AddSUPERVISOR();

 AddEVERYONE();

 AttachQueue();

 SetStatus();

 do
 {
  GetList();

  if (jobCount)
  {
   printf("Number of jobs in queue [%d]\n", jobCount);
```

```
  ServiceJob();

  printf(" end of job processing.\n");
  }

 } while (!kbhit()); /* end of do loop */

 DetachQueue();

} /* end of main() */
```

QCLIENT_DEMO

```
/********************************************************************
 *
 * Program Name:  QCLIENT.EXE
 *
 * Filename:      qc.c
 *
 * Version:       1.0
 *
 * Programmer:    John T. McCann
 *
 * Date:          October 4, 1990
 *
 */


/* START of include files */

#include <stdio.h>
#include <string.h>
#include <nxt.h>
#include <nit.h>
#include <nitq.h>
#include <nwmisc.h>
#include <signal.h>

/* END of include files */


/* START of defines, structures, and global variables */
```

```
#define Ofs(fp)      ((unsigned)(fp))
#define Seg(fp)      ((unsigned)((unsigned long)(fp) >> 16))

/*#endif*/


typedef union {
        struct {
                unsigned short Ax, Bx, Cx, Dx, Bp, Si, Di, Ds, Es,
                                FLAGS;
                } F;
        struct {
                unsigned char Al, Ah, Bl, Bh, Cl, Ch, Dl, Dh;
                } H;
            } Registers;

/* below is data structure used for IPX send/receive packets */
typedef struct
        {
        IPXHeader          Hdr;
        unsigned char      Data[546];
        } Packet ;


/* START of prototypes */

void DisplayError( int code, int routine);
void CreateQueueHere();
void AddSUPERVISOR();
void AddEVERYONE();
void AttachQueue();
void SetStatus();
void GetList();
void ServiceJob();
void MessageBy();
void SendMessage();
void DetachQueue();

/* Watcom prototypes for which I didn't have a .h file */
int  int86( int, Registers *, Registers *);
int  kbhit(void);

/* END of prototypes */
```

```
/* Global variables */

Registers Regs;
WORD       QueueType = 0x0303;
long       Qid;
WORD       jobCount, jobNumberList;
JobStruct  job;
int        Qhandle;
char       request[100];
char       QName[16] = "DEMO1";

/* START of procedures */

/*
¤
¤¤¤¤¤¤¤¤¤¤¤¤¤¤¤¤¤¤¤¤¤¤¤¤¤¤¤¤¤¤¤¤¤¤¤¤¤¤¤¤¤¤¤¤¤¤¤¤¤¤¤¤¤¤¤¤¤¤¤¤¤¤¤¤¤¤¤¤¤¤¤¤¤¤¤¤¤¤¤¤
¤
*/


void DisplayError( int code, int routine)
{

 printf("Error from ");

 switch (routine)
 {
  case 1: printf("StartJob");break;
  case 2: printf("QueueJob");break;
  case 3: printf("GetQid");break;

  default: printf("Unknown Procedure!");

 } /* end of switch */


 printf("-> ");

 switch (code)
 {
  case 150: printf("Server out of memory\n");break;
  case 153: printf("Directory Full\n");break;
  case 155: printf("Bad Directory Handle\n");break;
  case 156: printf("Invalid Path\n");break;
  case 208: printf("Queue Error\n");break;
  case 209: printf("No Queue\n");break;
```

```
    case 210: printf("No Queue server\n");break;
    case 211: printf("No Queue rights\n");break;
    case 213: printf("No Queue job\n");break;
    case 214: printf("No Job rights\n");break;
    case 217: printf("Station not server\n");break;
    case 218: printf("Queue halted\n");break;
    case 219: printf("Max Queue Servers reached\n");break;
    case 233: printf("Member already exists in property\n");break;
    case 237: printf("Property already exists\n");break;
    case 238: printf("Object already exists\n");break;
    case 239: printf("Invalid name\n");break;
    case 240: printf("Wildcard not allowed\n");break;
    case 241: printf("Invalid bindery security\n");break;
    case 245: printf("No object create privilege\n");break;
    case 247: printf("No propery create privilege\n");break;
    case 251: printf("No such property\n");break;
    case 252: printf("No such object {Not a member of Q_USERS}\n");break;
    case 254: printf("Server bindery locked\n");break;
    case 255: printf("Bindery failure\n");break;

    default: printf("failure code <%x> is unknown\n",code);

 } /* end of switch */

} /* end of DisplayError() */
/*
¤
¤¤¤¤¤¤¤¤¤¤¤¤¤¤¤¤¤¤¤¤¤¤¤¤¤¤¤¤¤¤¤¤¤¤¤¤¤¤¤¤¤¤¤¤¤¤¤¤¤¤¤¤¤¤¤¤¤¤¤¤¤¤¤¤¤¤¤¤¤¤¤¤¤¤
¤
*/
void StartJob()
{
 int cc;

 memset(&job.targetServerIDNumber, 0xFF, 4);
 memset(&job.targetExecutionTime, 0xFF, 6);
 job.jobType=0;
 job.jobControlFlags=0;
 memset(&job.textJobDescription, 0, 50);
 memset(&job.clientRecordArea, 0, 152);

 cc=CreateQueueJobAndFile(Qid, &job, &Qhandle);

 if (cc) DisplayError(cc, 1);

} /* end of StartJob() */
```

```
/*
¤
¤¤¤¤¤¤¤¤¤¤¤¤¤¤¤¤¤¤¤¤¤¤¤¤¤¤¤¤¤¤¤¤¤¤¤¤¤¤¤¤¤¤¤¤¤¤¤¤¤¤¤¤¤¤¤¤¤¤¤¤¤¤¤¤¤¤¤¤¤¤¤¤¤¤¤¤¤¤
¤
*/
void QueueJob()
{
 int cc;

 cc=CloseFileAndStartQueueJob(Qid, job.jobNumber, Qhandle);

 if (cc) DisplayError(cc, 2);

/* Note that some versions of the Novell C Library have the call
   implemented incorrectly, so, it might not work...but newer revisions
   of the library should be ok */

} /* end of QueueJob() */
/*
¤
¤¤¤¤¤¤¤¤¤¤¤¤¤¤¤¤¤¤¤¤¤¤¤¤¤¤¤¤¤¤¤¤¤¤¤¤¤¤¤¤¤¤¤¤¤¤¤¤¤¤¤¤¤¤¤¤¤¤¤¤¤¤¤¤¤¤¤¤¤¤¤¤¤¤¤¤¤¤
¤
*/
void WriteNETQ()
{
 Regs.F.Ax = 0x4000;
 Regs.F.Bx = Qhandle;
 Regs.F.Cx = strlen(request);
 Regs.F.Ds = Seg(request);
 Regs.F.Dx = Ofs(request);

 int86(0x21, &Regs, &Regs);

 Regs.F.Ax = 0x3E00;
 Regs.F.Bx = Qhandle;

 int86(0x21, &Regs, &Regs);

} /* end of WriteNETQ */
/*
¤
¤¤¤¤¤¤¤¤¤¤¤¤¤¤¤¤¤¤¤¤¤¤¤¤¤¤¤¤¤¤¤¤¤¤¤¤¤¤¤¤¤¤¤¤¤¤¤¤¤¤¤¤¤¤¤¤¤¤¤¤¤¤¤¤¤¤¤¤¤¤¤¤¤¤¤¤¤¤
¤
*/
void GetQid()
{
```

```
 int cc;

 cc=GetBinderyObjectID(QName, QueueType, &Qid);

 if (cc) DisplayError(cc, 3);

} /* end of GetQid() */
/*
 ¤
 ¤¤¤¤¤¤¤¤¤¤¤¤¤¤¤¤¤¤¤¤¤¤¤¤¤¤¤¤¤¤¤¤¤¤¤¤¤¤¤¤¤¤¤¤¤¤¤¤¤¤¤¤¤¤¤¤¤¤¤¤¤¤¤¤¤¤¤¤¤¤¤¤¤¤¤¤¤¤
 ¤
*/
void GetMsg()
{
 char msg[100];
 int  stn;

 printf("Please enter the station number to send a message to: ");
 scanf("%d",stn);

 printf("\n Please enter your message, up to 56 characters:");
 printf("\n To abort, just press ENTER with no message");
 printf("\n->");
 scanf("%s",msg);

 msg[56]=0;

 if (strlen(msg))
 {
  memcpy(request,&stn,1);

  memcpy(&request[1], msg, strlen(msg));

  WriteNETQ(request, strlen(request));
 }
 else
 {
  printf("\nMessage submittal aborted...");
 }

} /* end of GetMsg() */
/*
 ¤
 ¤¤¤¤¤¤¤¤¤¤¤¤¤¤¤¤¤¤¤¤¤¤¤¤¤¤¤¤¤¤¤¤¤¤¤¤¤¤¤¤¤¤¤¤¤¤¤¤¤¤¤¤¤¤¤¤¤¤¤¤¤¤¤¤¤¤¤¤¤¤¤¤¤¤¤¤¤¤
 ¤
*/
```

```
main()
{

 GetQid();

 printf("The Queue ID for the Queue [%s] is [%08lX]\n",QName,Qid);

 StartJob();

 GetMsg();

 QueueJob();

} /* end of main() */
```

PART 2

Protocol Considerations

NetWare provides many different mechanisms that allow your application to communicate with workstations on the network. The method of communication depends on the type of data that you need to relay, the speed with which that data needs to get to its destination, how important it is that the destination receives the data, and whether the communications used need to be compatible with non-NetWare networks.

Reasons for communicating include synchronization of activities, data passing, and recognition of services available. Operations such as program-to-program communications or interprocess communications can be achieved via IPX and SPX. IPX and SPX enable a truly distributed processing environment to exist for Novell LANS.

Chapter 5 provides an overview of communication protocols found within the NetWare environment (for v2.1x, unless otherwise noted). Then goes on to discuss, in an abstract way, operations you can accomplish, ending with actual examples of communication routines.

Chapter 6 discusses protocols other than IPX/SPX, including Named Pipes.

IPX/SPX

As the distributed nature of LANs plays a greater part in the development of applications, means of distributing communication is increasingly important. Preferable means of communications are reliable and quick (usually in that order of importance). In the NetWare environment there are two readily available protocols meeting these desires: NetBIOS, developed by IBM, and SPX, a derivation of IPX using Xerox's SPP. IPX, a derivation of Xerox's IDP, is also available, but IPX has no built-in reliability measures.

While quite reliable, NetBIOS in the NetWare environment is slower than SPX but is often used for developing applications that will be usable on various networks other than NetWare. SPX, innate to the NetWare environment, is both reliable and quick. This chapter will focus on the native NetWare protocols, IPX and SPX.

A BIOSed View

Unlike NetBIOS, SPX (and IPX) are inherently aware of internetworks. All nodes on a NetWare LAN have two addresses: a group address, and a node address. The group address is really known as the internetwork (or simply, network) address in the NetWare environment. The internetwork address describes the physical cable run where the node is located, except under Novell's Star system where it indicates the actual file server. Except for the Star, it is possible that more than one file server may exist on the same internetwork address. Further, the internetwork address is defined in software only, whereas the node address is defined in hardware or firmware—with the exception of Token-Ring's local address definability.

IPX

NetWare's lowest, and fastest, level of communications is called Internetwork Packet eXchange (IPX). IPX is the protocol that the NetWare shell uses to communicate across the network. It is a point-to-point, connectionless protocol (datagram), meaning that your application does not have to establish an explicit link between itself and the receiver. IPX has a few disadvantages, though. Namely, it does not guarantee delivery of data, it does not guarantee that the data will be sequenced properly between transmissions, and it does not suppress the reception of duplicate packets of data. To further understand packets, see Appendix F.

In order to perform IPX communications, each side must prepare two special data structures—an Event Control Block (ECB) and an IPX Header. The ECB is used by the shell to keep track of IPX (and SPX) data packets as they are being transmitted and received. Information about communication status fields and where in memory the components of the IPX packet are located are contained in the ECB. The IPX Header is physically appended to the message before it is sent to its destination. The IPX Header is used by IPX to determine the message's length (546 bytes maximum), source address, destination address, socket, and which routine to call after a send or receive count.

Sockets are used to route IPX and SPX packets to different processes expecting messages running on the same workstation. Socket numbers range from 0 to 0xFFFF. Xerox and Novell have reserved socket numbers 0 to 0x3FFF for specific network services. Novell administers socket numbers from 0x8000 to 0xFFFF for "well known" serving processes. You can contact Novell to receive a dedicated socket number(s) for your application. The remaining numbers, 0x4000 to 0x7FFF, are called Dynamic Sockets and are available for use on demand by any application running on the network. You should be careful, however, when using Dynamic Sockets, since other applications on the network might already be using the same number in this range that you are, thereby causing unexpected results, such as those caused by receiving another application's IPX packets.

Let's look at how you can use IPX to monitor workstations and determine what their current status is. The basic steps involved in using IPX are :

- Allocate an ECB for each IPX send or receive you will perform.
- Allocate an IPX Header for each message that you will send or receive
- Fill in the required fields of the ECB and IPX Header.
- Send the IPX packet, or "listen" for an IPX packet to receive.

SPX

The next level of communications occurs through the services of Sequenced Packet eXchange (SPX). SPX is a connection-oriented protocol. When using SPX, two workstations form a link, or pipe, over which they communicate. SPX is slower than IPX (Novell claims a 5% penalty), but it overcomes IPX's deficiencies by providing guaranteed data delivery, packet sequencing, and duplicate packet reception suppression. Where IPX is fast, SPX is robust.

Your needs should determine which you use. For instance, if you are doing real-time information gathering, ask yourself whether the loss or replication of a couple packets will affect your operations significantly. Likewise, if you were passing database updates to a database engine you probably want a guarantee that the packet survives and is not duplicated. Now, it should be noted that although IPX has no built-in guarantees of packet delivery and duplicate packet suppression, you can program these into an application. This may be necessary if you intend for your application to be usable under v2.0a of NetWare, due to the varied levels under which SPX is supported for v2.0a. Specifically v2.01-4 of the ANETx shell is the only one to be trusted in any way. Version 2.01-4 of the ANETx shell has never been shipped with NetWare, but is offered on many NetWare-aware bulletin boards as well as Novell's own Netwire CompuServe forum.

Reasons for communicating include synchronization of activities, data passing, and recognition of services available. In other words, much ballyhooed operations such as program-to-program communications or interprocess communications can be achieved via IPX and SPX. IPX and SPX enable a truly distributed processing environment for Novell LANs.

Internal Operations of IPX/SPX

Besides being identifiable by its internetwork/node address a node can have up over 65,000 different sockets (see Novell's documentation for a discussion of the proper ranges to use). Like a mailbox, a socket is only viable if defined for use at the node. Using sockets (which is not optional) simplifies interprocess communication. If a message is received for socket Z and there is buffer waiting to receive on socket Z, the message will be accepted (and possibly trigger an Event Service Routine (ESR)). Otherwise, it will be rejected.

As an example, a socket, say A000h, is set up to receive new user requests and socket A001h is used for communications coming from known users. Here there are two sockets set up to receive messages, if a message is not addressed with a valid (that is, open with a listen buffering waiting) socket number it will not be recognized. Realize that sockets give you, the developer, the ability to readily "parse" your requests/messages by simply assigning different socket numbers to your processes.

One possible construction using sockets is multi-processing within a node. This multiprocessing (or even multitasking), can be achieved in at least two distinct ways. One environment has multiple applications executing concurrently, with each application assigned its own set of sockets. Another environment (more reasonable on PCs) uses TSRs, each with its own set of sockets to use. The second environment readily lends itself to the use of ESRs.

ESRs

Each buffer listening (as well as sending, after the send is completed) for a packet/message can have an ESR. The ESR is nothing more than a special procedure that is called by IPX. The ESR is triggered when a packet is received or upon successful completion of a send. Discussions here will focus on ESRs upon reception of a packet.

Executing much like an ISR, an ESR is used to do processing of some sort that may or may not involve the packet reception triggering the ESR. For instance, a TSR that does processing, such as popping-up a screen, may be triggered by an ESR receiving a packet. Further, the TSR may be activated by a certain keyboard sequence or by the receipt of a packet, the latter via some polling mechanism. Thus, the TSR may be activated by the ESR stuffing the keyboard with the proper key sequence. Or, as another possibility, the TSR could hook into the timer interrupt (1Ch) and simply poll the statuses of buffers awaiting a packet. Once a buffer shows that it has received a packet, processing will occur.

Having the buffer (awaiting a packet in this case) use an ESR, rather than polling its status, allows for the occurrence of a more asynchronous approach to program behavior. Instead of watching for something to happen (polling), the application simply waits to be woken up (ESR). Using the wakeup approach avoids overhead that would come while polling every X clock cycle, if not every cycle.

Since it is essentially an ISR, the ESR should not take too long to complete, as you'd expect in the design of any ISR. Here are some examples:

```
; upon entering the ESR:
; *interrupts will be disabled
; *AL register will have identity of who called
; 00h=called by AES
; FFh=called by IPX
; *ES:SI register pair will point at the calling ECB
; *All processor flags and registers except SS:SP are saved, so
; no reason to save them within the ESR
MOV AX,ES setup the DataSegment properly
MOV DS,AX
or
PUSH ES
POP DS
CLI ; make sure interrupts are disabled
RETF ; ending as all ESRs must return...RETF
note that NO register values or flags are RET'd by an ESR
```

Find me

Ways specifying nodes for communication range from knowing the address ahead of time to broadcasting a packet to all nodes on the current internetwork. The original Novell Asynchronous Communications Server (ACS) used the first approach. The applications that deal with the ACS server were plugged into the ACS's address plugged through SETUPACS. An IPX function that broadcasts to all nodes is invoked by setting the send-to-node address to all high values (FFFFFFFFFFFFh). Alternatively, NetWare's SAP may be used, which is discussed in Part 3, Server Applications: Vaps and NLMs.

Another means of finding node(s) is through NetWare's Get Connection Information call (E3h sub 16h). With this call, you can find the login name of the user at the node. One scenario would have the application search for a login name of ENGINE (or whatever name that is desired). But, use of IPX does not require that a node sharing in communication be actually logged into any network. Simply having the shell (IPX.COM) loaded is sufficient, so the Get Connection Information call may not be viable.

And, in the spirit of the ACS, an application can have a predefined list of known addresses that it uses. Developers can also create a bindery object (perhaps even dynamic) that is used as a known object type to start the search for communication nodes. The bindery object would be of some predetermined type, perhaps without a prearranged name (a wildcard search for names could be performed in lieu of knowing names ahead of time). The object(s) would then have a property that included its address (NET_ADDRESS) and perhaps some other critical application data.

IPX_Receive_Example in Turbo Pascal

```
{$R-}     {Range checking off}
{$B-}     {Boolean short circuiting off}
{$S+}     {Stack checking on}
{$I+}     {I/O checking on}
{$N-}     {No numeric coprocessor}
{$M 65500,16384,655360} {Turbo 3 default stack and heap}

Program IPX_Receive_Example;
```

```
(*
   This Turbo Pascal v4.0 example hows how to set up to receive an IPX
packet.
*)


Uses
   Crt,
   Dos;

Const Socket = $4848; { This is just a socket I defined at random }
      SC      = $5555;

CMD=2;

type

{ below is the normal layout of an IPX packet }
IPXBLOCK = record
              CheckSum : array[1..2] of byte;
              Length   : array[1..2] of byte;
              TransCtrl: byte;
              PacketTyp: byte;
              DestNetw : array[1..4] of byte;
              DestNode : array[1..6] of byte;
              DestSckt : array[1..2] of byte;
              SrceNetw : array[1..4] of byte;
              SrceNode : array[1..6] of byte;
              SrceSckt : array[1..2] of byte;
              mm       : array[1..2] of byte;
              My_Check : integer; { 2 bytes }
              Special  : array[1..6] of byte;
              DataBulk : array[1..538] of byte;
           end;
```

```
{ below is the normal layout of an ECB buffer }
ECBBLOCK = record
            Link     : array[1..2] of integer;
            ESRaddr  : array[1..2] of integer;
            InUse    : byte;
            ComplCode: byte;
            ScktNum  : array[1..2] of byte;   {must match IPXBLOCK}
            IPX_W_Spc: array[1..4] of byte;
            Driver_Sp: array[1..12] of byte;
            ImmdAddr : array[1..6] of byte;
            FragCnt  : array[1..2] of byte;
            FragAdr  : array[1..2] of integer;
            FragSize : array[1..2] of byte;   { Typically 576 }
                                              { note: the FragAdr
points at
                                                our IPXBlock and data.
                                              }
        end;


Get = record
      INh      : Array [1..4] of Byte; { InterNetNetwork}
      Host     : Array [1..6] of Byte; { InterNetHost   }
      Sckt     : Array [1..2] of Byte; { InterNetSocket }
      end;

Rcv = record
      Host     : Array [1..6] of Byte;  { InterNetHost   }
      end;

var
x,temp:integer;
tem :array[1..2] of byte absolute temp;

f    : get;
q    : rcv;
ipxs : ipxblock;
ecbs : ecbblock;
ipxr : ipxblock;
ecbr : ecbblock;
regs : registers;
```

```
Procedure Rcv_Packet;
{ This procedure sets up an IPX receive buffer and waits for an
incoming packet (to receive), alternatively the user could press a key
to terminate the program should no packet ever be received }

var
k:char;
x:integer;
Begin


With ECBr do
   begin
                ESRaddr[1]:=0;
                ESRaddr[2]:=0;   { no ESR used }
                temp:=SC;        { Socket to receive on }
                ScktNum[1]:=tem[1];
                ScktNum[2]:=tem[2];

                FragCnt[1]:=1;   { number of fragments expected }
                FragCnt[2]:=0;
                FragAdr[1]:=Ofs(IPXr);
 (* Note lo-hi ordering of IPX packet address *)
                FragAdr[2]:=Seg(IPXr);

                Temp:=576;
{ expected packet length (that will be received) }
                FragSize[1]:=Tem[1];
                FragSize[2]:=Tem[2];
   end;

Regs.Bx:=0;
Regs.Al  :=0;
Regs.Dx:=SC;
Intr($7A,Regs);

Writeln('After Open Socket, stat = ',Regs.Al);
Writeln('Assigned Socket is = ',Regs.Dx);


Regs.Bx:=4;
Regs.Es:=Seg(ECBr);
Regs.Si:=Ofs(ECBr);
Intr($7A,Regs);
```

```
Writeln('IPX Receive Completion Status is: ',ECBr.ComplCode);
Writeln('IPX Receive In Use Flag is: ',ECBr.InUse);

{ Note: When a packet is received, you will receive into your defined
IPX packet buffer space the originiating node's full internetwork
address and you will receive a viable Immediate Address in your ECB
buffer defined for that receive }




REPEAT
UNTIL (ECBr.InUse=0) or (keypressed);

If keypressed then
REPEAT
k:=ReadKey;
UNTIL (not keypressed);


Regs.Bx:=1;
Regs.Dx:=SC; (* CLOSE SOCKET *)
Intr($7A,Regs);

Writeln('CLOSE: IPX Receive Completion Status is: ',ECBr.ComplCode);
Writeln('CLOSE: IPX Receive In Use Flag is: ',ECBr.InUse);


writeln('Packet Received:');
For x:=1 to 3 do Write(IPXr.mm[x],',');
writeln;
For x:=1 to 3 do Write(chr(IPXr.mm[x]));


End; { Received Packet }


Begin

Rcv_Packet;

End.
```

IPX_Send _Example in Turbo Pascal

```
{$R-}     {Range checking off}
{$B-}     {Boolean short circuiting off}
{$S+}     {Stack checking on}
{$I+}     {I/O checking on}
{$N-}     {No numeric coprocessor}
{$M 65500,16384,655360} {Turbo 3 default stack and heap}


Program IPX_Send_Example;
(*
  This Turbo Pascal v4.0 example demonstrates how to send an IPX packet
*)



Uses
  Crt,
  Dos;

const  Socket = $5555;  { This is just a socket I more or less chose at
random }
type

{ below is the normal layout of an IPX packet }
IPXBLOCK = record
              CheckSum : array[1..2] of byte;
              Length   : array[1..2] of byte;
              TransCtrl: byte;
              PacketTyp: byte;
              DestNetw : array[1..4] of byte;
              DestNode : array[1..6] of byte;
              DestSckt : array[1..2] of byte;
              SrceNetw : array[1..4] of byte;
              SrceNode : array[1..6] of byte;
              SrceSckt : array[1..2] of byte;
              DataBulk : array[1..538] of byte; { just a data area }
           end;



{ below is the normal layout of an ECB buffer }
ECBBLOCK = record
              Link     : array[1..2] of integer;
```

```
               ESRaddr  : array[1..2] of integer;
               InUse    : byte;
               ComplCode: byte;
               ScktNum  : array[1..2] of byte;   {must match IPXBLOCK}
               IPX_W_Spc: array[1..4] of byte;
               Driver_Sp: array[1..12] of byte;
               ImmdAddr : array[1..6] of byte;
               FragCnt  : array[1..2] of byte;
               FragAdr  : array[1..2] of integer;
               FragSize : array[1..2] of byte;  { Typically 576 }
                                                { note: the FragAdr
                                                    points at the
                                                    IPX packet(s) }
        end;


Get = record
      INh        : Array [1..4] of Byte;   { InterNetNetwork }
      Host       : Array [1..6] of Byte;   { InterNetHost    }
      Sckt       : Array [1..2] of Byte;   { InterNetSocket  }
      end;

Rcv = record
      Host       : Array [1..6] of Byte;   { InterNetHost    }
      end;

var
temp:integer;
tem :array[1..2] of byte absolute temp;

f    : get;
q    : rcv;
ipxs : ipxblock;
ecbs : ecbblock;
ipxr : ipxblock;
ecbr : ecbblock;
regs : registers;
```

```
Procedure Send_Packet;
{ This procedure sets up an IPX packet and ECB buffer and then opens an
  IPX socket and sends the assembled packet and then closes the socket
}
var
x:integer;
Begin
Fillchar(IPXs,576,0); { null out these two fields }
Fillchar(ECBs,36,0);

 With IPXs do
    begin
              fillchar(CheckSum,2,0); { not using the CheckSum }
              temp:=34;
              Length[1]:=tem[1];      { set up length of packet }
              Length[2]:=tem[2];
              TransCtrl:=0;
              PacketTyp:=17; { Unknown packet type ... }

              DestNetw[1]:=$00;
              DestNetw[2]:=$00;
              DestNetw[3]:=$0;
              DestNetw[4]:=$00;

              DestNode[1]:=$ff;
              DestNode[2]:=$ff;
              DestNode[3]:=$ff;
              DestNode[4]:=$ff;
              DestNode[5]:=$ff;
              DestNode[6]:=$ff;

              temp:=socket;
              DestSckt[1]:=tem[1]; { set up the destination socket }
              DestSckt[2]:=tem[2];

              temp:=$0740;
              SrceSckt[1]:=tem[1]; { set up the source socket (really
                                     doesn't matter here) }
              SrceSckt[2]:=tem[2];

              DataBulk[1]:=72; {H}
              DataBulk[2]:=73; {I}
              DataBulk[3]:=33; {!}

      End; { of with }
```

```
With ECBs do
  begin
            ESRaddr[1]:=0;
            ESRaddr[2]:=0;   { no ESR here {}

            temp:=socket;
            ScktNum[1]:=tem[1]; { set up the socket, needs to match
that in IPX packet }
            ScktNum[2]:=tem[2];

            for x:=1 to 6 do ImmdAddr[x]:=$ff; { set up the Immediate
                                            Address}
                     { This address is important if your packet
                       is to go over any bridges, use the IPX Get
                       Local Target call to get the appropriate
                       Immediate Address }

                     { The following illustrates how you'd do a
                       Get Local Target Call
                       Regs.Bx:=2;
                       Regs.Es:=Seg(IPXs);
                       Regs.Si:=Ofs(IPXs.DestNetw[1]);
                       Intr($7A,Regs);
                     }

            FragCnt[1]:=1; { number of fragments, in lo-hi order,
                          compliments of Intel }
            FragCnt[2]:=0;
            FragAdr[1]:=Ofs(IPXs); { addrss of IPX packet, in lo-hi
                                order (offset-segment) }
            FragAdr[2]:=Seg(IPXs);

            Temp:=34;              { length of IPX packet, this length }
            FragSize[1]:=Tem[1]; { is always 30 bytes to cover the   }
            FragSize[2]:=Tem[2]; { standard IPX packet, any          }
                                 { additional size is used to "cover"}
                                 { your data portion of the IPX      }
                                 { packet                            }
  end;


Regs.Bx:=0;
Regs.Al  :=0;      (* OPEN SOCKET  0 *)
```

```
Regs.Dx:=Socket;

Intr($7A,Regs);

Writeln('After Open Socket, status =   : ',Regs.Al);
Writeln('Assigned Socket Number is =   : ',Regs.Dx);


Regs.Bx:=3;
Regs.Es:=Seg(ECBs);
Regs.Si:=Ofs(ECBs);   (* SEND PACKET  3 *)
Intr($7A,Regs);

Writeln('Completion Code AFTER send is : ',ECBs.ComplCode);
Writeln('In Use Flag Stat After Send is:',ECBs.InUse);


Regs.Bx:=1;
Regs.Dx:=socket; (* CLOSE SOCKET  1 *)
Intr($7A,Regs);

End; { Send Packet }




Begin

Send_Packet;

End.
```

```
/******************************************************************
 *
 * Program Name:   IPXSR.EXE
 *
 * Filename:       ipx.c
 *
 * Version:        1.0
 *
 * Programmer:     John T. McCann
 *
 * Date:           October 5, 1990
 *
 */

/*
  This IPX example will open a socket, set up a receive buffer and send
  a broadcast (destination address of 0xFFFFFFFFFFFF) to the local
  network and will then receive a message from itself...

  This code uses the Novell C library
*/


/* START of include files */

#include <stdio.h>
#include <string.h>
#include <nxt.h>
#include <nit.h>
#include <nwmisc.h>
#include <signal.h>

/* END of include files */

/* START of defines, structures, and global variables */

#define SOCKET_TO_USE 0x6868;
#define retriesAllowed 2 /* number of retries (IPXSend..) before aborting */
```

```
#if defined(__TINY__) || defined(__SMALL__) || defined(__MEDIUM__)
#define Seg(ptr) _DS
#define Ofs(ptr) (unsigned)(ptr)
#else
#define Ofs(fp)        ((unsigned)(fp))
#define Seg(fp)        ((unsigned)((unsigned long)(fp) >> 16))
#endif

typedef union {
        struct {
                unsigned int Ax, Bx, Cx, Dx, Si, Di, FLAGS;
                } F;
        struct {
                unsigned char Al, Ah, Bl, Bh, Cl, Ch, Dl, Dh;
                } H;
            } Registers;

/* below is data structure used for IPX send/receive packets */
typedef struct
        {
        IPXHeader           Hdr;
        unsigned char       Data[546];
        } Packet ;


ECB     ECBs, ECBr;   /* ECB's for IPX send and receive */
Packet  IPXs, IPXr;   /* IPX buffers for IPX send and receive */

Registers Regs;

int timeOut; /* how long in ticks (~55ms each) for receiving a packet*/

/* END of defines, structures, and global variables */


/* START of prototypes */

void doIPXsetup();
void doIPXwait();
void resendAbort();
void rcvPacket();
```

```
/* Watcom prototypes for which I didn't have a .h file */
int   getche( void );
int   getch( void );
int   int86( int, Registers *, Registers *);
void exit (int);
int   kbhit(void);

/* END of prototypes */


// START of procedures


void SendPacket()
{
int SR;

   doIPXsetup();

   sprintf(IPXs.Data,"From Stn [%d]", GetConnectionNumber());

   rcvPacket();

   printf("\nWould you to Send (1) or Receive (2) a message :");
   scanf("%d", &SR);

   if (SR==1) /* if sending, otherwise just wait */
    IPXSendPacket(&ECBs);
   else
    printf("\nWaiting...");

   doIPXwait();

   printf("\nReceived: [%s]",IPXr.Data);


} /* end of SendPacket */
/*
 ¤
 ¤¤¤¤¤¤¤¤¤¤¤¤¤¤¤¤¤¤¤¤¤¤¤¤¤¤¤¤¤¤¤¤¤¤¤¤¤¤¤¤¤¤¤¤¤¤¤¤¤¤¤¤¤¤¤¤¤¤¤¤¤¤¤¤¤¤¤¤¤¤¤¤¤¤¤¤¤¤¤
 ¤
*/
void doIPXsetup()
{
```

```
/* This procedure will
   Initialize IPX (C library) and memory areas,
   Open a socket
   Get the intermediate address to use when communicating a known node
   Set the time out value, used for resending "lost" requests
   Initialize IPX send and receive areas */

BYTE status;
WORD socket, mySocket;
int  result;
char myAddress[10];

  status=IPXInitialize();
  if (status != 0)
  {
   printf("Unable to Initialize IPX interface, aborting...\n\7");
   exit(4);
  }

  socket=SOCKET_TO_USE;

  result=IPXOpenSocket(&socket, 0x00); /* open short lived socket */

  if ( (result) && (result!=0xff) ) /* 0xff means already open, that's
ok*/
  {
   printf("\nFAILED: result of IPX open [%x], exiting to system\n\7",result);
   exit(5);
  }
/* below zeroes out the ECB and IPX areas */
  memset(&ECBs,0, sizeof(ECBs));
  memset(&IPXs,0, sizeof(IPXs));
  memset(&ECBr,0, sizeof(ECBr));
  memset(&IPXr,0, sizeof(IPXr));

  ECBs.socketNumber = socket;

  ECBs.fragmentCount = 1;
  ECBs.fragmentDescriptor[0].address = &IPXs;
  ECBs.fragmentDescriptor[0].size = 52; /* just a random size */

  IPXs.Hdr.packetType = 4; /* not entirely necessary to set... */
```

```
   GetInternetAddress(GetConnectionNumber(),
                      &IPXs.Hdr.destination.network[0],/* receives our
                                                          network addr */
                      myAddress, &mySocket);

   printf("\nDestination network [%02X%02X%02X%02X]",
         IPXs.Hdr.destination.network[0],IPXs.Hdr.destination.network[1],
         IPXs.Hdr.destination.network[2],IPXs.Hdr.destination.network[3]);

   memset(&ECBs.immediateAddress[0], 0xFF, 6); /* you might use
                                                  GetLocalTarget() to
                                                  ascertain the
                                                  immediateAddress
                                                */

   memcpy(&IPXs.Hdr.destination.socket, &socket, 2); /* this socket */

   memset(&IPXs.Hdr.destination.node[0], 0xFF, 6); /*
destination=everyone*/

   ECBr.socketNumber  = socket;
   ECBr.fragmentCount = 1;
   ECBr.fragmentDescriptor[0].address = &IPXr;
   ECBr.fragmentDescriptor[0].size    = 576; /* big enough to receive
                                                largest size allowed */

   timeOut = 40; /* one second = 18.7 ticks */

} /* end of doIPXsetup */
/*
 ¤
 ¤¤¤¤¤¤¤¤¤¤¤¤¤¤¤¤¤¤¤¤¤¤¤¤¤¤¤¤¤¤¤¤¤¤¤¤¤¤¤¤¤¤¤¤¤¤¤¤¤¤¤¤¤¤¤¤¤¤¤¤¤¤¤¤¤¤¤¤¤¤¤¤¤
 ¤
*/
void doIPXwait()
{
/* This procedure waits for the "receive" ECB (ECBr) to "hear"
   something, which is denoted by ECBr.inUseFlag becoming equal to 0
   if the loops below "timeout" then the request is sent again, perhaps
   it was lost in transit or the reply was lost in its transit

   timeOut contains amount of time, in system clocks (~55ms each) to
   wait before resending request
   all requests are presumed to be from the ECBs variable
*/
```

180

```
unsigned int stime,time,TimeOut, resends;

  resends=time=0;
  TimeOut=timeOut; /* the global variable timeOut has to be signed, for
                      our calculation below it has to be unsigned,
                      hence use of TimeOut */

  stime=IPXGetIntervalMarker(); /* get start time interval */

  while (ECBr.inUseFlag)
  {
   time=IPXGetIntervalMarker(); /* get current time interval */
   IPXRelinquishControl();       /* let the driver do some work */

   /* below indicates we had a time out, resend request */
   if (((time-stime)>TimeOut) && (ECBr.inUseFlag))
   {
    resends++;
    IPXSendPacket(&ECBs);        /* send again */

    stime=IPXGetIntervalMarker();/* get start time interval, again */
   }

   if (resends>=retriesAllowed) resendAbort(); /* quit, too many
retries*/

  } /* end of while (ECBr.inUseFlag) */

} /* end of doIPXwait */
/*
 ¤
 ¤¤¤¤¤¤¤¤¤¤¤¤¤¤¤¤¤¤¤¤¤¤¤¤¤¤¤¤¤¤¤¤¤¤¤¤¤¤¤¤¤¤¤¤¤¤¤¤¤¤¤¤¤¤¤¤¤¤¤¤¤¤¤¤¤¤¤¤¤¤¤¤¤¤¤¤
 ¤
*/
void resendAbort()
{
/* This procedure is called only when communications have failed
   after several retries
*/

  printf("\nAborted, unable to communicate with anyone!\7");

  exit(11);
```

```
} /* end of resendAbort */
/*
 ¤
 ¤¤¤¤¤¤¤¤¤¤¤¤¤¤¤¤¤¤¤¤¤¤¤¤¤¤¤¤¤¤¤¤¤¤¤¤¤¤¤¤¤¤¤¤¤¤¤¤¤¤¤¤¤¤¤¤¤¤¤¤¤¤¤¤¤¤¤¤¤¤¤¤¤¤¤
 ¤
*/
void rcvPacket()
{
/* This procedure sets up the listen buffer then posts it for listening
*/

  ECBr.fragmentCount                 = 1;
  ECBr.fragmentDescriptor[0].address = &IPXr;
  ECBr.fragmentDescriptor[0].size    = 576;
  ECBr.socketNumber                  = SOCKET_TO_USE;
  IPXListenForPacket(&ECBr);

} /* end of rcvPacket */
/*
 ¤
 ¤¤¤¤¤¤¤¤¤¤¤¤¤¤¤¤¤¤¤¤¤¤¤¤¤¤¤¤¤¤¤¤¤¤¤¤¤¤¤¤¤¤¤¤¤¤¤¤¤¤¤¤¤¤¤¤¤¤¤¤¤¤¤¤¤¤¤¤¤¤¤¤¤¤¤
 ¤
*/
void main()
{

 SendPacket();

}



/*******************************************************************
 *
 * Program Name:  SPXSR.EXE
 *
 * Filename:      spx.c
 *
 * Version:       1.0
 *
 * Programmer:    John T. McCann
 *
 * Date:          October 5, 1990
 *
 */
```

```
/*
   This SPX example will prompt the user for the NetWare connection
   to make contact with and whether it will be sending or receiving
   the message....when using this code, run the station that will be
   receiving first because once it is waiting it will wait forever
   only if it receives a message or if your press a key will it stop
   the sending node will send and then wait briefly to see if it gets
   a return message then it returns to DOS...
*/



/* START of include files */

#include <stdio.h>
#include <string.h>
#include <nxt.h>
#include <nit.h>
#include <nwmisc.h>
#include <signal.h>

/* END of include files */

/* START of defines, structures, and global variables */

#define SOCKET_TO_USE 0x6868;

/* below is data structure used for IPX send/receive packets */
typedef struct
        {
        SPXHeader           Hdr;
        unsigned char       Data[546];
        } SPXPacket ;


ECB        ECBs, ECBr;   /* ECB's for IPX send and receive */
ECB        ECBr1, ECBr2;
SPXPacket  SPXs, SPXr;   /* IPX buffers for IPX send and receive */
SPXPacket  SPXr1, SPXr2;

int timeOut; /* how long in ticks (~55ms each) for receiving a packet*/
```

```
WORD SPXconnection, SR;

/* END of defines, structures, and global variables */


/* START of prototypes */

void doSPXsetup();
void doSPXwait();
void InitECBs();
void GetSetup();
void resendAbort();
void rcvConnection();
void exit (int);
int  kbhit(void);


/* END of prototypes */

/* START of procedures */

void SendPacket()
{
/*
   This is the controlling procedure, it calls all the other procedures
   in order to start/receive communications
 */
  doSPXsetup();

  sprintf(SPXs.Data,"From Stn [%d]", GetConnectionNumber());

  ECBs.fragmentDescriptor[0].size = 576; /* reset buffer size */
  SPXSendSequencedPacket(SPXconnection, &ECBs);

  if (SR==1) /* sending */
  {
   while ((ECBr1.inUseFlag) && (!kbhit()) && (ECBr2.inUseFlag))
   {
    IPXRelinquishControl();
   }

   if ((ECBr1.inUseFlag) && (ECBr2.inUseFlag))
   {
```

```
    printf("\nConnection not completed, status 1 [%X], status 2 [%X]",
            ECBr1.inUseFlag, ECBr2.inUseFlag);
    exit(3);
  }
} /* end of if SR==1 (sending) */


if (SR==2) /* just listening */
{
 while ((ECBr.inUseFlag) && (!kbhit()))
 {
  IPXRelinquishControl();
 }
 if (ECBr.inUseFlag)
 {
  printf("\nConnection not completed, status [%X]",ECBr.inUseFlag);
  exit(3);
 }

 memcpy(&SPXconnection,&ECBr.IPXWorkspace,2); /* get Connection ID */

} /* end of if SR==2 (listening) */

printf("\nSPX connection found to be [%X]",SPXconnection);

SPXSendSequencedPacket(SPXconnection, &ECBs); /* Send back a message
*/

while ( (ECBr1.inUseFlag) && (ECBr2.inUseFlag) && (!kbhit()) ) ;

printf("\nReceive Buffer [1]: [%s]  inUseFlag [%X]",
        SPXr1.Data,ECBr1.inUseFlag);
printf("\nReceive Buffer [2]: [%s]  inUseFlag [%X]",
        SPXr2.Data,ECBr2.inUseFlag);

SPXTerminateConnection(SPXconnection, &ECBs);

} /* end of SendPacket */
```

```
/*
 ¤
¤¤¤¤¤¤¤¤¤¤¤¤¤¤¤¤¤¤¤¤¤¤¤¤¤¤¤¤¤¤¤¤¤¤¤¤¤¤¤¤¤¤¤¤¤¤¤¤¤¤¤¤¤¤¤¤¤¤¤¤¤¤¤¤¤¤¤¤¤¤¤¤¤¤¤¤¤¤
 ¤
*/
void doSPXsetup()
{
/*
    This procedure will
    Initialize SPX (C library) and memory areas,
    Open a socket to send and receive on
    Get the intermediate address to use when communicating with another
      node that is "known", the example here uses broadcasts
    Set the time out value, used for resending "lost" requests
 */
BYTE status, majorRev, minorRev;
WORD socket, maxCon, availCon, timer;
int  result;

  status=SPXInitialize(&majorRev, &minorRev, &maxCon, &availCon);

  if (status != SPX_IS_INSTALLED)
  {
   printf("Unable to Initialize SPX interface, aborting...\n\7");
   exit(4);
  }

  socket=SOCKET_TO_USE;

  result=IPXOpenSocket(&socket, 0x00); /* open short lived socket */

  if ( (result) && (result!=0xff) ) /* 0xff means already open, that's ok*/
  {
   printf("\nFAILED: result of IPX open [%x], exiting to system\n\7",result);
   exit(5);
  }

  InitECBs();  /* zero out memory areas */

  GetSetup();  /* Get Connection to talk */

  GetTarget(); /* Get that Connection's Immediate Address */
```

```
   rcvConnection(); /* set up one listen for connection buffer and
                        two receive communications buffers */

   if (SR==1) /* 1= Send, i.e. do Establish Connection */
   {
    timer=status=0;

    status=SPXEstablishConnection( (BYTE) 255, (BYTE) 0,
               &SPXconnection, &ECBs);

    printf("\nSPXEstablishConnection Status [%x]",status);

    while (timer<20000)
    {
     timer++;
     if (!ECBs.inUseFlag) timer=63999;
     IPXRelinquishControl();
    }

    /* printf("\nAfter timer [%x]",ECBs.inUseFlag); */


    if (timer!=63999)
    {
     printf("\nUnable to make a connection, aborting...");
     exit(1);
    }

    if (ECBs.completionCode)
    {
     printf("\nSPX could not establish connection, code = [%x]",
               ECBs.completionCode);
     exit(14);
    }

    printf("\nConnection established.");

   } /* end of if SR==1 */

} /* end of doSPXsetup */
/*
 ¤
¤¤¤¤¤¤¤¤¤¤¤¤¤¤¤¤¤¤¤¤¤¤¤¤¤¤¤¤¤¤¤¤¤¤¤¤¤¤¤¤¤¤¤¤¤¤¤¤¤¤¤¤¤¤¤¤¤¤¤¤¤¤¤¤¤¤¤¤¤¤¤¤¤¤¤¤
 ¤
*/
```

```
void InitECBs()
{
/*
   below zeroes out the ECB and SPX areas and sets up the buffer to
   initiate communications with
 */

  memset(&ECBs,0, sizeof(ECBs));
  memset(&SPXs,0, sizeof(SPXs));
  memset(&ECBr,0, sizeof(ECBr));
  memset(&SPXr,0, sizeof(SPXr));
  memset(&ECBr1,0, sizeof(ECBr1));
  memset(&SPXr1,0, sizeof(SPXr1));
  memset(&ECBr2,0, sizeof(ECBr2));
  memset(&SPXr2,0, sizeof(SPXr2));

  ECBs.socketNumber  = SOCKET_TO_USE;

  ECBs.fragmentCount = 1;
  ECBs.fragmentDescriptor[0].address = &SPXs;
  ECBs.fragmentDescriptor[0].size = 42; /* buffer size MUST be 42 */

} /* end of InitECBs */
/*
 ¤
¤¤¤¤¤¤¤¤¤¤¤¤¤¤¤¤¤¤¤¤¤¤¤¤¤¤¤¤¤¤¤¤¤¤¤¤¤¤¤¤¤¤¤¤¤¤¤¤¤¤¤¤¤¤¤¤¤¤¤¤¤¤¤¤¤¤¤¤¤¤¤¤¤¤¤¤¤¤¤
 ¤
*/
void GetSetup()
{
/*
   NOTE that below we just prompt the user for a connection to
   communicate with and whether or not this instantiation of
   this application is the sender or the receiver
 */
WORD ConNum, result, mySocket;

  ConNum=SR=0;
  printf("\nPlease enter the connection number to connect to: ");
  scanf("%d",&ConNum);

  result= GetInternetAddress(ConNum,
                   &SPXs.Hdr.destination.network[0],
                   &SPXs.Hdr.destination.node[0], &mySocket);
```

```
  if (result)
  {
   printf("\nFAILED: result of GetInternetAddress [%x], ",result);
   printf("exiting to system\n\7");
   exit(5);
  }

  printf("\nDestination network [%02X%02X%02X%02X], result [%x] Con[%d]",
          SPXs.Hdr.destination.network[0],SPXs.Hdr.destination.network[1],
          SPXs.Hdr.destination.network[2],SPXs.Hdr.destination.network[3],
          result,ConNum);

  SPXs.Hdr.destination.socket=SOCKET_TO_USE; /* this socket */

  printf("\nWould you to Send (1) or Receive (2) a message :");
  scanf("%d", &SR);

} /* end of GetSetup */
/*
 ¤
¤¤¤¤¤¤¤¤¤¤¤¤¤¤¤¤¤¤¤¤¤¤¤¤¤¤¤¤¤¤¤¤¤¤¤¤¤¤¤¤¤¤¤¤¤¤¤¤¤¤¤¤¤¤¤¤¤¤¤¤¤¤¤¤¤¤¤¤¤¤¤¤¤¤¤¤¤¤¤¤
 ¤
*/
void GetTarget()
{
/*
   Get the Local Target address of the node to send to
 */
WORD result;
int  timeOut;

  result =IPXGetLocalTarget(&SPXs.Hdr.destination.network,
              &ECBs.immediateAddress[0],&timeOut);

  if (result)
  {
   printf("\nFAILED: result of IPX Get Local Target [%x], ",result);
   printf("exiting to system\n\7");
   exit(6);
  }

  printf("\nImmediate Address found to be [%02X%02X%02X%02X%02X%02X]",
          ECBs.immediateAddress[0],ECBs.immediateAddress[1],
          ECBs.immediateAddress[2],ECBs.immediateAddress[3],
          ECBs.immediateAddress[4],ECBs.immediateAddress[5]);
```

```
} /* end of GetTarget */
/*
 ¤
¤¤¤¤¤¤¤¤¤¤¤¤¤¤¤¤¤¤¤¤¤¤¤¤¤¤¤¤¤¤¤¤¤¤¤¤¤¤¤¤¤¤¤¤¤¤¤¤¤¤¤¤¤¤¤¤¤¤¤¤¤¤¤¤¤¤¤¤¤¤¤¤¤¤
 ¤
*/
void rcvConnection()
{
/*
  This procedure sets up the listen buffer for connection initiation
  and posts two buffers to listening for messages
 */

  ECBr.fragmentCount                 = 1;
  ECBr.fragmentDescriptor[0].address = &SPXr;
  ECBr.fragmentDescriptor[0].size    = 42;
  ECBr.socketNumber                  = SOCKET_TO_USE;
  SPXListenForConnection((BYTE) 0, (BYTE) 0, &ECBr);

  /* in use flag for SPXListenForConnection will be 0xF9 while it is
     waiting */

  ECBr1.fragmentCount                 = 1;
  ECBr1.fragmentDescriptor[0].address = &SPXr1;
  ECBr1.fragmentDescriptor[0].size    = 576;
  ECBr1.socketNumber                  = SOCKET_TO_USE;
  SPXListenForSequencedPacket(&ECBr1);

  ECBr2.fragmentCount                 = 1;
  ECBr2.fragmentDescriptor[0].address = &SPXr2;
  ECBr2.fragmentDescriptor[0].size    = 576;
  ECBr2.socketNumber                  = SOCKET_TO_USE;
  SPXListenForSequencedPacket(&ECBr2);

} /* end of rcvPacket */
/*
 ¤
¤¤¤¤¤¤¤¤¤¤¤¤¤¤¤¤¤¤¤¤¤¤¤¤¤¤¤¤¤¤¤¤¤¤¤¤¤¤¤¤¤¤¤¤¤¤¤¤¤¤¤¤¤¤¤¤¤¤¤¤¤¤¤¤¤¤¤¤¤¤¤¤¤¤
 ¤
*/
void main()
{

  SendPacket();

}
```

CHAPTER 6

Named Pipes and Other Methods

This chapter examines some of the protocols available for developers to use other than IPX/SPX. It begins with a discussion of Named Pipes, NetWare's mechanism for communication in OS/2 environments, and continues with a discussion of some of NetWare's built-in interprocess communication features

Named Pipes

Named Pipes originated in the OS/2 environment for interprocess communications between client-server applications on an OS/2-based network. Novell has created the interface that allows DOS clients to participate in transactions with OS/2-based server applications. Basically, an OS/2 process acts as a value-added server on the network.

Named Pipes are created and monitored by these processes. When a client requests information via a named pipe, the server process performs the desired transaction and returns the result over the Named Pipe to the requesting client. Typically, a DOS client will wait for the response from the serving process before continuing. The best aspect of using Named Pipes is that the client application does not need to know anything about the underlying method used for communications, unlike IPX and SPX, where the programmer must be intimately involved in the interaction between both sides of the communications link.

With the current implementation of Named Pipes in NetWare, only workstations running OS/2 can actually create a Named Pipe. DOS clients can only use Named Pipes that have been created. And since DOS clients cannot create Named Pipes (they can only use them), the usefulness of Named Pipes in the NetWare environment is limited, especially if there are no OS/2 workstations. This inability of DOS workstations to create Named Pipes is a pretty severe limitation for most developers. However, if the network will include OS/2 workstations, then using named pipes is viable.

The basic idea behind Named Pipes is exchanging data at a read/write level.

Just like the operations on a DOS file, reading and writing of the Named Pipe allows for data exchange. And, just like DOS files, named pipes exist in the file space of a network disk. The fact that Named Pipes are created with a special keyword, PIPE, as part of the "directory" path specified indicates Named Pipe files from others in the same file space.

For instance, in this OS/2 example code, an attempt to create a Named Pipe would be:

```
#define   NUM_CLIENTS   10   /* number of clients */
#define   PIPENAME      "\\PIPE\\DEMOPIPE"
HPIPE     pipeHandles[NUM_CLIENTS];

void far CreatePipe(ClientNum)
int ClientNum;
{
 USHORT openMode = 0x0002;      /* a duplex named pipe */
 USHORT pipeMode = 0x0010;      /* total number of instances allowed */
 LONG   timeOut  = 0;           /* timeout value to use, 0=default */
 USHORT cc;
 struct COMMBUFFER commBuffer;

  /* create an new instance of a named pipe  */
  cc= DosMakeNmPipe(PIPENAME, &pipeHandle[ClientNum], openMode,  pipeMode,
          sizeof(struct COMMBUFFER), sizeof(struct COMMBUFFER), timeOut);
 .
 .
 .
```

The DOS client might try to open the pipe with:

```
WORD connectionIDtoUse;  /* set to 1-8, points to the file server
                            connection to use */
char fileServerName[50]; /* big enough to house file server name */
struct COMMBUFFER *commBuffer, *outBuffer;
ULONG timeOut;
USHORT bytesRead, cc;

   GetFileServerName(connectionIDtoUse, fileServerName)
   sprintf(pipeName,"\\\\%s%s",fileServerName,PIPENAME);
                    /* PIPENAME is same as above #define */
```

```
timeOut = 10000L;                  /* time out after 10 seconds  */
do                                 /* send messages out the pipe */
{
    cc = DosCallNmPipe(pipeName,      (char *)commBuffer,
           (USHORT)sizeof(struct COMMBUFFER), (char *)outBuffer,
           (USHORT)sizeof(struct COMMBUFFER), &bytesRead,
           timeOut);
} while (cc == ERROR_PIPE_BUSY);
if (cc)
    printf("DosCallNmPipe Error : %d", cc);
```

.
.
.
.

NetWare Messaging Services

A simplistic but easy to use method of communications is NetWare's messaging services. This is the same set of routines that NetWare's send and broadcast commands use. These functions allow you to send messages, up to 59 bytes in length, to the active users of your applications. Messaging services also provide a simple pipe mechanism, available only on pre-NetWare 386 file servers to transparently send messages up to 126 bytes long to a user's workstation. Your application must be aware of this functionality so that it can manually receive the messages for its own use.

When using NetWare messaging services, you must first determine the connection IDs of the users that are running your application, since messaging services use this connection ID as the means of identifying the destination of your messages. The connection ID is the position of a user in NetWare's logged-in user table. Once you have the connection ID, you can perform either of the two types of message services.

In the following example, we will look at two different techniques. The first technique is a method for sending broadcast messages to all users in your application's group that are currently logged in. One drawback to this method is that users will be sent messages even if they are not using your application. So, you might want to create and maintain a second group only while your application is active.

```
/* GetCurrentGroupUsers

Description: This function builds a list of connection IDs of the users
that are members of GroupName and are currently logged in.

Parameters: char *GroupName - Name of the group
 int   *NumUsers  - Returns number of users
 int   *UserList  - Array of users' connection IDs

Returns: None
*/
void GetCurrentGroupUsers(char *GroupName, int *NumUsers,
                          int *UserList)
{
 int Result;      /* Function result */

  char ObjectName[OBJECT_NAME_LEN]; /* Name of connected objects */
  WORD ObjectType;                  /* Type of connected object */
  long ObjectID;                    /* Bindery ID of connected object*/
  WORD ConnectionNumber;            /* Current connection number */
  BYTE LoginTime[7];                /* Time object logged in */

    *NumUsers = 0;                  /* Initialize number of users to 0 */

 /* Check all 100 positions in the file server's connection table */
for (ConnectionNumber = 1;ConnectionNumber <= 100;++ConnectionNumber)
{

  /* Get the current information on this connection */
  Result =
GetConnectionInformation(ConnectionNumber,ObjectName,&ObjectType,
  &ObjectID,LoginTime);

  /* Check the result */
  if (Result == SUCCESSFUL &&        /* Call did not fail, */
   ObjectType == OT_USER &&          /* it's a user, and */
   IsMember(GroupName,ObjectName)) { /* a member of our group */

   /* Update our own connection list */
   *(UserList + *NumUsers) = ConnectionNumber;
   ++(*NumUsers);
  }
 }
}
```

```
/* SendMessageToGroupUsers

Description: This function builds a list of the users that are logged
in and members of GroupName, and then broadcasts Message to them.

Parameters: char *GroupName - The group to which to send Message
 char *Message - The message to send

Returns: None
*/
void SendMessageToGroupUsers(char *GroupName, char *Message)
{
    int Result;     /* Function result */
    BYTE ResultList[100];   /* Tells if Message reached connection */
    WORD UserList[100];   /* GroupName's active connections */
    WORD NumUsers;    /* Number of users in UserList */

    /* Get the list of current users */
 GetCurrentGroupUsers(GroupName,&NumUsers,UserList);

    if (NumUsers) {     /* There are member users logged in */

  /* Send the message */
  Result = SendBroadcastMessage(Message,UserList,ResultList,NumUsers);
 }
}

Example: SendMessageToGroupUsers("MY_DATABASE_USERS",
 "PLEASE QUIT, FILES ABOUT TO BE PACKED.");
```

The next technique uses NetWare message pipes. No, these are not Named Pipes, but are similar in how they are used. Message pipes can hold only 126 bytes of data, and the workstations involved must poll the shell for any messages that have been sent to it. Message pipes are useful for "quick and dirty" questions and commands between applications. A major drawback of using these pipes is that they must be reopened before each call to make sure that you have the latest list of targets. The example that follows details a function for sending data across a message pipe and one for retrieving data from a message pipe. Remember, message pipes only work with pre-NetWare 386 file servers.

```
/* OpenGroupMessagePipes

Description: This function performs the initial open of the
communication pipes between logged-in members of GroupName.

Parameters: char *GroupName - Name of application group

Returns: None.
*/

void OpenGroupMessagePipes(char *GroupName)
{
 int  Result;            /* Function result */
 int  NumUsers;          /* Number of active users */
 int  UserList[100];     /* Active users' connection IDs */
 BYTE ResultList[100];   /* Individual connection results */
 /* Get list of current users */
 GetCurrentGroupUsers(GroupName,&NumUsers,UserList);

 /* Open message pipes between this client and the user list */
 Result = OpenMessagePipe(UserList,ResultList,NumUsers);
}


/* CloseGroupMessagePipes

Description: This function closes the communication pipes between
logged-in members of GroupName.

Parameters: char *GroupName - Name of application group

Returns: None
*/
void CloseGroupMessagePipes(char *GroupName)
{
 int  Result;            /* Function result */
 int  NumUsers;          /* Number of active users */
 int  UserList[100];     /* Active users' connection IDs */
 BYTE ResultList[100];   /* Individual connection results */

 /* Get list of active users */
 GetCurrentGroupUsers(GroupName,&NumUsers,UserList);

 /* Close opened pipes between those users */
```

```
  Result = CloseMessagePipe(UserList,ResultList,NumUsers);
}

/* SendPipeMessageToGroup

Description: This function sends a "private" message to all logged-in
members of GroupName.

Parameters: char *GroupName - Name of application group
 void *Message - Data to send to group, must be ASCII characters from
0x20 to 0x7F

Returns: 0 == Success, !0 == Failure
*/
int SendPipeMessageToGroup(char *GroupName, void *Message)
{
 int  Result;              /* Function result */
 int  NumUsers;            /* Number of active users */
 int  UserList[100];       /* Active users' connection IDs */
 BYTE ResultList[100];     /* Individual connection results */

 GetCurrentGroupUsers(GroupName,&NumUsers,UserList);
 Result = OpenMessagePipe(UserList,ResultList,NumUsers);
 if (Result == SUCCESSFUL) {
  Result = SendPersonalMessage(Message,UserList,ResultList,NumUsers);
 }
 return(Result);
}

/* GetPipeMessage

Description: This function retrieves the oldest outstanding message and
its sender from this particular user's pipe.

 Parameters: void *Message - Message received
   int *Sender  - Connection ID of message sender

 Returns: 1 == Message Available, 0 == No messages
*/
int GetPipeMessage(void *Message, int *Sender)
{
 int  Result;

 Result = GetPersonalMessage(Message,Sender);
 if (Result == SUCCESSFUL && *Sender != 0) {
```

```
 Result = 1;
 } else {
 Result = 0;
 }
 return(Result);
}


/* RespondPipeMessage

Description: This function sends a response message to a connection
that sent a personal message to this user.

 Parameters: void *Message - Message received
    int  Sender - Connection ID to receive message

 Returns: 1 == Message sent, 0 == Message not sent
*/
int RespondPipeMessage(void *Message, int Sender)
{
 int  Result;
 int  User = Sender;
 BYTE Response;

 Result = SendPersonalMessage(Message,&Sender,&Response,1);
 if (Result == SUCCESSFUL && Response == 0) {
  Result = 1;
 } else {
  Result = 0;
 }
 return(Result);
}
```

Some examples of how you might use these functions include:

```
 OpenGroupMessagePipes("MY_GROUP");
  ...
 if (SendPipeMessageToGroup("MY_GROUP","REQ:APP?") == 0)
  ...
 if (GetPipeMessage(MyMessage,&Sender)) {
  if (strstr(MyMessage,"REQ:APP?") != NULL) {
   Result = RespondPipeMessage("RESP:APP?:PAYROLL",Sender);
  }
 }
  ...
```

```
CloseGroupMessagePipes("MY_GROUP");
```

The following two code snippets show how to SEND a message with MHS' SEAL and how to receive messages with MHS' UNSEAL. They are only code snippets and require Novell's MHS documentation for complete understanding, showing them here demonstrates one way which they can be used.

```
/*********************************************************************
 *
 * Program Name:   SEALDEMO.EXE
 *
 * Filename:       sealdemo.c
 *
 * Version:        1.0
 *
 * Programmer:     John T. McCann
 *
 * Date:           November 5, 1988
 *
 * NOTE: NO main() ROUTINE< Just example routines
 */

/* This is an example routine to produce a file for SEAL.EXE to operate
   on. Once SEAL has sucessfully "sealed" a message, it is sent to its
   recipient Note that there is no provision to send to multiple
   recipients, you must seal a different message for each destination

   BE SURE TO INCLUDE THE FOLLOWING TO PROPERLY SETUP YOUR ENVIRONMENT
   FOR SEAL'S (and UNSEAL) use:

   (inside the login script for a user:)

   dos set mv="ServerName/VolumeName:"

   The ServerName is to be replaced with your server's name and the
   VolumeName is to be replaced with the volume name that contains the
   MHS directories as they were setup
```

```
        R E M E M B E R :

        You will need the MHS documentation to further assist you in
        understanding this code

*/


doSeal()
{
    int ccode;
    FILE *handle;
    char destName[65];
    char destWorkGroup[65];
    char sealParameter[80];
    char sealedMCBpath[65];
    char copyString[255], tempbuf[1024], tempbuf1[255];
    char directory[65], MCBpath[255];
    char Tempfile[15], destination[40];

/*
 * This routine shows how to put together a message and seal it or send
 * it (or at least get it started) to the destination user
 *
 *
 * IMPORTANT
 * NOTE: You will want to have the documentation on putting together
 *       a message for SEAL to further understand this example
 *
 */

/* You might come up with a better filenaming scheme, but this isn't
   an example of how to come up with unique names, you could use the
   DOS call to do that...
 */

    strcpy (Tempfile, "seal.tmp");

    strcpy (directory, "Z:\\MAIL\\");
    strcat (directory, "MHSWORK");
    strcat (directory, "\\");    /* i.e. Z:\MAIL\MHSWORK\FILENAME. */

    strcpy (MCBpath, directory);
    strcat (MCBpath, Tempfile);
```

```
  handle = DOSCreate(MCBpath, 0xA0); /*creates with a Shareable handle*/
  fclose (handle);

  handle = fopen(MCBpath, "w");
  if (handle == NULL)
  {
    printf("Error Creating file for SEAL");
    fclose (handle);
  }
  else
  {

/* Some the variables below are setup other places, they are show here
   only to show you where you would include them, see the MHS
   documentation for more information on how to define these fields
 */

                                    /*  v--changed P to Allow */
  fprintf (handle, "MHS-1\n18\n0\nNNYNA\n%s\n", appName);

  fprintf (handle, "%s\n%s\n", orgName, orgWorkGroup);  /* origination
*/

  splitNameGroup (destination, destName, destWorkGroup);

  fprintf (handle, "%s\n%s\n", destName, destWorkGroup); /* destination
*/
  fprintf (handle, "%s\n", subject);
  fprintf (handle, "%s\n", attachPath);
  fprintf (handle, "\n\n\n\n1\n\n\n");/*the 1 in this line is the    */
                                     /*attach type look @ the end of*/
                                     /*this routine and change the  */
                                     /*line marked with "LOOK"   if */
                                     /*you change the "1"           */
  fprintf (handle, messageBuf);
  fclose (handle);

  strcpy (sealParameter, "-F");
  strcat (sealParameter, MCBpath);

  if (spawnlp (P_WAIT, "seal.exe", "seal", sealParameter, NULL))
  {
   printf("No Path to SEAL.EXE!");
   /* this above error is only a warning because we want to give the */
   /* user a chance to save his file...*/
```

```
    return(-1);
  }


/* After SEALING the message we go back and check to see what the
result
    was of the seal operation */


  handle = fopen (MCBpath, "r");
  fscanf (handle,"%s%s%s%s%s%s%s%s%s%s%s%s%s%s%s%s%s%s%s",
  tempbuf, tempbuf,
  tempbuf, tempbuf, tempbuf, tempbuf, tempbuf, tempbuf, tempbuf,
tempbuf,
  tempbuf, tempbuf, tempbuf, tempbuf, tempbuf, tempbuf, tempbuf,
tempbuf1);

 /*
  * LOOK
  *
  * the if statement below checks to see if a 1 was read in
  * 1 is NOT a valid error for the MCB, but 1 is the attachment type
used
  * by this application <see line with "LOOK" above>
  * and SOMETIMES on SOME machines under SOME versions of DOS, the
above
  * fscanf doesn't read everything it is expected to, so point is, if a
  * 1 is read in <49 in decimal or 31 in hex, yes the ASCII 1> that
  * means that the next line is the line that has the error indication
  * so, read in an additional string to get it...whew!
  */

  if (tempbuf1[0]==46)
    {
     /* read too far, above checks for a period "." */
      strcpy (tempbuf1,tempbuf);
    }


  if (tempbuf1[0]==49 && tempbuf1[1]==0)
    {
      fscanf(handle, "%s",tempbuf);
      strcpy (tempbuf1,tempbuf);
    }
```

```
fclose (handle);


if (tempbuf1[0] != 48) /* if error condition is not 0, 0=no error */
  {
      switch (tempbuf1[1])
      {
      case 56:

      /* error is 18 */

         printf("Illegal Named used in Seal\n");

      break; /* error 18 */

      case 57:

      /* error is 19 */

         printf("Illegal Hostname used in Seal\n");

      break; /* error 19 */

      case 48:

      if (tempbuf1[2]==50) /* error is 102 */
      {
         printf("No preferred application specified in Seal\n");
      }
      else
      {
         printf("Seal operation failed\n");
      }

      break; /* error 102 or anything starting with 10xxxx */

      default:
         printf("Seal Failed, in an unknown way\n");

      break; /* any error not specified above */

    } /*end of case */
  }
```

```
} /* end of doSeal */



splitNameGroup (nameGroup, name, workGroup)
  char *nameGroup;
  char *name;
  char *workGroup;

 /*
  * this routine determines the name and workGroup to use for the
  * sealing of messages
  *
  * nameGroup might be "USERJOHN@NOVELL"
  *
  */

 /*
  * R E M E M B E R :
  *
  * You will need the MHS documentation to further assist you in
  * understanding this code
  *
  */

{
 int i;

  if (nameGroup == NULL)
     {
        *name = 0;
        *workGroup = 0;
     }
     else
     {
        for (i = 0; i < 8; i++)
        {
          if ((*nameGroup == 0) ||
              (*nameGroup == '@') ||
              (*nameGroup == ' ')) break;
              *name++ = *nameGroup++;
        }
        *name = 0;
```

```
    while ((*nameGroup == ' ') || (*nameGroup == '@'))
          nameGroup++;    /* advance to the Work Group part */


      for (i = 0; i < 8; i++)
      {
        if ((*nameGroup == 0) ||
              (*nameGroup == ' ')) break;
                *workGroup++ = *nameGroup++;
      }
      *workGroup = 0;

   } /* end of else above */

} /* end of splitNameGroup (nameGroup, name, workGroup) */



/***********************************************************************
 *
 * Program Name:   UNSEALDM.EXE
 *
 * Filename:       unsealdm.c
 *
 * Version:        1.0
 *
 * Programmer:     John T. McCann
 *
 * Date:           November 5, 1988
 *
 * NOTE: NO main() ROUTINE< Just example routines
 */

/* This is an example routine to extract a file from the MHS system and
   read/use it.


   BE SURE TO INCLUDE THE FOLLOWING TO PROPERLY SETUP YOUR ENVIRONMENT
   FOR SEAL'S (and UNSEAL) use:

   (inside the login script for a user:)

   dos set mv="ServerName/VolumeName:"

   The ServerName is to be replaced with your server's name and the
   VolumeName is to be replaced with the volume name that contains the
```

MHS directories as they were setup

R E M E M B E R :

You will need the MHS documentation to further assist you in
understanding this code

```
*/

readMessages()
{
 char unsealUParm[255];
 char unsealAParm[255];
 char unsealDParm[255];
 char fileInfo[43];
 int  ccode;
 char tempdir[65],tempdir2[65];
 int  listWidth, stringLength, returnCode, syscall, loop;
 LIST *element;


/*
 * This routine uses several local variables to help in the reading of
 * messages, specifically this routine shows how to read new messages
 * all messages are UNSEALed into the specified directory
 *
 * this is to show how UNSEAL works
 */

 strcpy (tempdir, "Z:\\MAIL\\"); /* assuming Z: points at current server */
 strcat (tempdir, "\\MHSWORK");  /* could get current or default server */

 /* i.e., tempdir is "Z:\MAIL\MHSWORK", this is the directory which
    UNSEAL will deposit is messages in
  */

/* Some the variables below are setup other places, they are show here
   only to show you where you would include them, see the MHS
   documentation for more information on how to define these fields
 */

 strcpy (unsealUParm, "-U");
 strcat (unsealUParm, orgName);
 strcat (unsealUParm, " -D");
```

```c
      strcat (unsealUParm, tempdir);
      strcat (unsealUParm, " -A");
      strcat (unsealUParm, appName);


      if ((spawnlp (P_WAIT, "unseal.exe", "unseal", unsealUParm,
               unsealAParm, unsealDParm, NULL) < 0 ) && (errno == ENOENT))
       {
        printf("Unable to find path to UNSEAL into! aborting\n");
        return(-1);
       }

      strcat (tempdir, "\\");
      strcpy (tempdir2, tempdir);
      strcat (tempdir2, "*"); /* just an "*", old messages
                               will have *.exr extension */


      /* i.e., path is now "Z:\MAIL\MHSWORK\*"  */

      if (FindFirstFile (tempdir2, fileInfo, FA_NORMAL))
       {
        showMail(tempdir, &fileInfo[30]); /* fileInfo[30] is the filename
                                        found */
       }
      else
       {
        while (!FindNextFile(fileInfo))
          {
           showMail(tempdir, &fileInfo[30]); /* fileInfo[30] is the filename
                                           found */
          }
       }

} /* end of readMessages ()   */




showMail (Directory, FILEName)
 char *Directory;
 char *FILEName;

{
   char Users[40];
   char destName[9];
```

```
    char destWorkGroup[9];
    FILE *handle;
    char tempbuf[1024];
    char renamebuf[65], attach_dest[65], timeSent1[40], timeRecd1[40];
    char timeSent2[40], timeRecd2[40];
    char fileMove[255], fileN[64];
    int  aa, option, returnCode, loop;
    char MCBpath[255];
    char Tempfile[15];
    char directory[65];
    char one[2];
    char *MV;


    MV = getenv("MV");

/*
 * Opens up the mail and retrieves its contents
 */

    messageBuf[0] = destination[0] = subject[0] = attachPath[0] = 0;
    strcpy (tempbuf, Directory);
    strcat (tempbuf, FILEName);

    handle = fopen (tempbuf, "r");
    strcpy (renamebuf, tempbuf);

/*
 * R E M E M B E R :
 *
 * You will need the MHS documentation to further assist you in
 * understanding this code
 *
 */

    /* read 1st line of MCB and verify file is an MCB */
    fscanf (handle, "%s", tempbuf);
    if (strcmp (tempbuf, "MHS-1"))
     {
      fclose (handle);
      return(-1);
     }

    /* read and discard lines 2, 3, and 4 */
```

```
fscanf (handle, "%s%s%s", tempbuf, tempbuf, tempbuf);
fscanf (handle, "%s", tempbuf);

/* read line 5 of MCB and verify application name */
/* !!not!! being done, allows message to come from other apps to here
 * fscanf (handle, "%s", tempbuf);
 * if (stricmp (tempbuf, appName) && stricmp (tempbuf, "."))
 */

fscanf (handle, "%s%s", origination, tempbuf);   /* origination */
strcat (origination, " @ ");
strcat (origination, tempbuf);
fscanf (handle, "%s%s", destName, destWorkGroup);/* destination */

fgets (tempbuf, sizeof(tempbuf), handle);        /* flush \n */
fgets (subject, sizeof(subject), handle);

subject[strlen(subject) - 1] = 0;                /* remove \n */
fscanf (handle, "%s", attachPath);
if (!strcmp (attachPath, "."))
  attachPath[0] = 0;

if (attachPath[0])  /* if there is an attachPath, get the pathname */
 {
   strcpy (MCBpath, MV);
    a = 0; c = 1;
    while (a < sizeof (attachPath) )
      {
       c++;a=c;
       if (attachPath[c] == 0)
       {
         a = sizeof(attachPath)+2;
         /* get out of loop */
       }
       else
       {
         one[0] = attachPath[c];
         one[1] = 0;
         strcat (MCBpath, one);
       }
      }
  strcpy (attachPath, MCBpath);
 }

attach_dest[0] = 0; /* no attachment destination yet */
```

```
  /* read and discard lines 12, 13, 14, 15, 15.5, 16, 16.5, 17, 18 */
  fscanf (handle, "%s%s",tempbuf, tempbuf);
  fscanf (handle, "%s%s%s%s",timeSent1, timeSent2, timeRecd1,
timeRecd2);
  strcat (timeSent1, " ");
  strcat (timeSent1, timeSent2);
  strcat (timeRecd1, " ");
  strcat (timeRecd1, timeRecd2);
  fscanf (handle, "%s%s%s", tempbuf, tempbuf,tempbuf);
  fgets (tempbuf, sizeof(tempbuf), handle);  /* flush \n */
  fread (messageBuf, 1, sizeof (messageBuf), handle);
  fclose (handle);
  strcpy (tempbuf, renamebuf);

  strcat (renamebuf, ".EXR"); /* rename the UNSEALED file so we know we
                                 have read it */
  rename (tempbuf, renamebuf);


  b++; /* b is used to keep track of how many new messages have been
found */

  /* Here we could set up a DESTINATION for the UNSEALED message's
     Attached file, the variable used is attach_dest
   */

  strcpy(attach_dest,"\\ATTACHES\\FILENAME.HER"); /* remember to
                                                     replace with your
                                                     destination,
                                                     perhaps through
                                                     an input statment
                                                     of some type
                                                   */

  if (attach_dest[0]) /* if strlen is 0, then attach_dest[0] is 0 */
  {
    strcpy (fileMove, "NCOPY ");
    strcat (fileMove, attachPath);
    strcat (fileMove, " to ");
    strcat (fileMove, Directory);
    strcat (fileMove, "attach.tmp");
    strcat (fileMove, " >nul");

    a = system (fileMove);
```

```
    /* don't delete it yet */

    strcpy (fileMove, "COPY ");
    strcat (fileMove, Directory);
    strcat (fileMove, "attach.tmp ");
    strcat (fileMove, attach_dest);
    strcat (fileMove, " >nul");
    /* we do the copy in this way for two reasons:
     * 1. MHS puts the server name and volume on the front of the
     *    attach filename
     * 2. Ncopy can't copy to local drives' directory names, like:
     *    C:\DOS, Ncopy can copy just to C: but not to C:\+ some
     * directory name so, we copy the attach file to a temporary file,
     * then we copy that temporary file to the real destination
     * this alleviates us from having to strip off the server name and
     * volume name from the front of the attach filename...
     */
    a = system (fileMove);

    strcpy (fileMove, "DEL ");
    strcat (fileMove, Directory);
    strcat (fileMove, "attach.tmp");  /* get rid of temp file */
    strcat (fileMove, " >nul");
    a = system (fileMove);

  }

}    /* end of showMail(directory, fileName) */
```

PART 3

Creating Server Applications: VAPs and NLMs

The third major section of this book takes a look at the intricacies of creating Value Added Processes (VAPs) and NetWare Loadable Modules (NLMs). These programs are loaded into NetWare file servers and perform a variety of services. This introduction, which takes a look at the differences between VAPs and NLMs, is followed by a chapter on creating and testing VAPs, and one on creating and testing NLMs. These include sections on interVAP and interNLM communication, as well as guidelines for converting VAPs to NLMs.

What are Server Applications?

In the world of network computing there are, in general, two types of nodes, clients and servers. The client requests a service and the server receives the request. Then the server processes the request and potentially replies to the client. Nowhere is this more obviously apparent than in the interaction between a user workstation and a network file server.

The simple process of logging in involves the client requesting the login and the server doing the work necessary to allow or disallow the user login. To be sure, the client does some work itself to login, but without the server providing login functionality there would be no actual login. The whole concept of client/server computing involves providing services with optimal placement. How optimal the placement is will be discussed later in this chapter.

As you can see, client/server computing is nothing more than requestor and requestee, or, requestor of services and provider of services. Stepping down from the network environment, one can see principles of client/server computing taking place within a local workstation. Whenever you make a request to DOS you are requesting a service, thus you are a client. When DOS replies to you, fulfilling your request, it is the server or provider of services. So, whenever you have a program open a file (or make any of a number of other DOS calls) you have been involved in client/server-like computing.

Client/server computing is not strictly limited to nodes that are always clients or always servers. It is the side requesting a service that is termed the client and the side providing a service and reply (though replies are not always required) that is termed the server. For instance, with NetWare, user workstations are usually viewed as clients requesting services from a file server. There are at least two deviations to this. The first occurs when a file server makes a request of a workstation, for example, when a file server sends out a "watchdog" request. This request verifies that a workstation is still up. The receiving workstation is expected to return an "I'm alive" message, so in this case the file server acts as the client and the workstation acts as the server.

The second manner in which a workstation acts as the server is when it is participating in internodal communications. Internodal communications are made possible through communications programs, either your own or a third party product such as MAP ASSIST from Fresh Technology, which provides peer-to-peer disk drive access. The model viewed here is of two workstations communicating back and forth to achieve some goal. Thus one or more workstations act as clients and/or servers.

The method used to provide internodal communication is immaterial when considering who is a client and who is a server. The communications protocol used is merely a conduit for the internodal communications—aside from protocol-related issues (synchronization, timeliness, sequencing, etc.), it does not dictate which communications take place, just how they take place. The protocol used for client/server computing does not even have to be real-time. Here real-time is used to indicate that the client and server are both active and are using a protocol that requires them to exist concurrently for communications to occur. A client/server model might use IPX, SPX, NetBIOS, MHS, or any other desired communications protocol.

Distributing Clients and Servers

The matter of dividing processing between clients and servers can be simple. Sometimes it is immediately obvious which events should take place at the client and which at the server. In the worst case it is confusing and nontrivial. In many best-case scenarios, you will have placed tasks at the "end" (client or server) to maximize performance. Such placement will minimize network traffic. However, your goal may not be to maximize performance, though this is the primary advantage to client/server computing. Rather, your goal may be centralization of data or even fault tolerance. You can improve fault tolerance, for example, by having multiple nodes perform the same tasks. In any case, you optimize the performance of a client/server application when the task-sharing application generates the least amount of network traffic.

Generally, deciding upon roles (client or server) means determing how best to balance loads. For instance, in a network where all nodes are PCs, you would rarely have a server providing keyboard input verification for a client. This would be a waste of server resources because the client, presumably a PC, has enough time and power on its hands to provide the keyboard verification itself before sending it to the server for processing.

In addition to balancing loads, security requirements may determine the roles of clients and servers. For example, instead of a client reading a password file directly, and thus transmitting the data (whether encrypted or nonecrypted) across a network, the server could read the file (presuming the file is located at the server on a local device) and provide an encryption key for the client. This encryption key (especially a time-dependent key) could then be used by the client when it returns a password to the server for verification. Using this method a client never sends out a password or a direct encrypted/nonencrypted representation of it onto the network media.

When contemplating how to divide the tasks, consider a couple of items. First, you might place any task that is mundane/repetitive where the most data is gathered. For instance,you should set up the processing of keyboard entries at the machine where the entry took place. Another example is the sorting/indexing of a data file. If the file to be sorted is at the server, the server would be best suited to provide the sorting because of the lack of network traffic.

Also, for CPU-intensive tasks, you might find advantages in using a server that is not also a "normal" file server. The perceived advantage is that the real file server is not being tied up with CPU-intensive operations. The real file server is not best suited for doing CPU-intensive operations as it has many other tasks to perform. Thus, another "CPU-intensive server" would be more in line.

Also, try not to get caught in the trap of thinking that there needs to be a clean break between clients and servers. Their roles may be switched at any time; at one moment a machine might be acting as a client and the next moment it becomes a server. Again, the essential difference between clients and servers is this: Clients perform requests and servers provide services based on client requests which may or may not involve a reply.

Choosing the Communications Protocol

In the NetWare environment there are both real-time and nonreal-time communication options. These protocols include IPX, SPX, NetBIOS, Named Pipes, MHS and Queues. In the future there will be TCP/IP, Streams, and TLI, as well as others. Of these protocols, IPX, SPX, NetBIOS and Named Pipes are considered real-time, or interactive. The protocols are used when more or less immediate request/reply communications are needed. As noted in the section on communications, the fastest, but most error-prone, of these protocols is IPX. Problems with IPX include: packet (datagram) loss, packet duplication, and packet parcels arriving out of sequence. With minimal effort the interested developer could develop a system of "guaranteeing" IPX packet delivery. Essentially this method uses packet sequence numbers, return receipts (packets sent back to sender to acknowledge packet receipt) and IPX's Asynchronous Event Scheduler (see VAP Service Advertising example) to ensure packets are not lost by setting a timeout for receiving return receipts. Additionally, one could easily produce a "sliding window protocol" to allow one request to result in many replies. For instance, with SPX a reply is issued for each request. This results in a ping-like protocol which poorly accommodates slow communications links.

Novell's SPX provides guaranteed packet delivery and duplicate packet supression with minimal packet buffer overhead (12 bytes more than a similar IPX buffer) and time overhead (approximately 5% longer to send/receive packets). However, be cautious about using SPX as there are several versions of NetWare in which SPX does not function properly. Unfortunately, there is no detailed list of these problems other than that SPX shuts down and stops receiving. Thankfully, the problem seems dependent on each particular network's setup and is not a problem generally. SPX is relatively new for NetWare; it first appeared with NetWare v2.0a when using v2.01-4 of the ANETx (x=2,3) shell. (SPX is also in v2.01-x, x=1,2,3 of the ANETx shell but is not fully functional). Note that SPX occurs locally at a workstation and to the network file servers appears as IPX. That is, the servers do not see SPX—they see IPX being directly used by SPX to perform its operations. All of SPX's processing occurs at the local node (fileserver or workstation) and thus the version of SPX at the local node may be different for disparate nodes.

Before using NetBIOS developers should be implementing or planning to implement their application on a variety of network foundations. For instance, if developing strictly for NetWare LANs, NetBIOS would be an inappropriate first choice. The essential problem with choosing NetBIOS for a NetWare LAN is that NetBIOS is a generic communications protocol and because of this it has very low performance when compared to NetWare's native IPX and SPX protocols. In addition to having low performance, NetBIOS can require more work than do Novell's native protocols in achieving internodal communications. However, if developing your application for LANs other than NetWare, you might find NetBIOS is the only choice that works across all the network platforms you will encounter. Alternately, you might consider one of many development tools such as NetWise's RPC or PeerLogic's PIPES Platform.

Like NetBIOS, Named Pipes is a mechanism that can be used on LANs other than NetWare. However, unlike IPX and SPX, Named Pipes performs its peer-to-peer (i.e., internodal) communications at a higher level. For instance, with IPX and SPX, internodal communications takes place because each "side" knows the other's internetwork address. Thus, the nodes participating in IPX or SPX communications must know the physical address of each participating node. Just like NetBIOS, Named Pipes uses names to resolve the communications "tunnel". However, Named Pipes uses higher level read and write instructions instead of send and receive. Consequently, one of the limitations of Named Pipes is its limited functionality when compared to lower level protocols (i.e., IPX/SPX). But, for some applications, there may be little need for anything beyond read and write operations. One cautionary note: as of this writing Novell's Named Pipe implementation does not operate with Microsoft's Windows version 3.0.

Up to now, all the protocols mentioned are interactive—that is, both sender and receiver need to be concurrently active for communications to occur. Novell's Message Handling Service (MHS) behaves differently. Actually produced by Action Technologies, Inc., MHS provides a message engine, operating much like an E-mail system (i.e., store and forward). The messages produced are sent in an asynchronous fashion, meaning that the sender and receiver do not need to be present concurrently for communications to occur. And, like NetBIOS or Named Pipes, MHS uses names for addressing destinations for messages. But, unlike any protocol mentioned thus far, MHS requires someone to set up a specific MHS gateway. With the other protocols mentioned so far, the network itself (a shell may be needed at the local participating nodes) is used for the transport of messages and by the network's sheer existence, messages can be sent. Also, unlike any protocol mentioned thus far, MHS can function with any network available, as well as stand alone (no network).

One other method for achieving asynchronous message transfers in NetWare networks are Queues. With NetWare v2.1 and above, the NetWare Queues provide the ability for clients to prepare messages (jobs). In turn, these jobs are read (serviced) by Queue Servers (see Queue chapter for examples of Queue client and server). These Queue Servers need not be present when jobs are submitted to the queue. They need not be present because the NetWare file server acts as a repository for these "queued jobs." Remember, for current versions of NetWare, queues are server-based, not networkwide. This means a Queue Server will need to be attached to the proper server in order to service a specific queue. Note that NetWare Queues do not directly fit the peer-to-peer communications model.

In future releases of NetWare, the choice of protocols will be enhanced to include TCP/IP, Streams, TLI, NFS, etc. Novell's TCP/IP protocol is, as of this writing, under development and should be available sometime before 1992. Streams and TLI are currently available for NetWare/386, but only for applications at the file server. Because of the current unavailability of workstation partners for Streams and TLI, they are basically non-existent or at least not entirely viable.

Using Novell's SAP

Once you have decided the communications protocol, you might wonder how your clients will find the server(s). In the NetWare environment there is a simple protocol available. NetWare's vehicle to advertise services (provided by servers) is called the SAP or Service Advertising Protocol. Basically, it provides the ability to advertise a name—specifically, a server name. Thus, NetWare's SAP is an advertising protocol for servers. When a server uses the SAP, that server's name, type and internetwork address are placed in the bindery of each NetWare file server on the network. The server type is the same as a bindery object type. Every minute or two, a server using the SAP must re-advertise itself. If a server does not continually advertise itself its name is dropped from the bindery of each NetWare file server. Thankfully, the NetWare Library for DOS, VAPs and NLMs has an advertise service procedure ready to provide for your SAP needs. In addition, sample code is provided for VAPs to show how the SAP routine works.

Clients can query the SAP using several different methods. The ScanBinderyObject call from the C Library allows clients to search the bindery of their local file server in order to ascertain a particular server's existence or simply to find a server of a particular type. For instance, Novell's SLIST command goes out to the bindery of the current file server and retrieves a list of all bindery objects of type 0x0004. Type 4 is reserved to indicate NetWare file servers.

In addition to scanning the bindery to find server names, a client could directly listen to the SAP. Since the SAP uses IPX for its broadcasting a client could open a socket and listen for the server broadcasts. However, this method might take a while (a couple of minutes) to "hear" a selected server. But this method does not require a client to first attach to a NetWare file server. Once again the NetWare C Library for DOS provides procedures to listen to the SAP socket. Also, one could use a GetNearestServer call to locate a particular server type so long as the designated server is capable of responding to such calls. For those interested, the *NetWare System Interface Technical Overview* (pn# 100-000648-001) shows the necessary components for listening to the SAP.

Threads

In a multitasking or multithreaded environment, your application may make use of more than one process, also known as a thread or stream of execution. Each of these different threads can represent activities of a client or a server. And they *can* do both.

For the rest of this chapter, client/server computing will be used to indicate internodal communications, not communications between threads. Such commuications will be more specifically termed—take procedure calls, as one example.

Server applications, specifically those run at NetWare file servers, are created for a variety of reasons. Server applications can provide centrally-based services. That is, workstations can always have a place to go for requesting services. Also, server applications can perform some tasks more readily than a workstation can, for instance, accessing certain files where the client normally does not have access privileges. As mentioned earlier, server applications can provide more security for certain tasks than a client can. Also, server applications can lower processing overhead or other overhead (for instance, RAM) at the client. Additionally, the server offers an environment much more conducive to continually-run applications than non-servers. For instance, a network diagnostic utility that continually monitors the health of the network would best be run in a server. The server could be a file server or a dedicated workstation that might also be used for other tasks.

When creating server applications for NetWare, you will find two distinctly different file server environments for your applications. With NetWare versions 2.1 and above your application will be called a Value Added Process or VAP. When creating server applications for NetWare versions 3.x your application will be called a NetWare Loadable Module, or NLM.

Basic Differences Between VAPs and NLMs

The basic areas where there are differences in the initial coding between VAPs and NLMs are:

- Initializing
- Obtaining connections
- Loading/unloading
- Availability of APIs
- Communicating between processes
- Interfacing to the user at the console
- Debugging

The next two sections discuss these areas in more detail, first with a discussion of VAPs, followed by one on NLMs. For VAPs:

1) Up front there is a specific header that you *must* have laid out *exactly* as you are told. This header is used by the NetWare operating system when loading the VAP and has to be in Assembly form. The header could be produced with C code but it is easier to understand when viewed in Assembly language. See Figure 0.0 for a sample header

2) A VAP, if it wants any services that a connection would have, (with the exception of IPX/SPX-only traffic), has to "login" to the file server, thus:

   a. A VAP consumes a connection (or more than one). Each process or thread needing connection services must "log in."

   b. A VAP must have a predefined name, which can be a big hassle, especially if the account has to have a password and that password is subject to change. Note that VAPs may also be run in NetWare bridges. These bridges are a special type of server since they only route network traffic.

3) A VAP must be loaded at file server boot time, and it cannot be unloaded.

4) A VAP cannot perform half the functions that NLMs can.

5) A VAP cannot talk to another VAP (in the same server) without going through some contrived communications model, which will be demonstrated.

6) A VAP can offer keywords at the server console and has limited keyboard input/output abilities when compared to NLMs.

7) With VAPs, entry into the debugger is "one way" and only possible after the file server has abended.

For NLMs:

1) The header is contained in a preformed file from Novell called PRELUDE.OBJ. Just include it when linking your code.

2) If an NLM wants a connection, it just talks directly to the kernel. There are no wasted file server connections and the NLM doesn't have to worry about logging in. It has full "supervisor" rights, too. There is a way to login as a given user, too. Also, unlike VAPs, threads within an NLM can share the same login connection.

3) NLMs can be loaded and unloaded at will, including on their own. For instance, an NLM can load another NLM when it needs it and instruct the loaded NLM to unload itself when it's done.

4) NLMs have lots of other functions available to them, those built right into the operating system and C Libraries. When linking there is a .DEF file that has commands you want to import and export (commands are imported and exported so that you may use other NLMs functions and they can use yours). For instance, the CLIB is an NLM, that is, you just reference its calls in your IMPORT section and that way, when 10 NLMs that use the CLIB are loaded, they all use the same NetWare/386 CLIB rather than having the CLIB loaded 10 times (as would be the case with VAPs). The CLIB used is a Dynamically Linked Library (DLL) so each NLM is not self-contained. With VAPs there is no common DLL and as a result VAPs are often created with all called procedures linked into the executable VAP code. The .DEF file is used when the NLM is linked with the Novell NLMLINK utility or the WATCOM WLINK utility.

5) NLMs talk to other NLMs via commands defined in the EXPORTs and IMPORTs. This allows for a very simple messaging protocol. If you want to call another NLM, just call a function (procedure) within your C code.

6) An NLM running under NetWare v3.0 can easily offer keywords at the server console. With NetWare v3.1, offering commands is more complicated, and as of this writing we know of no such way to implement it. However, NLMs offer a complete set of input and output commands as well as the ability to do pop-up screens and various windowing effects.

7) With NLMs there is a full commmand-line debugger. The debugger can be entered at anytime during the server's operation. The debugger can even be entered after the server has abended.

All in all, writing NLMs is similar to writing a C program for DOS, except that it's compiled with a 386 complier and has a few unique things linked into its header. Writing a VAP is a little more trouble, not because of how difficult it is to write the code, but because of the sheer lack of features available in VAPs, compared to those available in an NLM.

CHAPTER 7

VAPs

Creating a VAP

Creating NetWare server applications has been possible since the release of NetWare/286 v2.1. With all subsequent 2.1x versions, Novell has provided a mechanism to third parties that allows server application development. These server applications are called Value Added Processes or VAPs. Coding a VAP is not extremely difficult, but a number of factors prompted Novell to replace VAPs with the more sophisticated NLMs in NetWare versions 3.0 and higher.

When first announced, VAPs sounded like a godsend to programmers everywhere. However, in reality, coding a VAP was not as easy as was hoped. And to make things worse, early on Novell lacked sufficient support personnel to assist in VAP development. Inadequate documentation served to further discourage potential VAP developers. Finally, VAP developers had to contend with Novell's buggy VAP libraries. Some of these libraries, (which can be used reasonably in the current v1.2 release) were coded so poorly that they ensured a VAP using them would never run properly. The first "third party" VAP was actually created by a Novell employee. Novell released a few VAPs, such as the Btrieve VAPs, Macintosh VAPs, and another that could lock the server keyboard.

VAPs must be loaded at server boot time—it is not possible to load a VAP after the server has been brought up. And it is not possible to unload a VAP while the server is up. This only makes VAP development more difficult and time consuming as the file server must be rebooted each time a VAP crashes the server or a new one needs to be loaded. And during VAP development, one or both of these can be regular occurrences. The next section provides coding guidelines for creating VAPs.

Two Code Parts

With VAPs there are two basic data/code portions: the VAP header and the rest of the VAP's code. The VAP header has a specific arrangement, and the order of items in the VAP header is important for proper loading. The header is shown in Figure 8-1. The header serves as a VAP's communication control, both to other VAPs and to the file server operating system. Through each VAP's header a VAP can search for other VAPs and initiate communications with them (discussed in a later section). Note that no more than 10 VAPs can be loaded concurrently.

```
;Sample VAP Header
Signature                       db      'NWProc' ;must be this
; the next four fields filled in by NET$OS at load time
NetWareShellServices      dd      ?
ProcessControlServices    dd      ?
ConsoleControlServices    dd      ?
IPXSPXServices            dd      ?
VAPConsoleHandler         dd      ConsoleHandlerCall
VAPDownHandler            dd      DownHandlerCall
VAPConsoleOrDownDataSegment dw    DGroup
VAPConnectionRequestFlag  dw      1 ; 1=No connection, 0=connection
VAPNameString             db      'Sample VAP v1.0',
                                  64-($-VAPNameString) dup(0)
VAPConsoleKeyWordCount     dw      1
VAPKeyword1               db      'SAM', 16-($-VAPKeyword1) dup(0)
VAPSignOnMessage          d       'Sample VAP v1.0 -RUNNING', 0
                          db      10-($-VAPSignOnMessage) dup(0)
```

Figure 7-1. Sample VAP Header in Assembly Languge

The VAP header can be created in Assembly or C. The example here is in Assembly, primarily because this method easily demonstrates the header's layout. The rest of a VAP's code can be in any language, though Assembly and/or C are the usual languages of choice. In this text Assembly and C will be used. And, to make things easier, all code will be for C's small memory model.

By doing this, all data will be in one segment and all code will be in one segment. Remember, it is possible to use other memory models.

Initialization Code and Beyond

There are two main code components to VAPs: initialization code and after-initialization code. The initialization code performs memory allocations and spawns processes, or creates threads. Spawning processes allows a VAP to "multitask" its operations. Representing a unit of execution, each process can act independently of other processes in that VAP or other VAPs. These two operations (memory allocations and spawning processes) can *only* occur during a VAP's initialization.

When a VAP has completed its initialization, it calls InitializationComplete. At this point the VAP will not have any of its processes executed until all VAPs being loaded have called InitializationComplete. However, the server will sometimes allow a VAP process to continue after that process has called InitializationComplete but other processes have not. In such cases, the server could crash, as there are certain server initializations that are not completed when the server commences VAP loading. One solution to this is to wait 45 seconds after the "Load VAPs?" prompt is presented before loading VAPs. With NetWare versions 2.15 and later this wait can be accomplished by the VAP WAIT 45 command. This command is placed in the file SYS:SYSTEM\SERVER.CFG. If new memory allocation or spawning of processes is attempted after a process has called InitializationComplete, the server will crash.

If Your VAP Never Calls InitializationComplete

You might think that never telling the operating system that your initialization is complete would be a neat trick to allow creation of new processes when needed. We tried this once. It seems the VAPs initialization goes out and uses memory from the server's cache pool, but the operating system isn't really aware of this. What happened was that my system became very unstable; files that I wrote to became scrambled, a copy would not copy the same way twice—in short, it was a mess. I resolved the situation by making sure I did an

InitializationComplete call as soon as I could. This meant setting up my processes (threads) and "getting out of there" (InitializationComplete).

VAP Processes and Login Connections

While in operation, a VAP usually requests file server operations. These operations are the same ones that a user performs from a workstation (opening a file, getting a list of connected users, reading the bindery, etc.). In terms of a VAP, a particular process, or user will be the entity requesting the operation. If a VAP never spawns any processes it will, by default, have one process. If this first process or one that was spawned needs file server services, the process will need to attach and/or login as some type of user, but not necessarily as a user object type (0x0001). For security reasons, non-user object types might be used to ensure user utilities, such as SYSCON, cannot be used to alter VAP login objects.

Each VAP process acts independently of all other VAP processes, and thus each process needs its own login. No two processes can share a login connection. Two or more processes could share a login connection of a "third" process that performs the actual services. However, you will need to devise a method of mutual exclusion so that the requests by the different processes are handled properly. Communications between the processes could be established by a global variable acting as a semaphore. When the semaphore is positive, the process must wait, for example. As you continue, you will find two or more processes might use the same login account, but the connection obtained by logging in cannot be shared without some sort of special development as previously mentioned. For instance, if two processes within a VAP need file server service access they would both login to the file server. That is, two file server connections would be used. And, just like user login connections, VAP process connections have independent connection information tables. For instance if a particular VAP process has a file opened, no other VAP process can share the file handle granted. Each VAP process will need to open its own file and, in turn, will receive a file handle 0 for the first file open. Unlike DOS, VAP file handles start with 0 and a file handle of 255 indicates an open error.

Consequently, a theoretical maximum of 254 files can be opened by a single VAP process.

VAP Writing and Testing

Writing VAPs is a balancing act. It involves linking a special header, which you create, to your code and keeping in mind the order of events that occur, such as the header, initialization code, and running code. Summarizing these events, the developer:

1) Initializes VAP parameters (done in the VAP's header)
2) Changes data segments from default of read-only to read-write
3) Initializes all processes (also known as threads)
4) Indicates to the operating system that all processes have been initialized
5) Begins the VAP's "regular" execution

Each event must occur at the right place or time. Attempts to do otherwise will most likely crash or bring down the file server. For instance, as previously mentioned, dynamic allocation of memory or spawning of processes must take place before the InitializationComplete is called.

VAP Debugging

Debugging a VAP while it is running in a file server is difficult at best. This section will provide a few strategies. First and foremost, despite Novell's instructions, developing a VAP on a NetWare bridge server in lieu of using a regular file server will not necessarily expedite VAP development. Unless your VAP will never run in anything but a NetWare bridge, you should develop your VAP on a file server. Why does this work best? Because the file sever offers an environment that is different from that of a bridge. For one thing, your VAP will most likely be run in a file server, especially if it is developed for commerical use.

When a VAP crashes a file server it can be difficult to determine which VAP crashed, though it will likely be yours if it is the only one. Sometimes, however it is not even your VAP that crashed the server. Sometimes your VAP will use memory that is in marginal condition or cause the operating system to use such memory resulting in a General Protection Interrupt (GPI) type Abend. Due to the inept debugger in the NetWare/286 operating system (compared to that of NetWare/386), finding the exact process that crashed the server can be much like tracking a needle in a haystack. For instance, if the server Abends you can use the following procedure to ascertain what probably caused the crash.

When the server Abends, type "deb" at the server console. Deb will not be echoed on the screen and a "*" should appear. If the dash appears type "i61" and <enter>. A return code should appear. Figure 4-2 lists error code ranges and their meanings.

Error Code Ranges	Possible Conflict
≤3F	Corrupted network operating system (solution: regenerate operating system), or VAP crash
40-7F	Problems with cards in the server i.e., network boards, graphics board, or disk controller
≥80	Memory problems in server RAM or RAM on network cards

Figure 7-2. Error Code Ranges

You can also type "?" and the Abend error message should reappear. When it reappears it may offer more information about the Abend. Sometimes when VAPs crash the Abend message will indicate the VAP or process (with process number in hexadecimal) that crashed the server. Unless you know all the VAPs that loaded before your VAP, it will be difficult to know what this process number means. But, if yours is the only VAP in the server, you can track the process by counting your processes starting with 0.

To enter the NetWare debugger programmatically put an Interrupt 3 (Int3) instruction sequence in your VAP. This is the breakpoint interrupt, when NetWare sees this interrupt it will automatically Abend the server (in NetWare/386 it will bring up the debugger). In this case, under NetWare/286 you would see:

Abend: Breakpoint interrupt. Power off and back on to restart.
Running Process: VAP #2

At this point you would type in "deb" and you should see:

NET$OS Debugger v2 *

Now, type "i61" and <enter>—you get back:

Port(0061) = 30 *

This number, 30, is in hexadecimal, and to us, it really doesn't mean much other than a VAP or a corrupted operating system crashed the server. It is doubtful that the operating system is corrupt in this case. If you then type a "?" and <enter> you might receive:

Running Process: VAP #2
Exception Error #0x0003

Offending Add. = 07A8:05B0

At this point you could use the "d" command to display the bytes at this offending address. For instance:

d 7a8:5b0

And, much like DOS's debug, you will see the data in "block" form. There is no debugger command to disassemble the bytes in the data block so that represented machine instructions are revealed. In fact, the only commands are **D** (display bytes at the specified address); **I** (read In a port's value); and **R** which displays the current values of the registers. Note that when using the **R** option, both the CS and IP registers are not listed. You could use DOS's DEBUG on your VAP and attempt to do a pattern match on the bytes shown at the crashed server. This could show you where in your code the server was when it crashed.

VAP Setup and Startup Code

The code below details the VAP setup and startup code.

```
;********************************************************************
;*
;* Program Name:   VAP_Setup_Module
;*
;* Filename:       vsetup.asm
;*
;* Version:        1.0
;*
;* Comments:       This is the setup and startup code for VAPs.
;*
;********************************************************************
    name          VAPSetUpAndStartModule

DGROUP  GROUP   _DATA

PGROUP  GROUP   _TEXT
    assume cs:PGROUP


;;;;;;;;;;;;;;;;;;;;;;;;;;;;;;;;;;;;;;;;;;;;;;;;;;;;;;;;;;;;;;;;;;;;;;
;; TEXT definitions
;;      Define header, ESR routines, Handler routines,
;;      and ProcessStart procedures
;;;;;;;;;;;;;;;;;;;;;;;;;;;;;;;;;;;;;;;;;;;;;;;;;;;;;;;;;;;;;;;;;;;;;;
_TEXT   segment public 'CODE'
    ;VAP definitions
    public NetWareShellServices, ProcessControlServices
    public ConsoleControlServices, IPXSPXServices

    ;IPX/SPX Definitions
    public  _VAPESRHandler
```

```
;SAP Definitions
public _SAPWaitESRHandler, _SAPAdvertiseESRHandler
;Handler front-ends
extrn  _ConsoleHandler: near, _DownHandler: near

;IPX/SPX ESR Externals
extrn  _SAPWaitESR: near, _SAPAdvertiseESR: near
extrn  _workESR: near


;VAP Header
Signature                       db   'NWProc'
NetWareShellServices            dd   ?
ProcessControlServices          dd   ?
ConsoleControlServices          dd   ?
IPXSPXServices                  dd   ?
VAPConsoleHandler               dd   ConsoleHandlerCALL
VAPDownHandler                  dd   DownHandlerCALL
VAPConsoleOrDownDataSegment     dw   DGroup
VAPConnectionRequestFlag        dw   1;No connection
VAPNameString                   db   'Sample VAP v1.0',
                                     64-($-VAPNameString) dup(0)

VAPConsoleKeyWordCount          dw   1
VAPKeyword1                     db   'SAM', 16-($-VAPKeyword1) dup(0)
VAPSignOnMessage                db   'Sample VAP v1.0 -RUNNING', 0
                                db   10-($-VAPSignOnMessage) dup(0)


VAPStart    proc    near
    mov     ax, DGroup
    mov     di, 1                   ;change data segment to data (read/write),
                                    ;default is read-only
    call    dword ptr cs:ProcessControlServices
    cli
    mov     ax, DGroup
    mov     ds, ax
    mov     es, ax
    mov     ss, ax
    mov     ax, OFFSET DGroup:MainStackEnd
    mov     sp, ax
    sti
    call    _MAIN ; call C code's main() procedure
VAPStart    endp
```

```
;;;;;;;;;;;;;;;;;;;;;;;;;;;;;;;;;;;;;;;;;;;;;;;;;;;;;;;;;;;;;;;;;
;;   Spawned Process front-ends
;;   These set the process up by assigning the segment registers
;;   and assigning a stack to the process.
;;;;;;;;;;;;;;;;;;;;;;;;;;;;;;;;;;;;;;;;;;;;;;;;;;;;;;;;;;;;;;;;;
;;   The following lines will change as YOUR VAP dictates.
;;   You will need to have you own names, etc.
;;
;;   Note that you will also need to change the KEYWORDs and the
;;   Stack names at the bottom of this file.
;;;;;;;;;;;;;;;;;;;;;;;;;;;;;;;;;;;;;;;;;;;;;;;;;;;;;;;;;;;;;;;;;
    ;Process definitions
    public _PVAPstatus

    extrn  _Main: near
    extrn  _FirstProcess: near

_PVAPstatus             proc near
    cli
    mov    ax, DGroup
    mov    ds, ax
    mov    es, ax
    mov    ss, ax
    mov    ax, OFFSET DGroup:FirstStackEnd
    mov    sp, ax
    sti
    call   _FirstProcess
_PVAPstatus             endp


;;;;;;;;;;;;;;;;;;;;;;;;;;;;;;;;;;;;;;;;;;;;;;;;;;;;;;;;;;;;;;;;;
;; Handler front-ends
;;;;;;;;;;;;;;;;;;;;;;;;;;;;;;;;;;;;;;;;;;;;;;;;;;;;;;;;;;;;;;;;;
    assume ds: DGroup

ConsoleHandlerCALL   proc   far
    mov    _Keyword, ax
    call   _ConsoleHandler ; procedure in Ccode
    ret
ConsoleHandlerCALL   endp


DownHandlerCALL      proc   far
    call   _DownHandler
    ret
DownHandlerCALL      endp
```

```
;;;;;;;;;;;;;;;;;;;;;;;;;;;;;;;;;;;;;;;;;;;;;;;;;;;;;;;;;;;;;;;;;;;;;;;
;; Event Service Routine front-ends
;;;;;;;;;;;;;;;;;;;;;;;;;;;;;;;;;;;;;;;;;;;;;;;;;;;;;;;;;;;;;;;;;;;;;;;


_SAPWaitESRHandler          proc    far
    mov     ax, DGroup
    mov     ds, ax
    push    es
    push    si
    call    _SAPWaitESR
    add     sp, 4
    ret
_SAPWaitESRHandler          endp



_VAPESRHandler              proc    far
    mov     ax, DGroup
    mov     ds, ax
    push    es
    push    si
    call    _workESR
    add     sp, 4
    ret
_VAPESRHandler              endp



_SAPAdvertiseESRHandler     proc    far
    mov     ax, DGroup
    mov     ds, ax
    push    es
    push    si
    call    _SAPAdvertiseESR
    add     sp, 4
    ret
_SAPAdvertiseESRHandler     endp
```

```
;;;;;;;;;;;;;;;;;;;;;;;;;;;;;;;;;;;;;;;;;;;;;;;;;;;;;;;;;;;;;;;;;;;;;;;;;;
;; Misc Procedures
;;  MSC stack check fake-out
;;  IPX Functions
;;;;;;;;;;;;;;;;;;;;;;;;;;;;;;;;;;;;;;;;;;;;;;;;;;;;;;;;;;;;;;;;;;;;;;;;;;

        public  __CHKSTK
        public  _IPXOpenSocket
        public  _IPXCloseSocket
        public  _IPXGetInternetworkAddress
        public  _IPXSendPacket
        public  _IPXListenForPacket
        public  _IPXScheduleIPXEvent
        public  _IPXCancelEvent
        public  _IPXGetLocalTarget
        public  _IPXRelinquishControl
        public  _IntSwap

__CHKSTK    proc    near
    pop     cx          ; get return offset
    sub     sp,ax       ; allocate stack space
    jmp     cx          ; return to cx
__CHKSTK    endp

;Parameters:
;   On Entry:  Pointer to socket to open
;              Socket Longevity
;   On Exit:   Error codes in AX
_IPXOpenSocket proc    near
    push    bp
    mov     bp, sp

    mov     bx, [bp+4]
    mov     dx, [bx]
    mov     ax, [bp+6]

    xor     bx, bx
    call    dword ptr cs: IPXSPXServices

    pop     bp
    ret
_IPXOpenSocket endp
```

```
;Parameters:
;    On Entry:  Socket Number
;    On Exit:   nothing
_IPXCloseSocket    proc        near
     push    bp
     mov     bp, sp

     mov     dx, [bp+4]

     call    dword ptr cs: IPXSPXServices

     pop     bp
     ret
_IPXCloseSocket    endp




;Parameters:
;    On Entry:  10 byte buffer
;    On Exit:   10 byte buffer will contain address
_IPXGetInternetworkAddress    proc near
     push    bp
     mov     bp,sp

     mov     ax, DGroup
     mov     es, ax
     mov     bx, [bp+4]
     mov     si, bx
     mov     bx, 09h
     call    dword ptr cs: IPXSPXServices
     push    ds
     pop     es

     pop     bp
     ret
_IPXGetInternetworkAddress endp
```

```
;Parameters
;   On Entry:  Pointer to ECB
_IPXSendPacket proc near
    push    bp
    mov     bp, sp

    mov     ax, DGroup
    mov     es, ax
    mov     bx, [bp+4]
    mov     si, bx
    mov     bx, 03h

    call    dword ptr cs: IPXSPXServices

    push    ds
    pop     es

    pop     bp
    ret
_IPXSendPacket endp

;Parameters
;   On Entry:  Pointer to ECB
_IPXListenForPacket proc near
    push    bp
    mov     bp, sp

    mov     ax, DGroup
    mov     es, ax
    mov     bx, [bp+4]
    mov     si, bx
    mov     bx, 04h
    call    dword ptr cs: IPXSPXServices
    push    ds
    pop     es

    pop     bp
    ret
_IPXListenForPacket endp

_IPXScheduleIPXEvent proc near
    push    bp
    mov     bp, sp
```

```
        mov     ax, DGroup
        mov     es, ax
        mov     bx, [bp+6]
        mov     si, bx
        mov     ax, [bp+4]
        mov     bx, 05h

        call    dword ptr cs: IPXSPXServices

        push    ds
        pop     es

        pop     bp
        ret
_IPXScheduleIPXEvent endp


;Parameters
;   On Entry:  Pointer to ECB
_IPXCancelEvent proc near
        push    bp
        mov     bp, sp

        mov     ax, DGroup
        mov     es, ax
        mov     bx, [bp+4]
        mov     si, bx
        mov     bx, 06h

        call    dword ptr cs: IPXSPXServices

        push    ds
        pop     es

        pop     bp
        ret
_IPXCancelEvent endp

;Parameters:
;   On Entry:  Pointer to 12 byte address
;              Pointer to 6 byte empty buffer
_IPXGetLocalTarget    proc    near
        push    bp
        mov     bp,sp
```

```
        mov     ax, DGroup
        mov     es, ax
        mov     bx, [bp+4]
        mov     si, bx
        mov     bx, [bp+6]
        mov     di, bx
        mov     bx, 02h

        call    dword ptr cs: IPXSPXServices

        push    ds
        pop     es

        pop     bp
        ret
_IPXGetLocalTarget    endp

;Parameters:
;   On Entry:  nothing
;   On Exit:   nothing
_IPXRelinquishControl proc    near
        mov     bx, 0Ah
        call    dword ptr cs: IPXSPXServices
        ret
_IPXRelinquishControl endp


;Parameters:
;   On Entry:  Parameter to swap
;   On Exit:   Returns swapped integer in AX
_IntSwap    proc    near
        push    bp
        mov     bp, sp
        mov     ax, [bp+4]
        xchg    ah, al
        pop     bp
        ret
_IntSwap    endp

_TEXT       ends
```

```
;;;;;;;;;;;;;;;;;;;;;;;;;;;;;;;;;;;;;;;;;;;;;;;;;;;;;;;;;;;;;;;;;;;;
;; Data definitions
;; Define all stacks for all processes and also define keyword variable
;;;;;;;;;;;;;;;;;;;;;;;;;;;;;;;;;;;;;;;;;;;;;;;;;;;;;;;;;;;;;;;;;;;;
_DATA       SEGMENT word public 'DATA'
    assume ds:DGROUP

    ;Stacks
    dw      2000 dup (0)
    MainStackEnd   label      word

    ;;;;;;;;;;;;;;;;;;;;;;;;;;;;;;;;;;;;;;;;;;;;;;;;;;;;;
    ;;  Here are the stacks appropiate for each process.
    ;;;;;;;;;;;;;;;;;;;;;;;;;;;;;;;;;;;;;;;;;;;;;;;;;;;;;
    dw      2000 dup (0)
    FirstStackEnd label      word

    ;Keyword that will be used in C program
    public _Keyword

    _Keyword   dw  0


_DATA       ENDS

    end     VAPStart
```

The following code is a sample C program that constitutes the VAPs initialization and normal execution:

```
;************************************************************************
;*
;* Program Name:     SAMPLE.VAP
;*
;* Filename:         sample.c

;* Version:          1.0
;*
;* Files Used:       sap.c vsetup.asm vsap.lib
;*
```

```
;**********************************************************************
    extern int    Keyword;
    unsigned      ConsoleProcess, FirstProcessID;
main()
{
    int       ccode
    void      PVAPstatus();

    VSpawnProcess( PVAPstatus);

    StartSAPOscillationRoutines( "SAMPLE_VAP", 4, 1010 );
    SetUpToReceive();

    ConsoleProcess = VGetProcessID();
    VInitializationComplete();
    while (1)
    {
     VSleepProcess();
     switch (Keyword)
     {
      case 0:
            VWakeUpProcess( FirstProcessID );
            break;
     }
    }
}

void FirstProcess()
{
    FirstProcessID = VGetProcessID();
    VInitializationComplete();
    while (1)
    {
     VSleepProcess();
     VConsoleError( "This would print out any status info you wanted." );
    }
}


ConsoleHandler()
{
    VWakeUp Process( ConsoleProcess );
    return (0);
}
```

```
DownHandler()
{
    VPrintString( -1, -1, "SAMPLE VAP is down.\n\r", -1 );
    return (0);
}
```

The following is a sample makefile to build a VAP:

```
COPT=-DMSC -C -AS -G2s -Fc -Zpi -0d
LOPT=/LINE /MAP
OBJS=vsetup.obj sap.obj sample.obj

.c.obj:
        cl $(COPT) $*.c

.asm.obj:
        masm $*.asm

vsetup.obj:    vsetup.asm makefile

sap.obj:       sap.c comm.h

sample.obj:    sample.c

sample.vap     $(OBJS)
        link $(LOPT) $(OBJS),sample,,svap;
```

The following file is a library of calls defined for the VAP interface. It is written in MASM 4.0 assuming SMALL MSC 4.0 code (or MSC 5.0). Turbo C works too.

```
;********************************************************************
;*
;* Program Name:  VAP_PRIMITIVES
;*
;* Filename:      vap.asm
;*
;* Version:       1.0
;*
;* Comments:      This file is a library of calls defined for the VAP
;*                interface. Written in MASM 4.0 and assuming SMALL
;*                MSC 4.0 code (or MSC 5.0).—-Turbo C works too
;*
;********************************************************************
        name    VAPLibraryModule

PGroup  group   _TEXT
        assume cs: PGroup

_TEXT   segment public 'CODE'

        public  _VAllocateSegment
        public  _VChangeToDataSegment
        public  _VSpawnProcess
        public  _VInitializationComplete
        public  _VKillProcess
        public  _VChangeProcess
        public  _VDelayProcess
        public  _VSleepProcess
        public  _VWakeUpProcess
        public  _VConsoleError
        public  _VGetProcessID
        public  _SetEStoDS
        public  _VAPAttachToFileServer

        extrn   ProcessControlServices: dword
```

```
AllocateSegment                equ    0
ChangeToDataSegment            equ    1
ChangeSegmentToCode            equ    2
DeclareSegmentAsData           equ    3
DeclareExtendedSegment         equ    4
SpawnProcess                   equ    5
SetPassThroughShellMode        equ    6
InitializationComplete         equ    7
KillProcess                    equ    8
ChangeProcess                  equ    9
DelayProcess                   equ    10
GetProcessID                   equ    11
SleepProcess                   equ    12
WakeUpProcess                  equ    13
SetHardwareInterruptVector     equ    14
GetInterruptVector             equ    15
SetInterruptVector             equ    16
CalculateAbsoluteAddress       equ    17
SetExtendedProcessorError      equ    18
ConsoleError                   equ    19
GetFileServerName              equ    20
AttachToFileServer             equ    21
MapFileServerNameToNumber      equ    22


_VAllocateSegment:
        push    bp
        mov     bp, sp
        mov     ax, [bp + 2 + 2]              ; paragraph amount
        mov     di, AllocateSegment
        push    es
        jmp     ProcessControlServicesCALL

_VChangeToDataSegment:
        push    bp
        mov     bp, sp
        mov     ax, [bp + 2 + 2]              ; segment value
        mov     di, ChangeToDataSegment
        push    es
        jmp     ProcessControlServicesCALL
```

```
_VSpawnProcess:
        push    bp
        mov     bp, sp
        mov     cx, [bp + 2 + 2]            ; process entry
        mov     dx, ds                      ; process data segment
        mov     bx, cs                      ; assume near
        mov     bp, cs
        mov     di, SpawnProcess
        push    es
        jmp     ProcessControlServicesCALL

_VInitializationComplete:
        push    bp
        mov     di, InitializationComplete
        push    es
        jmp     ProcessControlServicesCALL

_VKillProcess:
        push    bp
        mov     di, KillProcess
        push    es
        jmp     ProcessControlServicesCALL

_VChangeProcess:
        push    bp
        mov     di, ChangeProcess
        push    es
        jmp     ProcessControlServicesCALL

_VDelayProcess:
        push    bp
        mov     bp, sp
        mov     dx, [bp + 2 + 2]            ;delay amount
        mov     di, DelayProcess
        push    es
        jmp     ProcessControlServicesCALL

_VSleepProcess:
        push    bp
        mov     di, SleepProcess
        push    es
        jmp     ProcessControlServicesCALL
```

```
_VWakeUpProcess:
      push   bp
      mov    bp, sp
      mov    bx, [bp + 2 + 2]          ; sleeping process ID
      mov    di, WakeUpProcess
      push   es
      jmp    ProcessControlServicesCALL

_VConsoleError:
      push   bp
      mov    bp, sp
      mov    si, [bp + 2 + 2]          ; display error on console
      mov    di, ConsoleError
      push   es
      jmp    ProcessControlServicesCALL


_VGetProcessID:
      push   bp
      push   es
      mov    di, GetProcessID

ProcessControlServicesCALL proc    near
      call   dword ptr cs:ProcessControlServices
      pop    es
      pop    bp
      ret
ProcessControlServicesCALL endp

_VAPAttachToFileServer        proc    near
      push   bp
      mov    bp, sp

      mov    ax, [bp+4]
      mov    si, ax
      mov    di, 15h
      call   dword ptr cs:ProcessControlServices
      xor    ah, ah
      xor    dh, dh
      mov    si, [bp+6]
      mov    [si], dx

      pop    bp
      ret
_VAPAttachToFileServer        endp
```

```
;;;;;;;;;;;;;;;;;;;;;;;;;;;;;;;;;;;;;;;;;;;;;;;;;;;;;;;;;;;;;;;;;;;;;;
;        ConsoleControlServices Calls
;;;;;;;;;;;;;;;;;;;;;;;;;;;;;;;;;;;;;;;;;;;;;;;;;;;;;;;;;;;;;;;;;;;;;;

        public  _VClearScreen
        public  _VPrintString
        public  _VReadKeyboard
        public  _Interrupt3
        extrn   ConsoleControlServices: dword

_Interrupt3     proc    near
        int     3       ; breakpoint Interrupt
_Interrupt3     endp

_VClearScreen proc      near
        push    bp
        mov     bp, sp
        mov     di, 0                           ;0 is ClearScreen
        call    dword ptr cs:ConsoleControlServices
        pop     bp
        ret
_VClearScreen endp

_VPrintString proc      near
        push    bp
        mov     bp, sp
        mov     ax, [bp + 2 + 8]
        push    ax
        push    ds
        mov     ax, [bp + 2 + 6]
        push    ax
        mov     ax, [bp + 2 + 4]
        push    ax
        mov     ax, [bp + 2 + 2]
        push    ax
        mov     di, 1
        call    dword ptr cs:ConsoleControlServices
        mov     sp, bp
        pop     bp
        ret
_VPrintString endp
```

```
_VReadKeyboard proc    near
        push   bp
        mov    bp, sp
        mov    ax, [bp + 2 + 4]
        push   ax
        push   ds
        mov    ax, [bp + 2 + 2]
        push   ax
        mov    di, 2

        call   dword ptr cs:ConsoleControlServices
        mov    sp, bp
        pop    bp
        ret
_VReadKeyboard endp


;;;;;;;;;;;;;;;;;;;;;;;;;;;;;;;;;;;;;;;;;;;;;;;;;;;;;;;;;;;;;;;;;;;
;       Misc Calls
;;;;;;;;;;;;;;;;;;;;;;;;;;;;;;;;;;;;;;;;;;;;;;;;;;;;;;;;;;;;;;;;;;;

_SetEStoDS     proc    near
        push   ds
        pop    es
        ret
_SetEStoDS     endp

_TEXT   ends
        end
```

The following is an example of obtaining connection information for connection 1 with a VAP.

```
typedef struct {
   MyWord         Native;
   char           Func; /* Get Connection Info 16 */
   unsigned char Conct; /* logical connection #  */
   } ConCall;
```

```
typedef struct {
   MyWord            Native;
   unsigned char     ID[4];
   unsigned char     type[2];
   char              name[48];
   char              loginTime[8];
   } ConRply;

ConCall Cc;
ConRply Cr;
.
.
.
   regs.F.Ax = 0xE300;
   Cr.Native.wl = 0x00;
   Cr.Native.wh = 0x0C;
   Cc.Native.wl = 0x00;
   Cc.Native.wh = 0x02;
   regs.F.Es = Seg(&Cr);
   regs.F.Di = Ofs(&Cr);
   regs.F.Ds = Seg(&Cc);
   regs.F.Si = Ofs(&Cc);
   Cc.Func = 0x16;
   Cc.Conct = RQ;
   MsDos(33, &regs);

/* where my MsDos call did:*/


void MsDos(int a, Registers *regs)
{
   a = &regs->F.AX; /* loads up AX register with pointer to regs structure*/
   doDos();
}

/* where doDos did:*/

_doDos:
ShellCall proc near
   ;unsigned int Ax, Bx, Cx, Dx, Bp, Si, Di, Ds, Es, FLAGS;
      push  bp
      mov   bp, sp
      push  es
      push  ds
      mov   saveBP, ax
```

```
        mov   si, ax    ;address of regs.F.Ax
        mov   ax, [si]  ;ax
        mov   bx, [si+2] ;bx
        mov   cx, [si+4] ;cx
        mov   dx, [si+6] ;dx
        mov   bp, [si+8] ;bp
        mov   di, [si+12] ;di
        push  ax
        mov   ax, [si+16] ;es
        mov   es, ax
        mov   ax, [si+14] ;ds
        mov   si, [si+10] ;si
        mov   ds, ax
        pop   ax

        call  dword ptr cs:NetWareShellServices

        push  si
        push  di
        mov   si,saveBP  ;address of regs.F.Ax
        mov   [si],ax
        mov   [si+2],bx
        mov   [si+4],cx
        mov   [si+6],dx
        mov   [si+8],bp
        pop   di
        mov   [si+12],di
        mov   [si+14],ds
        mov   [si+16],es
        mov   di,si
        pop   si
        mov   [di+10],si ; don't care what DI and SI are on return

        pop   ds
        pop   es
        pop   bp

        ret
ShellCall endp

  in data segment:
    saveBP   dw   0
```

VAP-to-VAP Communication

When creating a VAP, you may wish to use the services of another VAP. Unfortunately, achieving interVAP communication is neither documented nor easily discovered.

Here is one method to achieve interVAP communication. Surely there are other ways, but this one works.

Some highlights of are method include those for the VAP providing the services. Because VAPs can search for other VAPs and receive back the segment which contains the searched-for VAP's header, the first change made is to the VAP's header. This change has two parts. First, a name is set up in the header, which will be ensure the proper VAP has been located. Second, a segment:offset pointer that points to a data area is defined. In turn, this new data area points to a procedure within the code that will be available to other VAPs.

For the VAP requesting the services, a search of all VAP headers is performed, searching for the name set up in the header of the VAP providing services. Next, the pointer in the VAP header is resolved to find the pointer to the procedure. Once this is resolved it is then possible to call the other VAP. Note that NetWare/286 can only accommodate the loading of 10 VAPs. Finally, note that the code examples presume the SMALL memory model. Now, on with the changes, first the VAP header of the VAP is modified, as shown in Figure 4-3 on the next page.

The main reason the address of our data structure is defined at compile/link time is the fact that the VAP header segment is always read-only. That is, the segment (actually segment descriptor in terms of 80286 protected mode operation) is always read-only and cannot be changed to read/write. The inability to be changed to read/write indicates that the VAP function call to change a segment from code (read-only) to data (read/write) will not work. In fact, the server will Abend with a General Protection Interrupt. Further, whenever there is an attempt to write to a read-only area of memory a TRAP 000D will occur, or Exception 000D in terms of NetWare's error messages.

```
;VAP Header
Signature                        db    'NWProc'
NetWareShellServices             dd    ?
ProcessControlServices           dd    ?
ConsoleControlServices           dd    ?
IPXSPXServices                   dd    ?
VAPConsoleHandler                dd    ConsoleHandlerCall
VAPDownHandler                   dd    DownHandlerCall
VAPConsoleOrDownDataSegment      dw    DGroup
VAPConnectionRequestFlag         dw    0; 0=connection needed
                                       ; 1=no connection needed
VAPNameString                    db    'Test VAP v1.00',
                                       64-($-VAPNameString) dup(0)
                                       ; pad with nulls
VAPConsoleKeyWordCount           dw    1
VAPKeyword1                      db    'TESTVAP',
                                       16-($-VAPKeyword1) dup(0)
                                       ; pad with nulls
VAPreserved                      db    0
VAPSignOnMessage                 db    'TEST VAP LOADED', 0
EntryJMP                         db    'JMPTBL' ;unique id
                                               ;could be any name
                                 dd    _JmpTbl ;will set up address
                                               ;of this data
                                               ;structure here
                                 dw    DGroup  ;address of data segment
```

Figure 7-3. Modified VAP Header

Next, set up the actual pointer to the procedure to be called as shown in Figure 7-4.

```
    _SETUPjmp:
    setupJmp proc near

            ; set up SEGMENT:OFFSET of procedure JmpTest() and
            ; that procedure's data segment

            mov     _JmpTbl, offset _JmpTest
            mov     _JmpTbl+2, cs

            mov     ax, DGROUP
            mov     _JmpTbl+4, ax

            ret

    setupJmp endp
```

Figure 7-4. Setting the Segment Offest Pointer

Figure 7-5 shows SETUPjmp being called. Remember to set up the Assembly call SETUPjmp as a public symbol so your C code can be linked with it.

```
    from within a C procedure:

    .
    .
    .
    /* Set up Address of JmpTbl */
        SETUPjmp();
        VInitializationComplete();/**/
    .
    .
    .
```

Figure 7-5. Calling SETUPjmp

```
    JmpTest()
    {
    ConsoleMessage("You rang?");

    /* Here you would do whatever you need to do, this is the
       procedure being called by another VAP*/

    /* what follows is a method to embed Assembly language commands
       in your C program*/

    asm  pop bp
    asm  ret far
    }
```

Figure 7-6. Using Assembly to Perform a Far Return

Note that in addition to the segment:offset pointer to the procedure to be called, the data segment is also saved. This is important, as the routine in the requesting VAP will need to ensure the data segment is properly defined when calling this procedure. Also note that this routine (SETUPjmp) is not actually needed. You might opt to define this procedure (JmpTest()) in the VAP header instead of the data area. Either way will work, but the way shown here is more versatile. That is, the situation might be altered. The VAP being called might instead call the other VAPs who are requesting services of this VAP. For the VAP providing services to call the other VAPs, it will need to know their addresses. Here, these VAPs requesting services could deposit their addresses within a data area (JmpTbl) of the VAP providing services.

Following is the procedure being set up by the SETUPjmp procedure. Be sure that this procedure does an RETF (far return). You might use embedded Assembly language commands to do this, as shown in Figure 7-6.

At this point the VAP providing services is completely set up. Now, there are things to prepare for the VAP requesting services.

First, do not perform any of these functions from a process that has not yet call InitializationComplete. If you do not wait for InitializationComplete you may not get proper addresses.

From within a C procedure:

```
.
.
.
int a,b,c,e,segment,offset,dseg;
char kk[255];
 /* first, get address of JMPTBL, start looking thru VAP Headers next,
    call it */

   VInitializationComplete();/**/
   a=b=e=0;
   while (a<10) /* remember, only have 10 VAPs numbered 0 thru 9 */
   {
     segment=VGetVAPHeader(a); /* see code below for this procedure's
                                  def */
     if (segment) /*if we get a Segment, a 0 is returned if no VAP found*/
     {
     e++; /* a counter to track how many VAPs have been found, optional*/
     b=FindJMP(segment, &segment, &offset, &dseg); /*find jmptbl address*/
     if (b) /* found it!, if b is !=0 then we found the VAP providing
             services */
     {
       sprintf(kk,"segment [%x] offset [%x] dataseg [%x]",
               segment,offset,dseg);
       ConsoleMessage(kk);
       CallJMP(offset,segment,dseg);

       ConsoleMessage("Should have just called VAP providing services");
       a=99; /* leave loop now */
     }
   }
   else
   {
    a=99; /* leave loop now */
   }
   a++;
 }

.
.
.
```

Now, for the VGetVAPHeader routine:

```
_VGetVAPHeader:
 GetHdr proc near
        push    bp
        mov     bp, sp
        mov     ax, [bp+4] ;VAP Header ID to get
        mov     di, 17h
        ; VAP segment is returned in AX, 0= no more VAPs
        call dword ptr cs:ProcessControlServices ; as defined in the
                                                 ; VAP header
        pop     bp
        ret
 GetHdr endp
```

Now, for the FindJMP routine:

```
_FindJMP:
 SearchForJMP proc near
        push    bp
        mov     bp, sp

        push    es
        push    si
        mov     ax, [bp+4] ;VAP Segment/Descriptor
        mov     es, ax

        mov     si, 9Ch ; look at offset 9Ch for our JMPTBL id, we
                        ; calculated this ahead of time, it could be
                        ; done via an OFFSET declaration, or, I could
                        ; do a string search through a range of memory
                        ; but doing that here would just make the
                        ; example unnecessarily complex this is why I
                        ; opted for this method

        cmp     word ptr es:[si  ], 'MJ'
        jnz     NotOurVAP

        cmp     word ptr es:[si+2], 'TP'
        jnz     NotOurVAP

        cmp     word ptr es:[si+4], 'LB'
        jnz     NotOurVAP
```

```
;got this far, found our VAP, the one providing services
push    bx  ;save these registers
push    cx

mov     ax,es:[si+6];ofs ;get segment:offset of the data structure
mov     bx,es:[si+8];seg ;that contains the actual pointers

mov     es, bx          ;set up es:si to point to data area
mov     si, ax

mov     ax, es:[si]    ;real offset of procedure
mov     bx, es:[si+2] ;code segment
mov     cx, es:[si+4] ;data segment

mov     si, [bp+6]
mov     [si], bx    ;return segment to calling procedure in VAP
                    ;requesting services

mov     si, [bp+8]
mov     [si], ax   ;return offset

mov     si, [bp+10]
mov     [si], cx   ;return data segment

pop     cx
pop     bx

jmp     VAPfound


NotOurVAP:
    xor     ax,ax ;return 0, not found
VAPfound:

    pop     si
    pop     es
    pop     bp
    ret
SearchForJMP endp
```

Next, the routine that will actually call the VAP providing services:

```
_CallJMP:
JmpToOtherVAP proc far      ;note this routine is defined as far
        push    bp
        mov     bp, sp
        push    ds

        push    si
        push    di
        push    es

        ; first we will take the segment:offset address to call in a
        ; data area that we can do a far call from

        mov     si, offset JmpTbl1  ; our internal data area to to a
                                    ; jmp from note that we could jump
                                    ; from [bp+4] address also, but to
                                    ; make things clearer, we didn't
                                    ; do that here
        mov     di, [bp+4]
        mov     [si], di     ;offset to jmp to

        mov     di, [bp+6]
        mov     [si+2], di   ;segment to jmp to
        ; now our internal data area, JmpTbl1, is set up in
        ; offset:segment set up the es: register to point to where the
        ; ds: register does then set up the ds: register to point to
        ; the data segment of the procedure being called (that
        ; procedure being in the VAP providing services)

        push    ds
        pop     es

        mov     ds, [bp+8]

        call    dword ptr es:[si]  ; call the VAP providing services
                                   ; be sure that the routine called
                                   ; does a RETF (far return) and not
                                   ; a RET (near return) when it
                                   ; returns to us
```

```
        pop     es
        pop     di
        pop     si
        pop     ds
        pop     bp

        ret

JmpToOtherVAP endp
```

What follows is the data definition for the VAPs. This is basically the same as shown earlier, but you will note the addition of the data areas used for this example.

```
_DATAS  SEGMENT word public 'DATAS'
        assume ds:DGROUP

        ;Stacks
        dw      2000 dup (0)
        MainStackEnd   label   word
;;;;;;;;;;;;;;;;;;;;;;;;;;;;;;;;;;;;;;;;;;;;;;;;;;;;;;
;;  Here are the stacks appropiate for each process.
;;;;;;;;;;;;;;;;;;;;;;;;;;;;;;;;;;;;;;;;;;;;;;;;;;;;;;
dw      2000 dup (0)
FirstStackEnd label   word
;Keyword that will be used in C program
public_Keyword

public  _JmpTbl

public  JmpTbl1

_Keyword        dw      0

_JmpTbl         dw      6 dup(0) ; could be larger to hold
                                 ; more addresses

JmpTbl1         dw      2 dup(0)

public  saveBP
```

```
saveBP          dw     0

_DATAS  ENDS


/* END */
```

Sample SAP Routines for a VAP

```
/***********************************************************************
 *
 * Program Name:  SAMPLE.VAP
 *
 * Filename:   sap.c
 *
 * Version:    1.0
 *
 * Files used: comm.h
 *
 * Comments: This is a "plug-in" sap module to do service advertising.
 *           Also the ESR for receiving service requests is here.
 *
 ***********************************************************************/
#include "comm.h"

/* We will keep this pointer around so as to keep track of the */
/* oscillating ECB.  We will need to know where it is later so we */
/* can cancel the event associated with that ECB. */
ECB             *DownECBPointer;

void            SAPWaitESRHandler();
void            SAPAdvertiseESRHandler();
void            SetUpToReceive();
void            workESR();
void            ResetESR();
void            VAPESRHandler();

IPXdata         RQ1;
SAPData         SAPDataEntity;
ECB             SAPECB, RECB1;
IPXPacke        SAPPacket, RIPX1;
char            USERS[100];
```

```
void StartSAPOscillationRoutines( ServerName, ServerType, ServerSocket
)
char            ServerName[48];
int             ServerType;
unsigned int    ServerSocket;
{
        /* Initialize the variables for the SAP IPXPacket. */
        /* Notice that I broadcast on socket 452h (The SAP Socket) */
        /* You need not have the socket open to send on the socket. */
        SAPPacket.PacketType = (unsigned char)4;
        SAPPacket.PacketLength = IntSwap( sizeof( IPXPacket ) );
        IPXGetInternetworkAddress( (unsigned char
            SAPPacket.Destination.Network );
        memset( SAPPacket.Destination.Node, 0xFF, 6 );
        SAPPacket.Destination.Socket = 0x5204;

        /* I initialize the SAP data packet. See the SAP chapter in
           Novell's technical overview. */
        SAPDataEntity.InfoType = IntSwap( 2 );
        SAPDataEntity.ServerType = IntSwap( ServerType );
        strcpy( SAPDataEntity.ServerName, ServerName);
        IPXGetInternetworkAddress( (unsigned char
            SAPDataEntity.Address.Network );
        SAPDataEntity.IntermediateNetworks = IntSwap( 1 );
        SAPDataEntity.Address.Socket = ServerSocket;

        /* Initialize the ECB. */
        SAPECB.ESRAddress = (char far *)SAPWaitESRHandler;
        SAPECB.InUseFlag = 0;
        SAPECB.FragmentCount = 2;
        SAPECB.ECBSocket = 0x5204;
        memset( SAPECB.ImmediateAddress, 0xFF, 6 ); /* broadcast*/.
        SAPECB.FragmentDescriptor[0].Address = (char far *)&SAPPacket;
        SAPECB.FragmentDescriptor[0].Size = sizeof (IPXPacket );
        SAPECB.FragmentDescriptor[1].Address = (char far
            &SAPDataEntity;
        SAPECB.FragmentDescriptor[1].Size = sizeof( SAPData );

        IPXSendPacket( &SAPECB );

}
```

```
void SetUpToReceive()
{
/* These ESRs are the ones that do the actual processing of user
   requests
 * they are on socket 4452h (in the dynamic socket range per Novell
 * Right now, one is setup, see comments above workESR()
 */
int x;

        for (x=0;x<101;x++) USERS[x]=0; /* null out user table */

        /* Initialize the ECB 1 */
        RECB1.ESRAddress = (char far *)VAPESRHandler;
        RECB1.FragmentCount = 2;
        RECB1.ECBSocket = 0x4444;
        RECB1.FragmentDescriptor[0].Address = (char far *)&RIPX1;
        RECB1.FragmentDescriptor[0].Size = sizeof (IPXPacket );
        RECB1.FragmentDescriptor[1].Address = (char far *)&RQ1;
        RECB1.FragmentDescriptor[1].Size = sizeof( IPXdata );

        IPXOpenSocket ( &RECB1.ECBSocket, 0xFF );

        IPXListenForPacket( &RECB1 );

} /* end of SetUpToReceive */




/* This ESR receives in a packet from a Node, that data portion of the
 * incoming packet contains:
 * byte Logical Node id (0-65h 0-101d)
 * byte Command (0=SIGN OFF, 1=SIGN ON, 2=GET STATUS, 3=SHOW USERS)
 *     -0, 1 return codes affirming operation, 0xA4 means ok
 *     -2 returns 0 if VAP is down(key device missing) or 1 if VAP is up
 *     -3 returns a list of LOGICAL connections currently using VAP
 *     -X a bad code returns FF
 *     NOTE: this VAP is made to work in a ONE SERVER environment for now
 *
 * an array of 100 bytes is maintained, if the entry is 1, connection in use,
 * if entry is 0, connection not in use
 */
void workESR ( rECB )
ECB            *rECB;
{
int            x;
```

```
VPrintString( -1, -1, "SAMPLE_VAP received request.\n\r", -1 );
if ((RQ1.data[0] > 0x65) || (RQ1.data[1] > 0x03) )
    {
      RQ1.data[0] = 0xFF; /* bad call, logical station too big */
    }
    else
    {
      switch (RQ1.data[1])
      {
       case 0:
       USERS[RQ1.data[0]] = 0; /* exit them from active list */
       RQ1.data[0] = 0xA4;
       break;

       case 1:
       USERS[RQ1.data[0]] = 1; /* add them to active list */
       RQ1.data[0] = 0xA4;
       break;

       case 2:
       RQ1.data[0]=1; /* report device is active for now */
       break;

       case 3:
       for (x=0;x<101;x++)
       RQ1.data[x] = USERS[x]; /*send back whole list of goodies*/
       break;
      }
    }

/* Send back reply and reset ESR */
RIPX1.PacketType = (unsigned char)4;
RIPX1.PacketLength = IntSwap( sizeof( IPXPacket ) );
for (x=0;x<4;x++)
RIPX1.Destination.Network[x] = RIPX1.Source.Network[x];
for (x=0;x<6;x++)
RIPX1.Destination.Node[x] = RIPX1.Source.Node[x];
RIPX1.Destination.Socket = 0x5555;

/* Users receive on socket 5555, VAP receives on 4444 */
```

```
        RECB1.ESRAddress = 0; /* NO ESR AFTER SEND! */
        RECB1.FragmentCount = 2;
        RECB1.ECBSocket = 0x5555;
        RECB1.FragmentDescriptor[0].Address = (char far *)&RIPX1;
        RECB1.FragmentDescriptor[0].Size = sizeof (IPXPacket );
        RECB1.FragmentDescriptor[1].Address = (char far *)&RQ1;
        RECB1.FragmentDescriptor[1].Size = sizeof( IPXdata );

        IPXSendPacket( &RECB1 );   /* send back reply */

        RECB1.ESRAddress = (char far *)VAPESRHandler;
        RECB1.ECBSocket = 0x4444;

        IPXListenForPacket( &RECB1 );


} /* end of workESR */


/* These two ESRs require some explanation. When the IPXSendPacket is
done above the ESR SAPWaitESR will be called This ESR will immediately
change the ESR to SAPAdvertiseESR and waits one minute.  In one minute
the SAPAdvertiseESR will be activated and it will change the ESR to
SAPWaitESR and then do a send packet.  These two ESRs will oscillate
back and forth thus doing SAP calls. */

void SAPWaitESR( wECB )
ECB            *wECB;
{
        wECB->ESRAddress = (char far *)SAPAdvertiseESRHandler;
        IPXScheduleIPXEvent( 60*18, wECB ); /* Every 60 Seconds */
}


void SAPAdvertiseESR( wECB )
ECB            *wECB;
{
        wECB->ESRAddress = (char far *)SAPWaitESRHandler;
        IPXSendPacket( wECB );
}
```

```
int StopSAPOscillationRoutines( ServerName, ServerType, ServerSocket )
char         ServerName[48];
int          ServerType;
unsigned int ServerSocket;
{
  SAPData    wDataEntity;
  ECB        wECB;
  IPXPacket  wPacket;


  /* First I will cancel the SAP oscillation ESRs. */
  IPXCancelEvent( &SAPECB );
  while (SAPECB.InUseFlag)
        ;

  /* Was the event cancelled?  FC means yes. */
  if (SAPECB.CompletionCode != 0xFC)
        return (-1);

  /* Now I will send out a IPX packet telling all that this
     server is down. */
  wPacket.PacketType = (unsigned char)4;
  wPacket.PacketLength = IntSwap( sizeof( IPXPacket ) );
  IPXGetInternetworkAddress( (unsigned char
     *)wPacket.Destination.Network );
  memset( wPacket.Destination.Node, 0xFF, 6 );
  wPacket.Destination.Socket = 0x5204;

  /* I initialize the SAP data packet. */
  /* Tell everyone that we are going down. (Thus the 16 intermediate
     networks) */
  wDataEntity.InfoType = IntSwap( 2 );
  wDataEntity.ServerType = IntSwap( ServerType );
  strcpy( wDataEntity.ServerName, ServerName);
  IPXGetInternetworkAddress( (unsigned char
     *)wDataEntity.Address.Network );
  wDataEntity.IntermediateNetworks = IntSwap( 16 );
  wDataEntity.Address.Socket = ServerSocket;
```

```
/* Initialize the ECB. */
wECB.FragmentCount = 2;
wECB.ECBSocket = 0x5204;
memset( wECB.ImmediateAddress, 0xFF, 6 );
wECB.FragmentDescriptor[0].Address = (char far *)&wPacket;
wECB.FragmentDescriptor[0].Size = sizeof (IPXPacket );
wECB.FragmentDescriptor[1].Address = (char far *)&wDataEntity;
wECB.FragmentDescriptor[1].Size = sizeof( SAPData );

IPXSendPacket( &wECB );
while( wECB.InUseFlag )
        ;

return (0);
}
```

The following is the Include file comm.h

```
/*****************************************************************
 *
 * Program Name:  SAP_Module
 *
 * Filename:      comm.h
 *
 * Version:       1.0
 *
 * Comments:      Typedefs and such for IPX and SPX communications.
 *
 *****************************************************************/
struct IPXAddress
{
    unsigned char     Network[4];    /* high-low */
    unsigned char     Node[6];       /* high-low */
    unsigned int      Socket;        /* high-low */
};

typedef struct IPXPacketStructure
{
```

```
     unsigned int          PacketCheckSum;          /* high-low */
     unsigned int          PacketLength;            /* high-low */
     unsigned char         PacketTransportControl;
     unsigned char         PacketType;
     struct IPXAddress     Destination;
     struct IPXAddress     Source;
} IPXPacket;

typedef struct IPXdataStructure
{
   unsigned char                          data[100];
} IPXdata;

typedef struct SPXPacketStructure
{
     unsigned int          PacketCheckSum;          /* high-low */
     unsigned int          PacketLength;            /* high-low */
     unsigned char         PacketTransportControl;
     unsigned char         PacketType;
     struct IPXAddress     Destination;
     struct IPXAddress     Source;
     unsigned char         ConnectionControl;
     unsigned char         DatastreamType;
     unsigned int          SourceConnectionID;       /* high-low */
     unsigned int          DestinationConnectionID;  /* high-low */
     unsigned int          SequenceNumber;           /* high-low */
     unsigned int          AcknowledgeNumber;        /* high-low */
     unsigned int          AllocationNumber;         /* high-low */
} SPXPacket;

struct ECBFragment
{
   char far              *Address;
   unsigned int          Size;                     /* low-high */
};

typedef struct ECBStructure
{
```

```
    unsigned int              Link[2];
    char far                  *ESRAddress;              /* offset-segment */
    unsigned char             InUseFlag;
    unsigned char             CompletionCode;
    unsigned int              ECBSocket;                /* high-low */
    unsigned char             IPXWorkspace[4];
    unsigned char             DriverWorkspace[12];
    unsigned char             ImmediateAddress[6];      /* high-low */
    unsigned int              FragmentCount;            /* low-high */
    struct ECBFragment        FragmentDescriptor[2];
} ECB;

typedef struct SAPDataStructure
{
    unsigned int              InfoType;
    unsigned int              ServerType;
    unsigned char             ServerName[48];
    struct IPXAddress         Address;
    unsigned int              IntermediateNetworks;
} SAPData;
```

VAP LOGIN Example

```
int ccode;
WORD connectionID; /* #typedef WORD unsigned int */
char serverName[50];
  ccode = VAPGetFileServerName(serverName);
  if (!ccode)
  {
  ConsoleDisplay("Unable to load Work VAP in bridge, must use File Server.");
  Bridge=1;
  }
  else
  {
   ccode = VAPAttachToFileServer(serverName,&connectionID); /* */
   Bridge=0; /* not a bridge */
```

```
/* Now perform login via the VAP DOS/Shell Services Interface */
  lc.Native.wh =0x0E;                /* packet length, low-high order */
  lc.Native.wl =0;
  lc.Func =0x14;                     /* login to file server */
  lc.ty.wh =0x00;                    /* object type */
  lc.ty.wl =0x01;                    /* 0001=User object type */
  lc.NL =8;                          /* Name Length */
  strcpy(lc.Name,"VAPLOGIN");        /* login account name */

  lc.Pass[9] =0; /* password length */
  strcpy(lc.Pass,"\x0"); /* password (NULL) */

  lr.Native.wh =1; /* return buffer length, low-high */
  lr.Native.wl =0;

  regs.F.Ax = 0xE300; /* Service Function class */

  regs.F.Ds = Seg(&lc); /* pointers to the request buffer */
  regs.F.Si = Ofs(&lc);

  regs.F.Es = Seg(&lr); /* pointers to the reply buffer */
  regs.F.Di = Ofs(&lr);

  MsDos(33,&regs); /* call Shell Services, see actual routine
                      at bottom of page 25 of this chapter*/
  if (!regs.H.Al)
  {
   ConsoleDisplay("Hey, here we are...LOGGED IN");
  }
  else
  {
   ConsoleDisplay("Could *NOT* login as user VAPLOGIN!");
  }
```

Note: These examples show an approach that does not use the NetWare C Library for accessing NetWare functions within a VAP. You can use Novell's C Libraries for VAPs instead. These libraries are included in the NetWare C Interface for DOS.

```
The following demonstrates how two processes within a VAP call each
other:

.
.
.
WORD MainProcess, ESRprocess; /* GLOBAL */
.
.
.
main()
{
.
.
.

   MainProcess = VGetProcessID();

   while (1) /* loop forever */
   {
     VSleepProcess();/* wait here till someone wakes us up,
                      ESRprocess in this case */

     /* when done, wake up this process */
   }

} /* end of main() */
.
.
.

void workESR ()
{
.
.
.
```

```
    ESRprocess = VGetProcessID(); /**/


    while (1) /* loop forever */
    {

       /* there would probably be some condition here which
          would trigger the waking up of MainProcess */

       VWakeUpProcess( MainProcess );
       VSleepProcess(); /* right after we wakeup MainProcess we'll
                           go to sleep, otherwise we would continue
                           to run */

    }

} /* end of workESR() */
```

CHAPTER 8

NLMs

Some of the advantages that NetWare provides include superior LAN management features, good security, and a dependable, mature product line that can be installed using a wide variety of hardware components. However, as important as these issues are, none of them would really matter if NetWare LANs didn't first possess superior performance. In fact, raw performance at its fundamental—almost generic—level is one of the key issues that sets one NOS apart from another and makes all of the other higher-level issues, like network management, meaningful.

In the world of operating systems, a large measure of performance is dictated by the control mechanisms in place. Something must control the order of processing. If there were infinite resources, such as unlimited CPU cycles, or unlimited RAM, then the notion of control would be less important. However, the various computer processes, or threads, which are the building blocks of programs, vie for the use of limited resources. Thus, in an operating system that is multithreaded, that is, running many threads in a concurrent manner, there is the need for some scheduling control so that no one thread dominates a single CPU's time or multiple CPUs' time. Whether the control is centralized or decentralized is determined by the process scheduler engine. This scheduler determines when processes will be allowed to execute, since they are competing for limited resources.

The processing that occurs in multitasking operating systems is based on one of two scheduling control models—a preemptive model or a nonpreemptive model. Most multi-tasking operating systems, such as OS/2 and UNIX, are preemptive operating systems. NetWare 386, however, is a nonpreemptive operating system. To better understand why the Novell architects chose this scheduling environment for NetWare 386, it is necessary to first understand the logic behind both environments.

What is Preemption?

Within the domain of preemptive control, the operating system itself provides each thread with access to the CPU. However, preemptive scheduling dictates that the operating system may "kick" any process off the CPU at any time in order to allow another thread to run. This process is known as context switching. In general, each thread is given a certain amount of time to execute, but this amount of time is rarely indicated to the thread.

The purpose of stopping and restarting threads is to give all currently operating threads more or less equal CPU time. (Note, however, that different schedule privilege levels may be defined for individual threads.) By fulfilling this purpose, all of the threads are given a chance to run in a timely manner.

However, ensuring that all processes have a certain amount of time in which to execute produces a great deal of system overhead. The requirement for additional CPU cycles can slow the execution of the actual operating system code as well as any external code.

Additionally, when different threads interact with each other, there is the need to synchronize their data areas. That is, when threads communicate with one another, they must do so in a synchronized fashion or risk defeating their communications. A lack of synchronization could yield data that is invalid when accessed by different threads.

In a preemptive environment, each different shared data area or structure is synchronized. That is, there is a different lock for each data structure and their shared data areas may be locked. A lock would ensure that the memory is not changed while the lock-owning thread is "asleep." Indeed, each access to shared data regions needs to be synchronized with locks.

But, why synchronize memory at all? The major reason why a preemptive operating system has the need for memory locking is that in most cases, the thread has no idea at what point in its processing it was stopped and subsequently restarted. And, because a thread does not actually know when it will be put to sleep, it must protect the shared areas of memory it is dealing with to ensure their integrity. Without the synchronization of memory, shared data areas could become corrupted. This synchronization is the most important difference between preemptive and nonpreemptive operating systems.

Deadlocks

Most multiuser, or preemptive, operating systems provide semaphores as the lock control method. Semaphores are flags used to limit how many tasks can use or change a resource at the same time. These locks are necessary since the threads, not knowing when they will be preempted, need to access shared data and receive coherent data. However, the basic preemptive model allows for the possibility of a deadlock. The term deadlock refers to the situation where two processes are stuck in a tight loop while waiting for the other to free up resources needed to continue processing; a deadlock implies a lack of synchronization. The methods that the operating system allows to control or synchronize data areas may ensure that a deadlock will not occur, but, in most multiuser operating systems, deadlock is possibile.

As an example of a deadlock scenario, consider two threads, A and B. They both need to lock data areas 1 and 2 to perform their tasks. When they attempt to lock either data area and cannot, they fall asleep in order to wait for a previously asserted lock to be released.

There are many other examples of deadlock situations, but this one is simple enough to point out the potential problem that any operating system may encounter. In a preemptive operating system, however, where locks on shared data regions are practically required, it is more likely to occur. Not only that, but the enforcement of these locks and their subsequent unlocks only eats up CPU time, thus downgrading performance.

Nonpreemption and NetWare 386

By choosing nonpreemption as the scheduling model, the NetWare 386 architects removed a costly barrier to performance—namely, the need for all threads to perform locks on shared memory. This prerequisite is removed because nonpreemption means that threads are not unknowingly put to sleep at any time. Only in the rare instance when a thread makes a call to another thread that may possibly fall asleep (for example, when accessing from disk, which can be slow) would a thread be put to sleep. But, because the thread is making a call to another thread that may possibly fall asleep, that calling thread is presumed to know it has a possibility of sleeping. For instance, if a thread makes a disk read request of another thread, as opposed to a faster cache read request, the calling thread should presume it may fall asleep while the read request is fulfilled and make proper preparations for its shared data areas. The proper preparations might include locking the memory (with NetWare 386, threads perform their locking via semaphores), or ordering the disk read request so that it occurs after the thread has completed its use of the shared memory.

However, in NetWare 386's nonpreemptive environment, threads are allowed to run to completion. That is, a thread is active until the operation is complete. This way a thread can access shared data regions in a continuous manner. Guaranteed access is possible because the thread will only be put to sleep when it explicitly desires that or when it makes a call to another thread which may be put asleep. Once a thread makes a call to another, that calling thread will wait there until the called thread returns. If the called thread goes to sleep, so does the calling thread.

And, because threads are allowed to run to completion and access to shared memory can be trusted (that is, a thread will not unknowingly be put to sleep), a nonpreemptive operating system is almost entirely freed from the requirement of memory synchronization; almost all data accesses can be performed without synchronization.

Remember that NetWare 386 currently supports only a single CPU at a time; there is no multiprocessor support. Therefore, when one thread is running, that is it. There are no other threads running until that thread falls asleep or is terminated.

How would multiprocessor support work in a nonpreemptive environment? Certainly, there would be a need for some sort of shared memory locking. While one option in the multiple CPU scenario is for locks on shared memory to be in the operating system software, an arguably better option is locating locking responsibility in the hardware itself. That is, when one CPU is accessing a region of memory, no other CPUs would be allowed access to that area. But NetWare's answer to this problem is still sometime in the future.

Nonpreemption Bottlenecks

Because the NetWare 386 operating system does not force preemption on its threads, a thread can "run away" with CPU time. When creating NLMs, developers must build safeguards into their code, that is, to allow for sleeping threads. However, if their threads are short or they call routines that may put the threads to sleep, you may not need to insert preemption. If they have sizable loops, where the thread may dominate the CPU for more than 380milliseconds (ms), then it is imperative to insert a thread sleep period through such procedures as delay, Thread Switch, and Suspend Thread.

NetWare 386 v3.1 can notify a user at the file server console when a thread occupies more than 380ms of continuous CPU time. The preemptive environment places execution threads in a defensive position, one where they must constantly be on guard against changes to their shared memory. These changes may occur while a thread has been "unknowingly" put to sleep by the operating system. Therefore,in case they are put to sleep, all processes using shared memory must synchronize, or lock, that memory—the primary drawback of preemption. Also, with individual locks on different shared data areas, deadlocks can occur. The payoff of preemption, however, is that all threads get an equal amount of time to execute (depending on scheduling privilege levels) and no one thread can monopolize the CPU.

With access to shared memory being a common occurrence in a NetWare 386 file server, nonpreemption puts execution threads in the offensive position of being able to ensure, without mandatory locking, that their shared data remains coherent. This assurance is the result of a thread being able to run until it knowingly sleeps. The major downfall of nonpreemption is the possibility that a thread may monopolize CPU time. When this occurs, developers can make simple changes to their code to reduce the amount of continuous CPU time that their threads use. The payoff of nonpreemption is that all threads run more quickly, and there is less overhead when switching operations between threads.

You can spot which NLM is the offending thread only by the name immediately following the date and time stamp. In this case, the name is "NetWare v3.1 Tes0," which is derived from the module name. If you type MODULES at the file server console prompt, you will see the names of all the modules installed. Look for one whose name matches or starts out the same as the name you see next to the time stamp, less the number, in this case 0. This number indicates the thread number within that module that is using more than 380ms of CPU time.

Interestingly, when a thread is using quite a bit of CPU time, it may not be reflected by the MONITOR.NLM's Utilization field. However, the file server will still be sluggish. This anomaly has been noted when testing certain procedures that were developed explicitly to use more than 380ms of CPU time.

Creating NLMs

For programmers who have struggled developing VAPs, a NetWare Loadable Module (NLM) provides a lucid, relaxed environment that makes writing server-based applications easier than ever before. For instance, an NLM can be developed very quickly, from initial design to code completion including the parallel development of a workstation or client application that uses the NLM's services.

Novell's rich set of APIs is primarily responsible for facilitating NLM development. Numbering more than 600, the available APIs can, by and large, do it all—from bit manipulation to managing execution threads. Novell's Development Products Division in Austin, Texas is responsible for turning these APIs into the NetWare 386 C Library. The Watcom 386 C Compiler is the current compiler of choice for developing NLMs. For Assembly-language coders, the PharLap 386 assembler provides the basis for code assembly.

Obtaining Connections

An NLM seeking a connection talks directly to the kernel without wasting any file server connections and without worrying about logging in. And your NLM has full supervisor rights, too. The call reads:

```
SetCurrentConnection(0);
```

It allows an NLM to talk directly to the kernel without logging in. The connection number zero indicates talk "directly." If you need to log in you can do so arbitrarily; there is no prerequisite "connection needed" flag as required in a VAP's header. Plus, multiple threads can share the same login connection.

PROFILE.NLM

PROFILE.NLM is a utility produced by Nu-Mega Technologies that provides the ability to break down the NetWare 386 file server CPU utilization figure, as shown by MONITOR.NLM, into individual components. In NetWare 386, these components correspond to NetWare Loadable Modules (NLMs) and the file server operating system. Essentially, these components are groups of threads, or processes. The threads are grouped per NLM, with the additional group of those threads belonging to the file server operating system. And these distinctive groups of threads facilitate the tracking of CPU resources. In addition, the operating system must schedule all threads for execution, which provides an additional "handle" on these threads, making them easier to track.

When in action, PROFILE.NLM displays the name of each module (NLM) that is being tracked. This list should be about the same as the list seen when you type modules at the file server console. It is possible, however, that some of the NLMs reported by modules will not appear on the PROFILE.NLM listing. There are two possible reasons why an NLM might be absent from this list:

1) No threads in that NLM have been active since PROFILE.NLM was initiated.
2) The threads in the NLM are only active when called by another NLM.

For example, if the NLM has an extension of .dsk, .lan, or .nam, it is usually excluded from the list since these NLMs are, for the most part, only active when called by server.exe. The reason why these "called upon" NLMs are not visible to PROFILE.MLN will be explained more fully in the discussion of the CHECK.NLM utility a little later.

PROFILE.NLM provides the following information for each NLM that it recognizes:

- Maximum continuous CPU time used in milliseconds (CPU time slice)
- Total accumulated CPU time in HH:MM:SS format
- Average amount CPU time slice used
- Percentage of CPU used

Note that the CPU time figures reflect the time elapsed since PROFILE.NLM was last loaded or reset, not the amount of time since the NLM was loaded or active.

Also note that NLMs using more than 380milliseconds (ms) of contiguous CPU time are considered "misbehaved" because they do not relinquish control of the CPU often enough. With NetWare 386 v3.1, the SET-able option

Set Display Relinquish Control Alerts = ON

will display an alert at the file server console anytime any thread in any NLM uses more than 380ms of contiguous CPU time. PROFILE.NLM can then be used to reveal further information about the offending thread, such as the precise amount of time that the thread is continuously using CPU time.

In addition to these tidbits, PROFILE.NLM offers more detail about each thread within each NLM on a subsequent screen. Here, each thread of the NLM is listed and the same four indicators detailed. If the thread is named, you will see that thread name listed. Otherwise, the thread's name will be displayed as the name of the NLM with the addition of 0, 1, 2, etc. These numbers indicate the thread number.

CHECK.NLM

Some NLMs implemented in NetWare 386, such as Novell's CLIB.NLM, are slightly more difficult to track. Specifically, these are NLMs that are implemented as TSRs, in that they are only active when they are called upon by another NLM. When a thread or threads of one of these "TSR-NLMs" is activated by another NLM, these threads inherit the calling NLM's processing time and effectively become part of that NLM.

To help track which areas of memory an NLM is actually using, Nu-Mega offers the CHECK.NLM utility. CHECK.NLM is loaded with the target NLM as a command-line option, and detects whenever that NLM accesses memory outside of its domain. This is possible because CHECK.NLM runs the chosen NLM in Ring 3. For more information concerning Ring 3, see the Appendix. The CHECK.NLM runs in the background using less than 1% of CPU time. Note that, in the current version, CHECK.NLM can only be loaded once; hence you can monitor only one NLM at a time.

If an NLM does access memory that is supposedly out-of-bounds, CHECK.NLM halts the NLM's execution and pops up a window indicating that an Illegal Access has occurred. Also in that window is the name of the NLM, the name of that NLM's offending thread, the code offset into the NLM that has performed an illegal memory read or write, the access type (read or write), the nearest code symbol (procedure name) and the address that was being illegally accessed. Next, you are presented with several options, including: Add, Mark, Ignore, Log, Off, Enter Debugger, and Abort NLM.

By selecting the Add option, you indicate that it is acceptable for the NLM to access that particular out-of-bounds address. For instance, early versions of CHECK.NLM indicated an illegal memory access whenever an NLM retrieved the system time. This access is deemed illegal because the NLM must read a memory area outside of its memory to get the time. Thus, if you know that the area is being accessed to retrieve the system time, you could use the Add option to indicate that this memory address access is acceptable and should not be reported again in the current session. Note that this information is not saved for use at a different load time. Also note, in the released version of CHECK.NLM, it does not consider accessing the system time to be an exception.

By selecting the Mark option, you indicate that the access is truly illegal, causing that area of memory to be flagged read-only so no further corruption can occur. Subsequent accesses to an area of memory that has been marked will not trigger further pop-up windows. At the end of the NLM's execution, all of the "marks" will be recorded to a .log file, which is written to the current directory of the file server's DOS drive; the file name preceeding the .log extension will be that of the NLM. Note that it is possible to configure CHECK.NLM to recognize memory access ranges that are legal.

The Ignore option causes the illegal access to be treated as if it never occurred. And, if that same access occurs again, CHECK.NLM will use another pop-up window to signal that event, just like the first occurrence of this out-of-bounds access.

The Log option is very similar to the Mark option. With the Log option, however, the illegal memory access is logged (just as with Mark), but the memory area is not write-protected (meaning, it is not flagged read-only). Otherwise, the Log option works just like the Mark option.

The Enter Debugger option stops all file server processing and brings up the NetWare 386 debugger.

The Abort NLM option stops the offending NLM's execution and removes it from memory. Note that whenever an NLM is unloaded (normally or not) CHECK.NLM is also removed from memory.

Two additional options can be specified when loading CHECK.NLM. The first option is "/w," which turns off CHECK.NLM's memory restore option. This option is engaged when a memory area is overwritten by an illegal access. Specifying "/w" turns off the restoration of these memory areas, which is useful if you want the memory overwrite.

The second option is /p, which stops all file server processing until the memory access exception is acknowledged. If this option is not invoked, only the processing of the target NLM is stopped.

NLM Design Options

NLMs can have other functions. For instance, an NLM could be a disk or LAN driver, a name space, or a utility. In general, VAPs can only be utilities.

The interface for VADD (value-added disk drivers) and LAN drivers in NetWare v2.1x is very different from that of VAPs. For instance, VADDs and LAN drivers are linked with the operating system, while VAPs are loaded and are not ever cohesively linked with the OS.

Threads

Developing NLMs begins with the knowledge of C that most DOS, OS/2, and UNIX programmers have. Building upon this foundation, NLMs present DOS programmers with a new way to shape code execution, a way already familiar to OS/2 and UNIX devotees: multithreaded programming.

Representing an execution sequence, a thread (or process) can be easily initiated and terminated. For instance, the following statement begins a new thread:

```
StatusThreadID = BeginThread ( postStats, NULL, 4096, NULL );
// initiates screen updates of status information
```

The variable StatusThreadID is of type int, which (in the world of NetWare 386 and the Watcom 386 C compiler) is a 32-bit (four-byte) quantity. The procedure BeginThread is one of the APIs from the C library. Passed to BeginThread are the name of the procedure to start as a new thread (postStats); a pointer to a thread stack (the first NULL) which BeginThread should allocate; the size of the stack (4096 in this case); and finally, pointer to an argument list (the second NULL). The // pattern is an ANSI C comment symbol indicating that everything else on that line is a comment.

Variables

Just as with VAPs, available to all threads within an NLM, including a new thread when it is spawned, are global variables. Also accessible are any local variables that the procedure being spawned has defined for itself. The local variables remain available only to that instantiation of the procedure being threaded. This means that for every instantiation of a procedure, it receives its own copy of the local variables defined. For operations requiring synchronization, such as updating a global counter, the C library provides EnterCritSec and ExitCritSec:

```
EnterCritSec();
I/O_Requests++;
```

```
// every time we pass here, an I/O request was processed
ExitCritSec();
```

Once a thread within an NLM has entered a critical section (EnterCritSec), only that thread will be scheduled for execution time. No other threads in that NLM will receive CPU time until ExitCritSec is executed, allowing once again the scheduling of CPU time for other threads within that NLM. Note that no two threads in the same NLM can be in critical sections concurrently. But a thread could enter a critical section and never leave. Thus it is important to:

1) Have pairs of EnterCritSec and ExitCritSec

2) Limit how long the critical section monopolizes that NLM's execution time

Limiting the amount of time (instructions) that an NLM is in a critical section will facilitate the execution of other threads within the NLM.

Spawning of threads can occur anywhere, from the main() execution thread to a thread initiating a new thread of itself. Threads can run forever, and threads can terminate themselves. When all threads within an NLM are terminated or done executing, the NLM is automatically unloaded by NetWare 386. However, terminating the initial thread with ExitThread(-1), does not unload the NLM—even if it's the last thread to run. The result is a library of functions callable by other NLMs. Also note that a procedure may be run only as a thread (a thread initiated by BeginThread), and/or may be called as a normal procedure. Thus a procedure—such as a clock routine that updates itself on a screen—may simply be spun off as a thread once, then continue to spin and run forever. Or that same clock code, in a different data space (different parameters received), may be called to spontaneously update the time on a particular screen.

Loops and the Delay API

As a thread runs, it may, from time to time, be involved in loops. Whether such loops are for loops or eternally running loops (while, do while, and so on), there is the inherent risk of monopolizing CPU time for all processes, including

NetWare 386 processes. Use of the delay(x) API available in the C library prevents these loops. The following is an example of delay:

```
while (Reqptr.status)
// wait for a request to be received
{ delay(loopTimeDelay); }
```

Once past a number, the delay function causes the thread from which the function is called to sleep for x milliseconds. (Alternately, you can use the ThreadSwitch routine.) While the thread is sleeping, it is not scheduled for processor time. This requirement results from the nonpreemptive NetWare 386 environment.

Cleaning Up Listen Requests

If you are coding for IPX or SPX, it is important to remember that outstanding listen requests are not "cleaned up" when a thread is terminated. The only time such requests are cleaned up is when the NLM itself is unloaded, since the unload function performs a total cleanup. However, before a function or thread terminates, it must ensure that any listen requests it had posted using memory space from its local memory variables are cancelled. If the memory space used for the listen requests belongs to the global memory space (global within that NLM), there is no such worry. If an outstanding "local" listen request is not cancelled when a thread terminates (unless IpxClosedSocket is used), and a packet is received for that listen buffer, there is no way to tell what will happen next. Most likely, the file server will become unstable, since memory once dedicated to handling the listen has become part of another NLM or file server process or file server cache memory. To prevent the occurrence of such an event, allocation of all memory space for listen requests could be globally defined. Then, that memory will exist until the NLM is terminated, unless the memory is freed. If the memory is freed then the same problem of an unstable server can result. (In addition to global definitions, any memory allocated with malloc, calloc, or realloc is also defined as global.) Note that all IPX and SPX conventions of NetWare 386 act largely like their counterparts in OS/2. This includes the queue structures that the OS/2. IPX, and SPX functions provide for queueing of packet buffers, just like their counterparts in OS/2.

Using Memory

Gone are the bounds of 8086-style programming. If you require a megabyte of RAM for a data structure, simply allocate it. NetWare 386's use of a flat memory model eliminates the restrictions associated with segmented memory. Consequently, the combined code and data size of an NLM can be anything that fits into available memory. The only feature lacking in NetWare 386 is virtual memory, where memory is swapped to and from a disk drive. Virtual memory embedded in the operating system, however, would require significant additional run-time overhead and is subsequently not a feature of NetWare 386 (though NLMs can load and unload other NLMs). Also, if virtual memory were to be a feature, and if it were actually used, any cache RAM would most likely be dominated by the pages being swapped in and out of memory. Thus, the decision to exclude virtual memory was a prudent one.

Screen APIs

Further promoting NLM development are the C library's screen I/O APIs. Not only can you pop up screens and use color, but you can control pages and pages of screens. An NLM is free to have as many different screens as it desires so long as there is available memory. There could be debug, status, and inquiry screens, as well as logon, authorization, control screens, among others. In programming screens, it is important to write data to the screen judiciously. Given the overhead associated with writing to screens, their updating should be as infrequent as possible to minimize the effect on overall file server performance, which can be considerable. (Receiving input from the keyboard, however, requires no such caution.)

Putting It All Together

As mentioned earlier, you can program NLMs the same way under DOS. Most NetWare workstation APIs are available to NLMs.

Once your code is compiled, it's time to link it. The linking process might be a little different from what you're used to, but it's easy to perform. The NetWare 386 v3.1 SDK includes an NLMLINK utility (to be replaced with the WLINK utility in newer SDK releases) that takes a .DEF (definition) script file and links it together. This linking is special in that an NLM is not fully linked until NetWare 386 loads it. So the resulting NLM file is not intended to be a fully executable program. The Novell-supplied PRELUDE.OBJ file is linked with the main() procedure's OBJ file, or whatever procedure you define. PRELUDE sets up the NLM environment by:

- Allocating and initializes internal data structures
- Creating a screen for use by the NLM
- Parsing command line parameters to pass into main() as argc and argv
- Starting a new thread to execute main()

NLM-to-NLM Communication

Also, procedures to be imported and exported are named at link time. Using the .DEF file and NLMLINK utility, an NLM can import (by procedure name and by use of C's external definition descriptor) procedure calls from other NLMs. For instance, Novell supplies a Btrieve NLM that can be called directly by another NLM that imports the btrv function. (See Figure 9-9, a snippet from the demonstration program, DEMO.C, included with the NetWare 386 v3.1 SDK.) Via the export function of NLMLINK, an NLM can export some or all of its procedures so they can be used by other NLMs running on the same server. Note that importing a name (in the .DEF file) that is called by the resulting NLM prevents an NLM from being loaded if the imported symbol is not available. If the imported procedure name does not exist when the NLM is loaded, the NLM will not be loaded. However, if a name is imported, but is not called anywhere in the NLM, then the NLM can be loaded without regard to that name's availability. Additionally, the C library itself is an NLM. All C library API calls made by an NLM are defined as external procedures. This means that all NLMs use the same C library code. The NetWare/386 CLIB NLM is implemented as a Dynamic Link Library (DLL). Likewise, your NLM will not have to be recompiled or relinked if there is a change in the C library, unless there is a new function that your NLM intends to use. Because the C library is a DLL, there is no replication of code between NLMs as far as their use of the C library is concerned; the overall effect is that memory is saved.

The Btrieve NLM requires the use of your NLM's stack for its operations, and the stack size of 8,192 bytes (the default for NLMLINK) is adequate for this purpose. Additional stacks may be required if your C code was compiled with stack-passing conventions (/3s with Watcom C) rather than the default register conventions (/3r with Watcom C) or if your NLM calls other NLMs that use your stack. The output parameter prescribes the name of the resulting NLM while the input parameter indicates the .OBJ files to be linked. The import parameter describes the procedure names to be imported. CLIB.IMP is a file, as the @ sign indicates. Within CLIB.IMP are the names of all procedures available to be imported from the C library. Additionally, the procedure name btrv is designated to be imported. This procedure is exported by the Btrieve NLM. Once your NLM is successfully produced with NLMLINK, it is ready for loading and possible debugging with NetWare 386.

Communicating Between Processes

As previously mentioned, NLMs talk to other NLMs via commands defined in the EXPORTs and IMPORTs. This allows for the existence of a very simple messaging protocol. If you want to call another NLM, just call a function (procedure) within your C code.

Sample of NLM-to-NLM Communications

This program was necessitated by Novell's improper handling of the _SendBroadcastMessage procedure in its NetWare CLIB v3.1 (although in the NetWare CLIB v3.0 this problem is corrected). To provide a patch, this NLM intercepts calls to _SendBroadcastMessage and redirects them to SendBroadcastMessage.

```
#pragma aux cdecl "*" parm caller []\
        value struct float struct routine [eax]  modify [eax ecx edx fs gs]

#define WORD unsigned short
#define BYTE unsigned char

#pragma aux cdecl _SendBroadcastMessage;
#pragma aux cdecl SendBroadcastMessage;

int _SendBroadcastMessage( char *__message, WORD *__connectionList,
                     BYTE *__resultList, WORD __connectionCount);

int SendBroadcastMessage( char *__message, WORD *__connectionList,
                     BYTE *__resultList, WORD __connectionCount);

/* The actual procedure */
int _SendBroadcastMessage( char *__message, WORD *__connectionList,
                     BYTE *__resultList, WORD __connectionCount);
{
    return(SendBroadcastMessage( __message, __connectionList,
                          __resultList, __connectionCount ));
}

main()
{
  DestroyScreen( GetCurrentScreen() );/**/
  ConsolePrintf("\nNetWare/386 v3,1 CLIB correction NLM, 7/30/90\n");
  ConsolePrintf("References to _SendBroadcastMessage are now rerouted
            to SendBroadcastMessage")
  ExitThread(-1); /* remain in memory, sort of like a TSR under DOS */
```

The .DEF file used is:

```
description    "NetWare v3.1 SendBroadcastMessage patch NLM"
stack          16384
output         SENDPAT
input          sendbro prelude
import         @clib.imp
export         _SendBroadcastMessage
```

Notice the "export" option used. Defined here is the procedure name(s) to make available to other NLMs.

Writing and Testing NLMs

The file server is a performance-bound engine that, when heavily taxed, will not performs as well Be careful not to program everything for file server execution. First ascertain the needs of a server-based NLM. Keep in mind that the most efficient distributed computing occurs when the pieces of an application are placed where they are most required as well as where they perform best. I hope this look at NLM coding will show you just how readily your applications can be retrofitted for execution as NLMs.

Writing and testing an NLM is more refined and less complex than writing a VAP. NLMs still require a special header, but it is supplied by Novell. It's called PRELUDE.OBJ, and is linked into the code. Unlike VAPs, NLMs do not specially order processes. You can dynamically allocate memory and create threads (the same as spawning processes with VAPs) at any time. The only initialization code is found in PRELUDE.OBJ and does not need to be called; merely linking it with your code will ensure its initialization.

Debugging an NLM is also more pleasant than debugging VAPs for several reasons. First, NetWare/386 offers a full debugger. Second, the debugger can be entered at any time, not just when the server crashes or the breakpoint interrupt is called. Also, NLMs can be loaded and unloaded any time the server is up. To enter the NetWare/386 debugger press the following keys at the file server. Be sure to hold them all down in this order:

Right Shift, Left Shift, Left Ctrl, Left Alt, Esc

You might have to press down this key combination a couple of times to get into the debugger. Once you get there the screen will appear something like:

```
Break at 0000DB8E because of Keyboard request
EAX = 000834E4 EBX = 00083040 ECX = 00AAAA4 EDX = 0009E6D8
ESI = 000853BC EDI = 00083040 EBP = 0000000 ESP = FFF8CBCC
EIP = 0000DB8E FLAGS = 00000206 (PF IF)
0000DB8E FA CLI
# _
```

At this point you have a full debugger at your disposal. Figure 8-7 lists the commands available in the debugger. To repeat for your file server, type H at the # prompt.

Figure 8-1. Debugger Commands

b	breakpoint commands (see HB help screen)
c	address change memory in interactive mode
c address=number(s)	change memory value to the specified number(s)
c address="text"	change memory to the specified text ASCII values
d address {count}	dump memory for optional count length
REG=value	change the specified register to the new value where REG is EAX, EBX, ECX, EDX, ESI, EDI, ESP, EBP or EIP
f FLAG=value	change the FLAG to value (0 or 1) where FLAG is CF, AF, ZF, SF, IF, TF, PF, DF or OF
g {break address(s)}	begin execution at current EIP and set temp break(s)
h	display this help screen hb display breakpoint help screen he display expression help screen
i{B;W;D} PORT	input byte, word, or dword from PORT (default is byte)
m start {L len} byte(s)	search memory for pattern
n symbolName value	define new symbol with value
o{B;W;D} PORT=value	output byte, word, or dword value to PORT

p	proceed over the next instruction
q	quit and exit back to DOS
t or s	single step
u address {count}	unassemble count instructions starting at address
v	view file server screens
z	expression evaluates the expression
?{address}	If symbolic information has been loaded, the closet symbols to address (default is EIP) are displayed

The d, m, p, s, t, and u commands can be continued or repeated by entering a carriage return at the # prompt

Figure 8-1. Debugger Commands (continued)

b	display all current breakpoints
bc number	clear the specified breakpoint
bca	clear all breakpoints
b = address {condition}	set a execution breakpoint at address
bw = address {condition}	set a write breakpoint at address
br = address {condition}	set a read/write breakpoint at address

Figure 8-2. Breakpoint Commands

If a breakpoint condition is specified, the condition will be evaluated when the break occurs. If the condition is not true, then execution will resume immediately without entering the interactive debugger mode. A breakpoint condition can be any expression. For a description of possible expressions, see the HE help screen. There are four breakpoint registers, allowing a maximum of four breakpoints to be set at the same time. These breakpoints can be permanent breakpoints set using the B command or temporary breakpoints set using the G command. In addition the P command will also set a temporary breakpoint if the current instruction cannot be single-stepped.

Grouping Operators

These operators (), [] and { } have precedence 0. The grouping operators can be nested in any combination. Note that "size" is a data size specifier B, W, or D. (expression) causes expression to be evaluated at a higher precedence. [size expression] causes expression to be evaluated at a higher precedence and then uses expression as a memory address. The bracketed expression is replaced with the byte, word or double word at that address.{size expression} causes expression to be evaluated at a higher precedence and then uses expression as a port address. The braced expression is replaced with the byte, word or double word input from the port. In the order of symbol, description, precedence, unary operators are: !, logical not, 1; -, 2',39,'s complement, 1;-, 1', 39, 's complement, 1.

Binary operators					
*	multiply	2	>	greater-than	5
!=	not-equal-to	6	/	divide	2
<	less-than	5	&	bitwise AND	7
%	mod	2	>=	greater-than or equal-to	5
^	bitwise XOR	8	+	add	3
		bitwise OR	9	-	subtract	3
<=	less-than or equal-to	5	&&	logical AND	10
>>	bit shift right	4	||	logical OR	11
<<	bit shift left	4	==	equal-to	6

Figure 8-3. Binary Operators

Ternary operators are: expression 1, ? expression 2, expression 3. If expression 1 is true then the result is the value of expression 2, otherwise the result is the value of expression 3.

All numbers are entered and shown in hex format. You can use register, flag, and symbol values in addition to numbers.

Registers: EAX, EBX, ECX, EDX, ESI, EDI, ESP, EBP and EIP
Flags: FLCF, FLAF, FLZF, FLSF, FLIF, FLTF, FLPF, FLDF and FLOF

With the NetWare/386 debugger you can set breakpoints either by address or symbolically, using procedure names as symbols. To access symbolic names in your NLM, use the keyword DEBUG in your .DEF file used when linking.

For further information on service and utility NLMs, the NetWare 386 v3.1 SDK (Software Developer's Kit), and the NetWare 386 C Libraries, contact the Novell Development Products Division in Austin, Texas at (512) 346-8380.

The following code shows how to use Btrieve from within a NLM.

```
// This file contains the items specific to conversing with
// the Btrieve NLM.
// This file is part of DEMO.C which is included with the 3.1 SDK

// Below are all the specifics necessary for interaction with the
// Btrieve NLM

// Prototypes of functions that call the Btrieve NLM
int createBtrieveFile();
int openBtrieveFile();
int insertBtrieveRecord(short int, Request_Packet *);
int closeBtrieveFile();

extern short int cdecl btrv (short int, void *, void *, short int *,
void *, short int);

#define B_CREATE 14
#define B_OPEN 0
#define B_CLOSE 1
#define B_INS 2
#define DUP 1
#define MOD 2
#define BIN 4
#define SEG 16
```

```
struct key_spec
{
short int key_pos;
short int key_len;
short int key_flag;
char not_use1[4];
char reserve1[6];
};

struct file_spec
{
short int rec_len;
short int page_size;
short int ndx_cnt;
char not_use2[4];
short int file_flag;
char reserve2[2];
short int pre_alloc;
struct key_spec key_buf[3];
};

struct client_rec
{
char network[4];
char node[6];
char in_out[1];
char timeStamp[7];
};

struct       file_spec      file_buf;
truct        client_rec     client_buf;
char         file_name[26] = "SYS:\\SYSTEM\\DEMO-NLM.BTV";
short int    status;
short int    buf_len;
char         key_buf[30];
char         clientBlock[128];

short int    BtrieveAlive;
// used to indicate if it is ok to call
// further Btrieve calls (in the insert and close functions)
```

```
int createBtrieveFile()
{
// This procedure attempts to create "our" Btrieve file if it does not
// exist, per normal Btrieve setup procedures, excepting that the
// file name (defined above) MUST be null terminated as it can not be
// terminated with a <space> character as it can be in the DOS version
// of Btrieve

file_buf.rec_len = 18;              // size of our record
file_buf.page_size =1024;           // page size
file_buf.file_flag= 0;
file_buf.ndx_cnt = 3;               // number of indexes

file_buf.key_buf[0].key_pos = 1;    // key 0 position
file_buf.key_buf[0].key_len = 10;   // key 0 length
file_buf.key_buf[0].key_flag = DUP; // key 0 is string+duplicates

file_buf.key_buf[1].key_pos = 11;   // key 1 position
file_buf.key_buf[1].key_len = 1;    // key 1 length
file_buf.key_buf[1].key_flag = DUP; // key 1 is string+duplicates


file_buf.key_buf[2].key_pos = 12;   // key 2 position
file_buf.key_buf[2].key_len = 7;    // key 2 length
file_buf.key_buf[2].key_flag = DUP; // key 2 is string+duplicates

buf_len = sizeof(file_buf);
status=btrv(B_CREATE,clientBlock,&file_buf,&buf_len,file_name,0);

return(status);
} /* end of createBtrieveFile */



int openBtrieveFile()
{
// This procedure attempts to open "our" Btrieve file


 buf_len = sizeof(client_buf);
 status = btrv (B_OPEN, clientBlock, &client_buf, &buf_len, file_name,
 0);
```

```
if (status) BtrieveAlive=0; else BtrieveAlive=1;
// above (BtrieveAlive) is set to indicate if the Btrieve
// file was successfully opened

return(status);

} /* end of openBtrieveFile */

int insertBtrieveRecord(short int inOut, Request_Packet *RP)
{
// This procedure receives a variable (inOut) indicating if
// this is a record for an client entering the game (0) or
// for a client leaving the game (1)
// Also, a pointer to the representative IPX buffer is passed so that
// the network and node address information may be retrieved

// the record layout is as follows:
// name              byte count
// Network Address   4
// Node Address      6
// inOut             1
// timeStamp         7
// the final field, timeStamp is retrieved the clib time function
time_t timer;           // long time value
struct tm *timeStruct; // standard C time
structure

 timer = time(NULL);
 timeStruct = localtime (&timer);

 memcpy(&client_buf.network[0],&RP->Hdr.source.network[0], 10);

 memcpy(&client_buf.in_out,&inOut,1);

 memcpy(&client_buf.timeStamp[0],&timeStruct->tm_year, 1);
 memcpy(&client_buf.timeStamp[1],&timeStruct->tm_mon+1,1);
 memcpy(&client_buf.timeStamp[2],&timeStruct->tm_mday, 1);
 memcpy(&client_buf.timeStamp[3],&timeStruct->tm_hour, 1);
 memcpy(&client_buf.timeStamp[4],&timeStruct->tm_min, 1);
 memcpy(&client_buf.timeStamp[5],&timeStruct->tm_sec, 1);
 memcpy(&client_buf.timeStamp[6],&timeStruct->tm_wday, 1);

 buf_len = sizeof(client_buf);
```

```
  if (BtrieveAlive)
   status = btrv (B_INS, clientBlock, &client_buf, &buf_len, key_buf,
   1);

  return(status);

} /* end of insertBtrieveRecord */


int closeBtrieveFile()
{
// This procedure attempts to close "our" Btrieve file

 buf_len = sizeof(client_buf);

 if (BtrieveAlive)
   status = btrv (B_CLOSE, clientBlock, &client_buf, \ &buf_len,
   file_name,0);

 return(status);

 } /* end of closeBtrieveFile */
```

Renaming NetWare 386 v3.1 NLM Threads

Nu-Mega's PROFILE utility (discussed earlier in this chapter) has made it relatively easy to watch an NLM's individual threads. Unfortunately, when NLMs spawn threads, the threads are given almost meaningless names. The name is a concatenation of the NLM's name and a number. The first 16 characters are from the NLM's name and the 17th character is the number. If an NLM spawns more than 10 threads, then the first fifteen characters of the NLM's name are used, etc. Usually, the name doesn't mean much. Until Novell offers a useful way for naming NLM threads, I offer the following suggestions.

In renaming threads, a pointer to that thread's Process Control Buffer/Block (PCB) is derived. From this pointer an offset is added and, as a result, the area containing the thread name is located. Once located, a simple string copy operation renames the thread, possibly making it is easier to track an NLM's threads.

```
#include "stddef.h"
#include "sap.h"
#include "nwipxspx.h"
#include "time.h"
#include "conio.h"
#include "process.h"
#include "io.h"
#include "fcntl.h"
#include "nwsync.h"
#include "share.h"
#include "nwmsg.h"
#include "stdio.h"
#include "errno.h"

#include "NWENVRN.H"
static int TmpThread;

work1()
{
int a;

a=0;
 while (1)
  {
   delay(55);
   a++;
  }
}
/* end of work1() */


work2()
{
int a;

a=0;
 while (1)
  {
   delay(55);
   a++;
  }
} /* end of work2() */
```

```
int ChangeThreadName(int ThreadID, char *NewName); /* prototype */
ChangeThreadName(int ThreadID, char *NewName)
{
/* This procedure is passed the thread ID to rename and the new name to
   use, used when ThreadID is received from a call to BeginThread or
   BeginThreadGroup*/

int a,*Test;
char *y;

if (strlen(NewName)>17) NewName[17]=0; /* max len is 17 */

/* ThreadID is a virtual pointer to a structure which contains the
   pointer to the thread's PCB */

memcpy(&Test, &ThreadID, 4);

memcpy(&a, Test+3, 4);

printf("\na is [%lx]",a); /* pointer to process control block */

         /* add 0x1E to this PCB pointer */
a+=0x1E; /* for NetWare/386 v3.1, this is the offset into the
            process control block that defines the thread's name */

memcpy(&y, &a, 4);   /* point the variable y to the PCB thread name */

printf("\nwell, PCB thread name is [%s]",y);

strcpy(y,NewName);

printf("\nwell, now, PCB thread name is [%s]",y);

return 0;

} /* end of ChangeThreadName */


int ChangeThread0Name(int ThreadID, char *NewName);
ChangeThread0Name(int ThreadID, char *NewName)
{
```

```
int a,*Test;
char *y;
/* Used when ThreadID is received from GetThreadID() or BeginThread()*/

if (strlen(NewName)>17) NewName[17]=0; /* max len is 17 */

a=ThreadID;
a+=0x1E; /* for NetWare/386 v3.1, this is the offset into the
             process control block that defines the thread's name */

memcpy(&y, &a, 4);   /* point the variable y to the PCB thread name */

printf("\nwell, PCB thread name is [%s]",y);

strcpy(y,NewName);

printf("\nwell, now, PCB thread name is [%s]",y);

return 0;

} /* end of ChangeThread0Name */


main() {
int a,*Test;
char *y;
TmpThread = GetThreadID();
ChangeThread0Name(TmpThread, "Zapper 0 —But name waaay too long!");

TmpThread = BeginThreadGroup ( work1, NULL, 4096, NULL );
ChangeThreadName(TmpThread, "Eat out today");

delay(200); /* no special reason this is here */

TmpThread = BeginThreadGroup ( work2, NULL, 4096, NULL );
ChangeThreadName(TmpThread, "Rockets 101");

delay(10000); /* no special reason this is here */

}
```

The following NLMs are two that use the NetWare C libraries. As these are included with Novell's Software Developer's Kit v3.1, I cannot include the full program. Thus, you may notice some procedures that are referenced but missing from these examples.

```
*******************************************************************
*
 * Program Name:   CLIENT.EXE
 *
 * Filename:       client.c (DOS)
 *
 * Version:        1.0
 *
 * Programmer:     John T. McCann
 *
 * Date:           June 28, 1989
 *
 * Copyright (c) 1989 Novell, Inc.
 */

// This is the client portion of the Novell demonstration NLM.
// This client module acts as a game module, which is one of the many
// possibilities the demonstation NLM could be used for, this game module
// is one of the more entertaining methods of utilizing the demonstation
// NLM's services

// The game itself is played on a physical playing grid defined at the NLM.
// At any one time, this client module only displays a 60x20 chunk of that
// physical playing field. When the walls of the viewing grid
// correspond to the physical walls of the playing field,
// double lines are seen. Otherwise, only a single line is seen.
// At all times the current client is displayed as a "happy face", that
// way the user of this client may know which "player" is theirs.
// Also, when the game first starts, the client's player will be
// motionless.  However, once a direction is selected (with an arrow
// key) motion will be continuous in the direction of the last arrow
// pushed.  As the client's player moves about the grid it leaves a
// track, or wall, this track serves as a crash point, the physical
// walls of the grid are also crash points.  Points are accumulated for
// surviving another client's removal from the game whether they merely
// escaped from the game or they crashed.

// Due to the inclusion of this program with the v3.1 SDK, I am not
// able to reproduce the full code, I will reproduce a few procedures
// used to talk with the NLM
```

```
// START of defines, structures, and global variables

#define GameServerType 0x4087 // bindery type of game services we request
#define retriesAllowed 2    // number of retries (IPXSend..) before aborting
#define namesAllowed 10     // number of game servers that we can "hold"


#if defined(__TINY__) || defined(__SMALL__) || defined(__MEDIUM__)
#define Seg(ptr) _DS
#define Ofs(ptr) (unsigned)(ptr)
#else
#define Ofs(fp)        ((unsigned)(fp))
#define Seg(fp)        ((unsigned)((unsigned long)(fp) >> 16))
#endif


// START of procedures

void findGameServers()
{
// This procedure builds an array of all known game servers
char   searchName[48];
WORD   searchType;
long   searchID;
char   serverName[48];
WORD   objectType;
char   hasProp[1];
char   objectFlag[1];
char   objectSecurity[1];
int    ccode;

// set up for bindery scan

  strcpy (searchName,"*"); // wildcard search
  searchType = GameServerType;
  searchID   = -1L;

  namesFound = -1;
  ccode = 0;

  while (ccode==0)
  {
```

```
        namesFound++;
        ccode =
        ScanBinderyObject(&searchName,searchType,&searchID,&serverName, \
                     &objectType,&hasProp,&objectFlag,&objectSecurity);

        strcpy(names[namesFound].Name, serverName);

        if (namesFound>=namesAllowed) ccode=1; // leave now, unable to
                                               // accept further names
     } /* end of while ccode==0 */

} /* end of findGameServers */




void connectToGameServer(int s)
{
// This procedure receives a variable, s, that "points" to the game
// server to attempt communications with
//
// First, an attempt to enter game is performed, if accepted an
// IPX socket is opened as specified by game server, this socket is
// to be used for "in game" requests to the game server
char serverName[48];
WORD serverType;
char propName[16];
int  segNum;
BYTE propVal[128];
BYTE moreSeg;
BYTE propFlag;

int ccode;

  printf("Attempting to connect to game server %s...",names[s].Name);

  strcpy(serverName, names[s].Name); // copy over game server name
  serverType=GameServerType;        // object type of game server
  strcpy(propName, "NET_ADDRESS");  // property to read
  segNum=1;                         // read 1st segment of property

  ccode=ReadPropertyValue(&serverName, serverType, &propName, segNum, \
                   &propVal, &moreSeg, &propFlag);
```

```
if (ccode!=0)
{
 printf("\n\7Warning, unable to ascertain Game Server address, exiting...");
 exit(3);
}

memcpy(&gameAddr[0],&propVal[0],12); // move address found to global
                                    // variable for future reference
doIPXsetup();

IPXs.Data[0] = 00;
IPXs.Data[1] = 01; // request to enter game

IPXs.Data[2] = 1;  // player type 1

IPXListenForPacket(&ECBr);
IPXSendPacket(&ECBs);

doIPXwait();

if (IPXr.Data[0]==0xf0) // 0xf0=already in game
{
 printf("\nPreviously in game, removing old connection, retrying...");
 IPXs.Data[0]=1;
 IPXs.Data[1]=0xFF;    // request to leave game

 rcvPacket();
 IPXSendPacket(&ECBs);
 doIPXwait();

 IPXs.Data[0] = 00;
 IPXs.Data[1] = 01; // request to enter game
 IPXs.Data[2] = 1;  // player type 1

 rcvPacket();
 IPXSendPacket(&ECBs);
 doIPXwait();
}
```

```
  if ((IPXr.Data[0]) && (IPXr.Data[0]!=0xf0))
  {
   printf("\nReply received: Failed:%x\n",IPXr.Data[0]);
   exit(7);
  }
  else
   printf("Connected!\n\n");

  memcpy(&InGameSocket, &IPXr.Data[46], 2); // store inGame socket

  memcpy(&X,&IPXr.Data[34],4); // store initial X,Y,Z coordinates
  memcpy(&Y,&IPXr.Data[38],4); // received from game server
  memcpy(&Z,&IPXr.Data[42],4);

  ccode=IPXOpenSocket(&InGameSocket, 0x00); // open short lived socket

  if ( (ccode) && (ccode!=0xff) ) // 0xff means already open, that's ok
  {
   printf("\nFAILED: result of IPX open game [%x], exiting to system\n\7",ccode);
   exit(5);
  }

} /* end of connectToGameServer */




void doIPXsetup()
{
// This procedure will
// Initialize IPX (Clibrary) and memory areas,
// Open a socket which corresponds to the game server's "request line",
// Get the intermediate address to use when communicating with game server
// Set the time out value, used for resending "lost" requests
// Initialize IPX send and receive areas
BYTE status;
WORD socket;
int  result;

 status=IPXInitialize();
 if (status != 0)
 {
  printf("Unable to Initialize IPX interface, aborting...\n\7");
  exit(4);
 }
```

```
memcpy(&socket,&gameAddr[10],2); //set up socket number of game server

result=IPXOpenSocket(&socket, 0x00); // open short lived socket

if ( (result) && (result!=0xff) ) // 0xff means already open, that's ok
{
 printf("\nFAILED: result of IPX open [%x], exiting to system\n\7",result);
 exit(5);
}

// below zeroes out the ECB and IPX areas
memset(&ECBs,0, sizeof(ECBs));
memset(&IPXs,0, sizeof(IPXs));
memset(&ECBr,0, sizeof(ECBr));
memset(&IPXr,0, sizeof(IPXr));

ECBs.socketNumber  = socket;

result=IPXGetLocalTarget(&gameAddr[0],&ECBs.immediateAddress[0],&timeOut);
if (result)
{
 printf("\nFAILED: result of IPX Get Local Target [%x], ",result);
 printf("exiting to system\n\7");
 exit(6);
}

timeOut=timeOut*20; // increase time out, this will be used to
                    // determine when to resend a packet

ECBs.fragmentCount = 1;
ECBs.fragmentDescriptor[0].address = &IPXs;
ECBs.fragmentDescriptor[0].size = 52;

  IPXs.Hdr.packetType = 4;
  memcpy(&IPXs.Hdr.destination.network[0], &gameAddr[0], 12);

  ECBr.socketNumber  = socket;
  ECBr.fragmentCount = 1;
  ECBr.fragmentDescriptor[0].address = &IPXr;
  ECBr.fragmentDescriptor[0].size    = 576;

} /* end of doIPXsetup */


void doIPXwait()
```

```
{
// This procedure waits for the "receive" ECB (ECBr) to "hear" something,
// which is denoted by ECBr.inUseFlag becoming equal to 0
// if the loops below "timeout" then the request is sent again, perhaps
// it was lost in transit or the reply was lost in its transit

// timeOut contains amount of time, in system clocks (~55ms each) to
// wait before resending request
// all requests are presumed to be from the ECBs variable
//
unsigned int stime,time,TimeOut, resends;

   resends=time=0;
   TimeOut=timeOut; // the global variable timeOut has to be signed, for
                    // our calculation below it has to be unsigned,
                    // hence use of TimeOut


   stime=IPXGetIntervalMarker(); // get start time interval

   while (ECBr.inUseFlag)
   {
    time=IPXGetIntervalMarker(); // get current time interval
    IPXRelinquishControl();        // let the driver do some work

    // below indicates we had a time out, resend request
    if (((time-stime)>TimeOut) && (ECBr.inUseFlag))
    {
     resends++;
     IPXSendPacket(&ECBs);         // send again
     stime=IPXGetIntervalMarker();// get start time interval, again
    }

    if (resends>=retriesAllowed) resendAbort(); //quit, too many retries

   } // end of while (ECBr.inUseFlag)

}   /* end of doIPXwait */




void rcvPacket()
{
// This procedure sets up the listen buffer then posts it for listening
```

```
// this procedure only posts for listens pertaining to in game requests

  ECBr.fragmentCount                  = 1;
  ECBr.fragmentDescriptor[0].address  = &IPXr;
  ECBr.fragmentDescriptor[0].size     = 576;
  ECBr.socketNumber                   = InGameSocket;
  IPXListenForPacket(&ECBr);

} /* end of rcvPacket */


void willItRun()
{
// This procedure will try to set the lock mode to 1 (default is 0)
// then it will try to get the lock mode (which was just set to 1)
// if the lock mode is not 1, then NetWare is not loaded
// This is by no means a complete test of NetWare's existence, but
// is sufficient to prevent a user on an unnetworked PC from running
// this utility and hanging their PC
int  ccode; // holds completion code

  ccode=SetLockMode(1); //set lock mode to 1, Advanced NetWare

  ccode=GetLockMode();

  if (ccode!=1)
  {
   printf("\nSorry, this utility requires Advanced NetWare, aborting.");
   exit(20);
  }

} /* end of willItRun */


// END of procedures
```

Now, some sample code from the DEMO.NLM example.

```
/*********************************************************************
 *
 * Program Name:   DEMO.NLM
 *
 * Filename:       demo.c (NLM)
 *
 * Version:        1.0
 *
 * Programmer:     John T. McCann
 *
 * Date:           June 28, 1989
 *
 * Copyright (c) 1989 by Novell, Inc.
 *
 *
 *
 * SAP/Requestor/Control NLM
 * with exported calls to Btrieve NLM
 *
 * The purpose of these "module" is multi-fold
 *
 * First, there is the SAP broadcaster, its purpose is to advertise
 * our "server's" services to the other servers in the network
 * our server will show up in other file server's bindery as type
 */
#define SAPobject_type 0x4087
#define RequestSocket 0x6666
/*
 * the SAP is started up in the main() routine because it is itself
 * a routine from the CLIB, more notes concerning its usage are
revealed
 * in the code where it is called
 * note: workstations/clients will find our service by querying their
 * file server's bindery for objects of type designated above in the
 * #define SAPobject_type
 *
 * next, the doRequest process is started, its purpose is to receive
 * requests coming in from workstations and to qualify them
 *
 * requests are split into two parts, both a byte in size
 * 1) request class, currently 0 and 1 are defined,
 *    0 means the request is not coming from nodes using NLM
 *    1 means the request is coming from a node using NLM
```

```
 * 2) request code within class
 *
 */
#define InGameSocket 0x7777
/*
 * if the node is not found (using NLM), then the maximum number of
 * connections is check, if the current number of connections(players)
 * is the same as the maximum then a return code of 0x00FF is sent
 * back to the node to indicate that the NLM is not accepting more
 * users at this time
 */
#define MaxConnections 0x0A  // USER SELECTABLE!




// START of structures
typedef struct
{
 IPX_HEADER             Hdr;       // 30 bytes
 unsigned char          Req[2];    // request is always first
 unsigned char          Data[544]; // defined for known maximum size,
                                    // if buffer received is bigger
                                    // than what is reserved for it we
                                    // risk the very likely event of
                                    // trashing memory (note: I've had
                                    // this exp. on the PC side of
                                    // IPX.may not hold now) so, this
                                    // is a concern even though
                                    // oversize packets are supposed to
                                    // be cut off...
} Request_Packet;

 // note, int and long and long int are all the same, 4 bytes


// START of procedures

void doRequests()
{
// This procedure is called from main() and it:
// Draws the console management screen,
// Initiates a thread which monitors the in game requests
// Opens an IPX socket to handle incoming requests
// Posts a listen buffer to handle incoming requests
```

```
// then, this module "sits and spins" waiting for an incoming
// request to arrive, upon such time, it verifies the request
// and calls routines to complete the requests received

int ss,sd;  // ss is used to store the status of some calls and sd is
            // used as loop control
Request_Packet Req_Pckt;
IPX_ECB         Reqptr;
WORD            ReqSocket;
long            Connection;
int             BigThreadID;
int             StatusThreadID;

  reDrawMainConsole();

  BigThreadID = BeginThread ( doBigRequests, NULL, 4096, NULL );
  // initiates Big thread manager

  StatusThreadID = BeginThread ( postStats, NULL, 4096, NULL );
  // initiates screen updates of status information

  ReqSocket=RequestSocket;
  ss=IpxOpenSocket(&ReqSocket);

  sd=0;
  while (sd<10)  // stay in this loop forever
  {
   sd=0; // stay in loop, use ALT-ESC to kill (UNLOAD is used to kill)
   Reqptr.fragList[0].fragAddress = &Req_Pckt;
   Reqptr.fragList[0].fragSize    = 576;
   Reqptr.fragCount               = 1;

   Reqptr.next      = 0;   // initialize
   Reqptr.prev      = 0;
   Reqptr.semHandle = NULL;
   Reqptr.queueHead = NULL;

   ss=IpxReceive(ReqSocket, &Reqptr);

   while (Reqptr.status) // while status is not 0, i.e. no packet receieved
   {
    delay(loopTimeDelay);
   }

   NewRequests++; // everytime we pass here, a new request is received
```

```
   switch (Req_Pckt.Req[0])
   {
     case 0: // Valid Request Class
             doSwitch(&Req_Pckt, &Reqptr);
             break;
    default: // Invalid Request Class
             doReply(0x00ff, &Req_Pckt, &Reqptr);
             break;
   } // end of switch

   // will sit and spin here, servicing incoming requests
   // (rather than returning)

  } // end of while sd<10

 // the IPX close (below) is never executed, this is just to show that
 // this is where it would be closed, when the NLM is unloaded, this
 // socket and any waiting IPX receives will be closed and dismantled
 ss=IpxCloseSocket(RequestSocket);

} /* end of doRequests */

void doReply(unsigned short Reply, Request_Packet *RP, IPX_ECB *RECB)
{
// This procedure sends a reply to the client that is communicating
// with this NLM on the out of service socket, that reply might
// indicate acceptance into the NLM
Request_Packet Rep_Pckt;
IPX_ECB        Repptr;
WORD           RepSocket;
int            ss;

 gotoxy(0,8);
 printf("Reply Sent [%4x]\n",Reply);

 Repptr.fragList[0].fragAddress = &Rep_Pckt;
 Repptr.fragList[0].fragSize    = 30+60; //big enough to hold data returned
 Repptr.fragCount               = 1;

 Repptr.next = 0;
 Repptr.prev = 0;
 Repptr.semHandle = NULL;
 Repptr.queueHead = NULL;
```

```
memcpy(&Repptr.immediateAddress,&RECB->immediateAddress,6);
memcpy(&Rep_Pckt.Hdr.dest.network[0],&RP->Hdr.source.network[0], 10);
memcpy(&Rep_Pckt.Req[0],&Reply, 2);
Rep_Pckt.Hdr.packetType = 4; // Packet exchange packet
RepSocket=RequestSocket;
memcpy(&Rep_Pckt.Hdr.dest.socket[0],&RepSocket,2);

memcpy(&Rep_Pckt.Data[0],&RP->Data[0],52); // copy over the 50 byte reply

ss=IpxSend(RepSocket, &Repptr);

} /* end of doReply */


void startClock( void )
{
// This procedure is spawned by main() and runs continously, updating
// the time on the main screen, the amount of time it waits between
// updates can be altered to lessen its affect on overall performance
// (such as updating every 5 seconds (5000ms))
int row, col;          // holds current x,y screen location
time_t timer;          // long time value
struct tm *timeStruct; // standard C time structure
static char *days[]=
{
 "Sun","Mon","Tue","Wed","Thu","Fri","Sat"
};

 while (row!=(row+1))  // stay in loop
 {
  row=wherey(); col=wherex();
  // get the time into the full time structure
  timer = time(NULL);
  timeStruct = localtime (&timer);
  gotoxy(55,22);
  printf ("%s %2d-%2d-%4d ", days[timeStruct->tm_wday],
    timeStruct->tm_mon+1, timeStruct->tm_mday, timeStruct->tm_year+1900);
  printf ("%2d:%02d:%02d",
    timeStruct->tm_hour, timeStruct->tm_min, timeStruct->tm_sec);
  gotoxy(col,row);
  delay(1000);  // wait one second before looping again
 }

} /* end of startClock */
```

```
//   @@      @@    @@@@@   @@@@@@  @@    @@
//   @@@@ @@@@  @@    @@    @@     @@@   @@
//   @@ @@@ @@  @@@@@@@    @@     @@ @@ @@
//   @@      @@  @@    @@    @@     @@  @@@@
//   @@      @@  @@    @@  @@@@@@  @@    @@

main( int argc, char *argv[] )
{
// This is the main procedure, it is called first and it is able to
// accept parameters from the command line that initiates it, just like
// a C program at a DOS, OS/2 or UNIX workstation
int loop, loop1,loop2,block;
int clockThread;


 loop=openBtrieveFile();        // try to open the Btrieve file
 if (loop)
 {
  loop=createBtrieveFile();    // establish the Btrieve file, if needed
  if (loop)
  {
   ConsolePrintf("\n\7**WARNING** unable to create Btrieve file");
   ConsolePrintf(", error = [%d]\n\7",loop);
  }
  else
   ConsolePrintf("\n\7Btrieve database was created successfully.");

  loop=openBtrieveFile();
  if (loop)
  {
   ConsolePrintf("\n\7**WARNING** unable to open Btrieve file");
   ConsolePrintf(", error = [%d]\n\7",loop);
  }
 }

 if (!loop) ConsolePrintf("\nBtrieve database opened successfully.");

 eptr = AdvertiseService( SAPobject_type, MyName, RequestSocket);
 // service type, *name, socket
 // Service type refers to the bindery object type that this
 // service will be stored under, in this case, 0x4087 (arbitrary)
 // or 16519 in decimal
```

```
//
// *name is simply the name of the service/server, up to 47 chars
// that are NULL terminated
//
// socket is the socket that we are declaring for the purpose of
// receiving requests...note that this is broadcast with SAP
// (Service Advertising Protocol) which means this packet info goes
// out to socket 0x452, the SAP socket
//

} /* end of main() */

// END of procedures
```

Interfacing to the User at the Console

"Interactively" is the best way to describe how NLMs deal with console commands. Rather than specifying to the operating system exact keywords to watch for, the NLM hooks itself into the server process (NetWare/386 v3.0) that analyzes the command line.

If the server process doesn't understand the command line entered, it passes the challenge to the next "parser" in the process. If your NLM is one of these parsers, it has the chance to identify the command line, as long as no other parser ahead of it has claimed the command line for itself.

NLMs also offer a wide assortment of screen and I/O management APIs that represent tremendousgains in file server console presentation over VAPs. The following code shows how one would define a process that would hook into the command line parser for NetWare/386 v3.0. Remember, this is for NetWare 386 v. 3.0 only.

```
#include <nwtypes.h>
struct commandParserStructure
{
   struct commandParserStructure *Link;
   LONG (*parseRoutine)(
     LONG screenID,
     BYTE *commandLine);
} identifyMeParserStruct;
```

```
extern void RegisterConsoleCommand(
        struct commandParserStructure *newCommandParser);
extern LONG UnRegisterConsoleCommand(
        struct commandParserStructure *commandParserToDelete);

LONG identifyMeParser( LONG screenID, BYTE *commandLine );
void DeregisterIdentifyMe( void );

identifyMe()
  {

  identifyMeParserStruct.parseRoutine = identifyMeParser;
  RegisterConsoleCommand( &identifyMeParserStruct );

  return 0;
  }

LONG identifyMeParser( LONG screenID, BYTE *commandLine )
  {

  if (strcmp(commandLine,"TEST")==0)
  {
    ConsolePrintf("Hello, you just typed TEST!\n\7");
    return 0; // 0 means that I identified this command line
            // and parsing is to stop now
  }
  else    return 1;  // 1 means that I was unable to identify this
                     // command line and to pass parsing responsibility
                     // to next parser (if there is one, but that is for
                     // the operating system to decide
  }

void DeregisterIdentifyMe( void )
  {
  UnRegisterConsoleCommand( &identifyMeParserStruct );
  }
```

The .DEF file for this NLM would look like this:

```
description "TEST Command parser"
input    testme
output   testme
import   RegisterConsoleCommand
         UnRegisterConsoleCommand
```

```
            @clib.imp
start       identifyMe
exit        DeregisterIdentifyMe
```

Here you see that start indicates the first procedure, which will start the NLM (instead of main() being the first). The exit procedure shown above is in lieu of using the AtUnload procedure call. AtUnload is a CLIB API; it defines a procedure to call when the NLM is being unloaded. AtUnload still could be used, thus allowing more than one exit procedure to be called.

A special note here: When this command parser is being run it does not belong to any one thread (of an NLM). You must use SetThreadGroupID() if you wish to access your NLM's screen(s), such as through the use of printf(). In the above example, using ConsolePrintf() outputs directly to the console screen and does not require the use of SetThreadGroupID().

CHAPTER 9

Converting VAPs to NLMs

First, why convert at all? Neither NetWare version allows the other's server processes (VAPs for v2.1x, NLMs for v3.x) in its territory. VAPs are usable only with NetWare v2.1x, and NLMs are usable only with NetWare v3.x. Functionally, it is very possible to have a NLM do everything a VAP can do and more. It can be incredibly difficult if not impossible to make a VAP do everything an NLM can.

Beginnings

As mentioned in the Introduction to Part 3, the major areas where there are differences in the initial coding between VAPs and NLMs are:

- Initializing
- Obtaining Connections
- Loading/unloading
- Availability of APIs
- Communicating between processes
- Interfacing to user console
- Debugging

Leading the Changes

Differences are apparent right up front in the initialization of VAPs and NLMs. In VAPs there is a "rigid" structure that basically entails:

1) Initializing VAP parameters (done in the VAP's header)
2) Changing data segments from default of read-only to read-write
3) Initializing all processes (also known as threads)
4) Indicating to the operating system that all processes have been initialized
5) Beginning the VAP's "regular" execution

With NLMs there is no such rigid structure. About the only thing you might do is indicate a procedure to run whenever the NLM is unloaded. This "run at unload time" procedure is tagged by AtUnload(), as shown in Figure x.x.

```
AtUnload(That_s_it);

.

.

.

That_s_it()
{
  ConsolePrintf("This NLM is no more\n\7");
}
```

Figure 9-1. "Run at Unload Time" Procedure

Note that VAPs too have an unload procedure, known as the DownHandler procedure. It is specified in the VAP's header and is called when the file server is DOWNed.

Essentially, you can picture an NLM's operation as if it were a program running under OS/2. The implication is that the NLM can obtain "processes" whenever it so desires (and there is available memory), and it can remove those processes at any time.

Charting a course for converting your VAP to an NLM is not an imprecise process. In general, most functions transfer right over. Specifically, if you use ConsoleDisplay() or ConsoleMessage() in your VAP you could simply type:

```
#define ConsoleMessage ConsolePrintf
#define ConsoleDisplay ConsolePrintf
```

You don't even bother with altering your actual code.

One nice benefit of ConsolePrintf (an NLM function) is the ability to specify embedded strings that define variables to print. For instance, in a VAP:

```
ConsoleMessage("Hi, this is a message");
```
is legal, but

```
ConsoleMessage("Hi %s, this is a message",login_name);
```
is not. With an NLM, however,

```
ConsolePrintf("Hi %s, this is a message",login_name);
```
is legal.

For VAPs, you could use

```
sprintf(stuff,"Hi %s, this is a message",login_name);
ConsoleMessage(stuff);.
```

Interestingly, in VAPs, ConsoleDisplay() and ConsoleMessage() do not allow for embedded "\n" or "\7" to work as you would normally think. In fact, they are ignored. However, both Console..() procedures include an implied "\n" at the end of the string being printed. In NLMs, ConsolePrintf() operates mostly like printf() and does not include a default of "\n" at the end of the string being printed.

The single biggest change in converting VAPs to NLMs involves user IDs and bindery object types. With VAPs we were using straight "DOS" calls to perform 95% of our NetWare API-based calls (non-C Library). In an NLM, to get connection information, you would follow the call in Figure 9-2 on the next page.

```
typedef struct
{
 unsigned char  ah,al,bh,bl;
}
 longs;
 unsigned char junkk[254], holdtemp;
 longs
    THEM;
    WORD      HangOut;
  HangOut=RQ;
GetConnectionInformation(HangOut,junkk,junkk,&THEM,junkk);
```

Figure 9-2. NLM Call to Get Connection Information

All the junkk fields receive data I don't "care" about. This example illustrates how you might ascertain the connection's user ID. Now, with the DOS-type call of the VAP, the ID was returned in "normal" high-low order, that is, had the SUPERVISOR been at the connection, the ID would have been one, or, more exactly, 00 00 00 01.

But with the CLIB for NLMs (as with those of the workstation), the ID is returned as if the receiving field was of type LONG. This means the value returned is in low-high order, so the SUPERVISOR would be 01 00 00 00.

Because of this I has to "re-orient" this data to remain consistent with my code:

```
holdtemp=THEM.al; THEM.al=THEM.bh; THEM.bh=holdtemp;
holdtemp=THEM.ah; THEM.ah=THEM.bl; THEM.bl=holdtemp;
```

Note, however, the 386 NLM CLIB provides a LongSwap() function that also reverses the orientation of the LONG variable.

```
long THEM;
THEM=LongSwap(THEM);
```

You may be wondering about the origin of the GetConnectionInformation() call. Unlike VAPs, NLMs access most of their functions via the CLIB NLM. That is, the CLIB NLM exports its functions for other NLMs to use. It is the only way to perform the NetWare-aware functions defined in CLIB. (Other, non-NetWare-aware, functions include thread management, screen I/O, bit test operations, and others.)

With VAPs, however, you can call ShellServices directly just as you can with DOS-based NetWare applications when calling Interrupt 21h. There is no such interface for NLMs; they must use the calls in the CLIB NLM. You really don't lose anything because of that; your coding is simplified, yet still effective.

The last big difference between VAPs and NLMs concerns IPX/SPX. In VAPs, calls to IPX/SPX are very similar to DOS calls. There are no significant differences. For NLMs, the calls to IPX/SPX are essentially the same; the event control block (ECB) structure, however, is radically different.

The ECB structure takes after that of the OS/2 Requestor's interface. The VAP's ECB and the NLM's ECB follow. However, to make use of the functionality of VAPs with the NLM ECB, you need not concern yourself with all the new fields. See the "Setting Up the ECBs" example later in this chapter—it performs the same functions. The "J" appended to the InternetAddressJ and IPX_HEADERJ structures modifies the NWIPXSPX.H file in the NetWare 386 Programmer's Workbench and expedites the initial conversion.

The VAP's ECB

```
struct ECBFragment
{
   char far              *Address;
   unsigned int          Size; /* low-high */
};

typedef struct ECBStructures
{
   unsigned int          Link[2];
   char far              *ESRAddress;/* offset-segment */
   unsigned char         InUseFlag;
   unsigned char         CompletionCode;
```

```
      unsigned int           ECBSocket;/* high-low */
      unsigned char          IPXWorkspace[4];
      unsigned char          DriverWorkspace[12];
      unsigned char          ImmediateAddress[6];/* high-low */
      unsigned int           FragmentCount;/* low-high */
      struct ECBFragment     FragmentDescriptor[2];
} ECBs;
```

NLM's ECB

```
typedef struct
{
   void                   *fragAddress;
   unsigned long          fragSize;
} ECBFrag;

typedef struct IPX_ECBStruct
{
/* Fields for use by CLIB */
   unsigned long       semHandleSave;
   struct IPX_ECBStruct **queueHead;
 /* Beginning of Native NW386 ECB */
   struct IPX_ECBStruct   *next;
   struct IPX_ECBStruct   *prev;
   unsigned short         status;
   unsigned long          semHandle;
   unsigned short         lProtID;
   unsigned char          protID [6];
   unsigned long          boardNumber;
   unsigned char          immediateAddress [6];
   unsigned char          driverWS [4];
   unsigned long          ESREBXValue;
   unsigned short         socket;
   unsigned short         protocolWorkspace;
   unsigned long          dataLen;
   unsigned long          fragCount;
   ECBFrag                fragList [1];
} IPX_ECB;
```

Setting Up the ECBs

```
/*First the preliminary defintions*/
#ifdef VAP
struct IPXAddress
{
   unsigned char  Network[4];  /* high-low */
   unsigned char  Node[6];     /* high-low */
   unsigned int   Socket;      /* high-low */
};

typedef struct IPXPacketStructure
{
   unsigned int        PacketCheckSum;         /* high-low */
   unsigned int        PacketLength;           /* high-low */
   unsigned char       PacketTransportControl;
   unsigned char       PacketType;
   struct IPXAddress   Destination;
   struct IPXAddress   Source;
} IPXPacket;
#endif

#ifdef NLM
typedef struct
   {
   unsigned char network[4];  /* high-low */
   unsigned char node[6];     /* high-low */
   unsigned char socket[2];   /* high-low */
   } InternetAddressJ;

typedef struct
   {
   unsigned short      checksum;     /* hi-lo */
   unsigned short      packetLen;    /* hi-lo */
   unsigned char       transportCtl;
   unsigned char       packetType;
   InternetAddressJ    dest;
   InternetAddressJ    source;
   } IPX_HEADERJ;
#endif

typedef struct IPXdataStructure
{
     unsigned char               data[100];
} IPXdata;
```

```
#ifdef VAP
ECBs          RECB[5];
#endif
#ifdef NLM
IPX_ECB       RECB[5];
#endif


IPXdata       RQ[5];


#ifdef VAP
IPXPacket     RIPX[5];
#endif
#ifdef NLM
IPX_HEADERJ   RIPX[5];
#endif
```

Actual Code Snippet of a VAP and NLM ECB Setup

```
#ifdef VAP
  RECB[x].ESRAddress[0] = 0;
  RECB[x].ESRAddress[1] = 0;
  RECB[x].FragmentCount = 2;
  RECB[x].ECBSocket = 0x1111;
  RECB[x].FragmentDescriptor[0].Address = (char far *)&RIPX[x];
  RECB[x].FragmentDescriptor[0].Size = sizeof (IPXPacket );
  RECB[x].FragmentDescriptor[1].Address = (char far *)&RQ[x];
  RECB[x].FragmentDescriptor[1].Size = sizeof( IPXdata );

  IPXListenForPacket( &RECB[x] );
#endif
#ifdef NLM
  RECB[x].next=RECB[x].prev=0;
  RECB[x].semHandle=NULL;
  RECB[x].queueHead=NULL;
  RECB[x].socket = 0x1111;
  RECB[x].fragCount = 2;
  RECB[x].fragList[0].fragAddress = &RIPX[x];
```

```
RECB[x].fragList[0].fragSize  = sizeof ( IPX_HEADERJ );
RECB[x].fragList[1].fragAddress = &RQ[x];
RECB[x].fragList[1].fragSize  = sizeof ( IPXdata );

ss=IpxReceive(0x1111, &RECB[x]); // is defined "int ss;"
#endif
```

Summing It Up

There are other changes to get used to when converting VAPs to a NLMs, but they are mostly insignificant for the first pass of the conversion. Primarily you will spend your time rewriting your calls to the operating system while the remainder of your code—adding numbers, performing comparisons, and so forth— stays the same.

Later, after you have the NLM performing the basics of VAP, you can focus on refining its rich features, including as thread management.

I hope this quick exercise in VAP-to-NLM conversion show you that it is eminently doable. With a little time, maybe some sweat, you will have your first conversion done and the knowledge that "you can do it" in your repertoire.

BABY_SYSCON

The following code is an interesting example. It lets a non-SUPERVISOR user create new users (though not with SUPERVISOR equivalence) from a script file without having to know the SUPERVISOR's account password. Basically, it shows how to keep up with changes to the SUPERVISOR password. You should be able to use its constructions and applied programming to benefit your own applications.

You'll be prompted for the SUPERVISOR password when you first use this utility (and whenever you change the password). When you type it in, it is stored in the bindery. It is *not* implanted in the program code itself, thus avoiding security issues.

Once you have inserted the password, run it by typing:

CREATEU inputfilename

First, CREATEU logs you out of the current server (after making sure your current drive letter is on a network volume), even if it is the login directory and you haven't logged in yet. It then logs you in as the supervisor. Make sure the file name you give it exists on a local drive or in the login directory of the current server. A local drive is the best place; that way, no one will see it (remember, this file will have passwords).

It then processes the input file and logs you out. You'll need to log yourself back into the server to reestablish yourself.

Included is the Will_It_Run procedure, which presents one way to check for the existence of a NetWare network.

The following is the include file INT10GDS.INC:

```
var
OriginalColors : Byte;


Function CurrentDisplayPage:Byte;
Begin

Hr2.AH := $0F;
Intr($10,Regs2);

CurrentDisplayPage := Hr2.BH

End;


Procedure ColorAnyway(Color:Byte; Length:Integer);
Begin

Hr2.BH:=CurrentDisplayPage;
Hr2.AH:=$09;
Hr2.AL:=$20;
Hr2.BL:=Color;
Regs2.CX:=Length;
Intr($10,Regs2);

End;

Procedure SaveCurrentColor;
Begin

Hr2.BH := CurrentDisplayPage;
Hr2.AH := $08;
Intr($10,Regs2);

OriginalColors := Hr2.AH;

End;
```

```
{$C-}
{$P128}
Program  BABY_SYSCON;

Const

 AnetInc = 'ANET Quick User Add, (c) 1988 Integrity Software.';
 AbEnd   = 'Abend: Your current drive must be a network drive to use
           this utility.';


Type

    Reg =  record
                 AX, BX, CX, DX, BP, SI, DI, DS, ES, FLAGS: INTEGER;
           end;

HalfRegtype = record
                 Al,Ah,Bl,Bh,Cl,Ch,Dl,Dh:byte
              end;

Long  = record
           ah,al,bh,bl:byte;
        end;

Word  = record
        WH,WL:byte
        end;


S128Bytes   = array [1..128] of Byte;

{*****************************************************************}


Word  = record
        WH,WL:byte
        end;



S128Bytes   = array [1..128] of Byte;

{*****************************************************************}
```

333

```
SecretCall = record
                Native     : Word;
                Func       : Byte;
                Flags      : Byte;
                security   : Byte;
                objtyp     : WORD;
                objname1   : byte;
                objname    : array [1..48] of byte;
              end;


SecretRply = record
                Native     : Word;
              end;



E317call  = record
                Native     : Word;
                GSI        : Byte;    {Get Server Info}
              end;



E317RPLY    = record
    Native    : Word;
    ServerName: array [1..48] of Byte;
    NetwareVer: Word;
    ConntSuppt: Word;
    ConntInUse: Word;
    MaxVols   : Word;
    Junk      : array [1..72] of Byte;
              end

{*****************************************************************}


SecretCall  = record
                Native     : Word;
                Func       : Byte;
                Flags      : Byte;
                security   : Byte;
                objtyp     : WORD;
                objname1   : byte;
                objname    : array [1..48] of byte;
              end;

SecretRply = record
```

```
                Native     : Word;
             end;


E317call   = record
          Native: Word;
          GSI   : Byte;    { Get Server Info }
           end;


E317RPLY   = record
     Native    : Word;
     ServerName: array [1..48] of Byte;
     NetwareVer: Word;
     ConntSuppt: Word;
     ConntInUse: Word;
     MaxVols   : Word;
     Junk      : array [1..72] of Byte;
           end;



E30call   = record
          Native  : Word;  { length }
          Func    : Byte;  { login }
          TY      : Word;  { type }
          NL      : Byte;  { Name Length }
          Name    : array[1..10] of byte; { SUPERVISOR }
          PL      : Byte;  { Password Length }
          Pass    : array[1..48] of byte; { password   }
          end;


E30rply   = record
          native  : Word;  { length }
          end;

chkcall   = record
             Native : Word;
             Func   : Byte;  { $46 = get my bindery     }
                             { access level}
             end;

chkrply   = record
             Native : Word;
```

```
            Mask    : Byte;
            ID      : Long;
            end;


{***********************************************************************}

e336cl    = record
              Native : Word;
              Func    : Byte;     { $36 for get object name }
              Unique : Long;      { unique ID for the object }
            end;


e336rp    = record
              Native : Word;
              Id      : long;      { same ID as above }
              objtyp : word;       { type of object      }
              name    : array [1..48] of byte;
            end;



e335cl    = record
              Native : Word;
              func    : byte;
              objtyp : word;       { type of object      }
              namel : byte;
              objname   : array [1..48] of byte;
            end;



PropCall  = record
                Native    : Word;
                Func      : Byte;      { func 0x3e }
                objtyp    : Word;
                objnamel  : Byte;
                objname   : array[1..512] of byte;
              end;

ReadPropertyc = record
                  Native : Word;
                  Func    : Byte;
                  ObjTyp : Word;
                  ObjNmel: Byte;
                  ObjName: array[1..200] of byte;
{segnum,prpnaml,prpnme}
                  end;
```

```
ReadPropertyr = record
                 Native : Word;
                 Data   : S128Bytes;
                 More   : Byte;
                 Flags  : Byte;
               end;



{****************************************************************}


E33dcall   = record
                 Native: Word;
                 Func  : Byte;     { 55 for search for users }
                 Last  : Long;     { make it -1 }
                 ObjTyp: Word;     { search for users 0001 }
                 ObjNml: Byte;     { 1 }
                 ObjNme: Byte;     { * }
               end;

E3REPLY2   = record
                 Native    : Word;
                 Id        : Long;
                 Objecttype: Word;
                 PropName  : array [1..48] of Byte;
               end;

type
st255=string[255];
e201rp   = record
             Native : Word;
             L      : Byte;                    { length of path      }
             name   : array [1..255] of byte;  { path specification }
           end;


e201cl   = record
             Native : Word;
             Func   : Byte;    { $01 for get base's path  }
             Source : Byte;    { source base, from C drive }
           end;


e200cl   = record
             Native : Word;
```

```
                    Func   : Byte;    { $00 for set base's path  }
                    Target : Byte;    { target base, from C drive }
                    Source : Byte;    { source base, from C drive }
                    L      : Byte;                 { length of path      }
                    name   : array [1..255] of byte; { path specification }
                    end;


var
e      : array[1..4] of st255;
regs   : reg;
hr     : halfregtype absolute regs;
regs2  : reg;
hr2    : halfregtype absolute regs2;

Lc:E30call;
Lr:E30rply;

llc    :   readpropertyc;
sc     :   secretcall;
sr     :   secretrply;
cc     :   chkcall;
cr     :   chkrply;
Pc     :   e33dCall;
Pr     :   e3reply2;
The    :   String[80];
save_base,
msgl   :   Integer;
fn     :   string[30];

wherep:string[80];

gc     :   e335cl;
nc     :   e336cl;
nr     :   e336rp;
e3c    :   e317call;
e3r    :   e317rply;
un,aa,passlen,
a,b,c  :   integer;
getc   :   e201cl;
getr   :   e201rp;
setc   :   e200cl;


save_path : e201rp;
```

```
cl:string[80];
nonzero,
access:boolean;

{$i int10gds.inc }
{[[[[[[[[[[[[[[[[[[[[[[[[[[[[[[[[[[[[[[[]]]]]]]]]]]]]]]]]]]]]]]]]]]]]]]]]]}
{[[[[[[[[[[[[[[[[[[[[[[[[[[[PROCS BELOW HERE ]]]]]]]]]]]]]]]]]]]]]]]}
{[[[[[[[[[[[[[[[[[[[[[[[[[[[[[[[[[[[[[[[]]]]]]]]]]]]]]]]]]]]]]]]]]]]]]]]]]}


Procedure MailBoxName(Byyte:byte);
var
st : string[5];
a, r, d, e:integer;

(*
/* this routine produces the UserID w/o leading 0's...for use in     */
/* finding the user's MailBox directory                              */
/*                                                                    */
/* Byyte is a byte that is passed to MailBoxName (this procedure)     */


/* the next line initializes some variables in this routine          */
   a = r = st[0] = 0;

/* the variables:
 * a    is used to hold the tenths part of the Byyte variable—if Byyte
 *      is 32, a is 2
 * r    is used to hold the remainder of the tenths part—if Byyte is 33,
 *      then r is 1 (33 mod 16 = 1)
 * d    holds the visual character value of the 'sixteenths' part of the
 *      hexadecimal number to be returned
 * e    holds the visual character value of the ones part of the hexa-
 *      decimal number to be returned
 * st   is a temporary hold area for the hexadecimal representation of
 *      the number to be returned
 * wherep (a global variable)
 *      holds the value of the complete hexadecimal number to be
 *      returned
 * nonzero (a global variable)
 *      a flag used to eliminate leading zeroes
 */

*)
```

```
Begin
 a := trunc(Byyte / 16);
 r := Byyte mod 16;
 fillchar(st,sizeof(st),0);
 d := 48; e := 48;
 if (a > 16) then a := 0;
 if (a > 9)  then d := 55;
 if (r > 9)  then e := 55;


 if ((Byyte >= $10) or (nonzero))
 then
 begin
  st[0]:=#2;
  st[1]:=chr(a + d);
  st[2]:=chr(r + e);
  st[3]:=#0;
 end
 else
 if ((r+e)<>48) then
 begin
  st[0]:=#1;
  st[1]:=chr(r + e);
  st[2]:=#0;
 end;

 if ( ( ((a+d)<>48) or ((r+e)<>48) ) AND ( ((a+d)<>0) or ((r+e)<>0)) )
 then
 nonzero := TRUE;

 wherep:=concat(wherep,st);

End;   {   /* end of procedure MailBoxName(Byyte) */ }




Function CurrentDrive : integer;
Begin
 Regs.AX := $1900;
 MSDos( Regs );
 CurrentDrive := (Regs.AX and $FF) + 1
End;
```

```
procedure Script;
var
filvar      :  text;
st          :  string[2];
a           :  real;
aa,r,d,e,i  :  integer;
hm          :  string[255];
ok          :  boolean;


BEGIN



if un=1 then
begin {first pass}

un:=99; {no more first pass}

     r   : = currentdrive-1;
   regs.AX: = $E900;
     Hr.Dl: = r;
     hr.dh: = $00;
      MsDos(Regs);
      r   : = hr.al;    { Path Base }
 save_base: = hr.al;

if (hr.ah in [1..2])  or  (hr.ah=129)then
begin

Regs.AX              := $E200;

getc.func            := $01;
getc.source          := R;
getc.native.wh       := $02;
getc.native.wl       := $00;
save_path.native.wh := $FF;
save_path.native.wl := $00;

  with Regs do
  begin
            DS    := Seg(getc);
            SI    := Ofs(getc);

            ES    := Seg(save_path);
```

```
                DI := Ofs(save_path);
   end;

     MsDos(Regs);     {  GET THE CURRENT DRIVE SPEC, SAVE IT  }

end

ELSE   begin
       Write(Abend);Writeln(#7,#7);
       Writeln('Error Status is ',hr.al);
       {restore}
       halt(0);
       end;

{ Writeln('After GET SAVE_PATH, the status was ',hr.al);   {}

setc.func      := $00;
setc.source    := $00;
setc.target    := save_base;
setc.l         := $04;

setc.name[1]   := $53;      { S }
setc.name[2]   := $59;      { Y }
setc.name[3]   := $53;      { S }
setc.name[4]   := $3A;      { : }

setc.native.wh := ($04+$04);
setc.native.wl := $00;
getr.native.wh := $FF;
getr.native.wl := $00;

  with Regs do
  begin

          DS := Seg(setc);
          SI := Ofs(setc);

          ES := Seg(getr);
          DI := Ofs(getr);

   end;

     MsDos(Regs);          { THIS SETS CURRENT STUFF TO SYS: }

{ Writeln('After SET the status was ',hr.al);      {}
```

```
End; {of if first pass}


pr.id.ah := nr.id.ah;
pr.id.al := nr.id.al;   { we just got the id }
pr.id.bh := nr.id.bh;
pr.id.bl := nr.id.bl;

fn:='\MAIL\';
nonzero:=FALSE;
fillchar(wherep,sizeof(wherep),0);

    MailBoxName(pr.id.ah);   (*/* put together the MailBox name      */*)
    MailBoxName(pr.id.al);
    MailBoxName(pr.id.bh);
    MailBoxName(pr.id.bl);

(*  fn:=concat(fn,st,chr(0){'\LOGIN'});*)
  fn:=concat(fn,wherep,chr(0));

{writeln('FN is [',fn,']');}

Regs2.AX:=$3900; {CREATE SUBDIRECTORY}
Regs2.DS:=Seg(fn);
Regs2.DX:=Ofs(fn)+1;

MsDos(REGS2);

{Writeln('after making the subdir = >',hr2.al,'<');}


End;{Script}


Procedure  COPY_SCRIPT;
var
fx:string[10];
fnn:string[50];
fhf,fht:integer;
buffer:array[1..16384] of byte;
done:boolean;
Begin

fx:='LOGIN.'^@;
pr.id.ah:=nr.id.ah;
```

```
pr.id.al:=nr.id.al;   { we just got the id }
pr.id.bh:=nr.id.bh;
pr.id.bl:=nr.id.bl;

fnn:='\MAIL\';
nonzero:=FALSE;
fillchar(wherep,sizeof(wherep),0);
    MailBoxName(pr.id.ah);
(*/* put together the MailBox name       */*)
    MailBoxName(pr.id.al);
    MailBoxName(pr.id.bh);
    MailBoxName(pr.id.bl);

  fnn:=concat(fnn,wherep,chr(0));

  Regs.AX:=$3B01; {set dir}
  REGS.DS:=Seg(fnn);
  Regs.DX:=Ofs(fnn)+1; {dir}
{ writeln('chg dir ',fnn);{}
  MSDOS(REGS);

  fnn[0]:=chr(ord(fnn[0])-1);
  fnn:=concat(fnn,'\LOGIN.',chr(0));

  REGS.AX:=$3D00; {READ ONLY}
  REGS.DS:=Seg(fx);
  Regs.DX:=Ofs(fx)+1; {file to copy}
  MSDOS(REGS);
  if regs.ax <6 then writeln('ERROR opening >',fnn,'<');{}
  fhf:=regs.ax;
{ writeln('reading ',fnn,'.');{}

  Regs.AX:=$3B02; {set dir}
  REGS.DS:=Seg(fn);
  Regs.DX:=Ofs(fn)+1; {dir}
{ writeln('chg dir ',fn);{}
  MSDOS(REGS);

  fn[0]:=chr(ord(fn[0])-1); {get rid of trailing NULL}
  fn:=concat(fn,'\LOGIN.',chr(0));

  REGS.AX:=$3C00; {CREATE}
  REGS.CX:=00;{create with normal attribs}
  REGS.DS:=Seg(fx);
  Regs.DX:=Ofs(fx)+1; {file to create}
```

```
  MSDOS (REGS);
  if regs.ax <6 then writeln('ERROR creating >',fn,'<>',regs.ax,'<');
{}
  fht:=regs.ax;

done:=false;

if (fhf<6) OR (fht<6) then DONE:=TRUE;

While NOT DONE do
Begin

    REGS.AX:=$3F40;
    Regs.BX:=FHF;
    Regs.CX:=$4000;
    Regs.DS:=Seg(buffer);
    Regs.DX:=Ofs(buffer);
    MsDOS(Regs);
{    writeln('WE READ [',regs.ax,'] bytes');{}
    if Regs.AX=0 then DONE:=TRUE;

    if NOT DONE then
    Begin
      Regs.CX:=Regs.AX;  {bytes to write}
      Regs.AX:=$4000;
      Regs.BX:=FHT;
      Regs.DS:=Seg(buffer);
      Regs.DX:=Ofs(buffer);
      MsDOS(Regs);
      if regs.ax = 0 then writeln('DISK FULL'#7);
    End;

END; {while not done}


if (fhf<6) or (fht<6) then
else
begin
 hr.AH:=$3E;
 Regs.BX:=FHF;
 MsDOS(REGS);
 hr.AH:=$3E;
 Regs.BX:=FHT;
 MsDOS(REGS);
end;
```

```
End; {copy_script}


Procedure AddPWD; {ADD PASSWORD}
var
q: byte;
Begin
{ llc   lr }



    llc.native.wh:=$ff;
    llc.native.wl:=0;
    lr.native.wh:=$ff;
    lr.native.wl:=0;
    llc.func:=$39; {ADD PROP to OBJECT}
    llc.objtyp.wl:=1;
    llc.objtyp.wh:=0;
    llc.ObjNmel:=   ord( e[1][0] );
    for a:=1 to llc.ObjNmel do
      llc.ObjName[a] :=    ord( e[1][a]); {CREATE NAME}

    q:=llc.ObjNmel+1;

    llc.ObjName[q]   := 0; {STATIC PROPERTY}
    llc.ObjName[q+1]:=$11; {read/write by anyone logged in}
    llc.ObjName[q+2]:=8;
    llc.ObjName[q+3]:=80;{PASSWORD}
    llc.ObjName[q+4]:=65;
    llc.ObjName[q+5]:=83;
    llc.ObjName[q+6]:=83;
    llc.ObjName[q+7]:=87;
    llc.ObjName[q+8]:=79;
    llc.ObjName[q+9]:=82;
    llc.ObjName[q+10]:=68;

With REGS do
Begin

  AX:=$E300;
  ES:=Seg(lr);
  DI:=Ofs(lr);

  DS:=Seg(llc);
```

```
   SI:=Ofs(llc);
End;

  MSDOS(REGS);
{  writeln('AFTER ADD PWD [',hr.al,']');{}
   if hr.al <> 0 then writeln('Unable to add password for ',e[1]);

     llc.ObjName[q]   := 2; {SET PROPERTY}


   with llc do
   begin
     objname[q+2]:=13;   {GROUPS_I'M_IN}
     objname[q+3]:=$47;
     objname[q+4]:=$52;
     objname[q+5]:=$4f;
     objname[q+6]:=$55;
     objname[q+7]:=$50;
     objname[q+8]:=$53;
     objname[q+9]:=$5f;
   objname[q+10]:=$49;
   objname[q+11]:=$27;
   objname[q+12]:=$4d;
   objname[q+13]:=$5f;
   objname[q+14]:=$49;
   objname[q+15]:=$4e;
   end;

With REGS do
Begin

  AX:=$E300;
  ES:=Seg(lr);
  DI:=Ofs(lr);

  DS:=Seg(llc);
  SI:=Ofs(llc);
End;

  MSDOS(REGS);
 { writeln('AFTER ADD GII [',hr.al,']');{}
   if hr.al <> 0 then writeln('Unable to add group for ',e[1]);

   with llc do
   begin
```

```
    objname[q+2]  :=15;    {SECURITY_EQUALS}
    objname[q+3]  :=$53;
    objname[q+4]  :=$45;
    objname[q+5]  :=$43;
    objname[q+6]  :=$55;
    objname[q+7]  :=$52;
    objname[q+8]  :=$49;
    objname[q+9]  :=$54;
    objname[q+10]:=$59;
    objname[q+11]:=$5f;
    objname[q+12]:=$45;
    objname[q+13]:=$51;
    objname[q+14]:=$55;
    objname[q+15]:=$41;
    objname[q+16]:=$4c;
    objname[q+17]:=$53;

  end;

With REGS do
Begin

  AX:=$E300;
  ES:=Seg(lr);
  DI:=Ofs(lr);

  DS:=Seg(llc);
  SI:=Ofs(llc);
End;

  MSDOS(REGS);
{  writeln('AFTER ADD SEQ [',hr.al,']');{}
  if hr.al <> 0 then writeln('Unable to add security for ',e[1]);




{-=-=-=-==-=-=-==-=-=-=-=-==-=-=-=-==-=-=-==-==-}

    llc.func:=$3E; {ADD PROP to OBJECT}

    llc.ObjNmel:=   ord( e[1][0] );
    for a:=1 to llc.ObjNmel do
      llc.ObjName[a] :=    ord( e[1][a]); {NAME}

    q:=llc.ObjNmel+1;
```

```
    llc.ObjName[q]   := 1; {SEGMENT}
    llc.ObjName[q+1]:= 0; {NO MORE}
    llc.ObjName[q+2]:=8;
    llc.ObjName[q+3]:=80;{PASSWORD}
    llc.ObjName[q+4]:=65;
    llc.ObjName[q+5]:=83;
    llc.ObjName[q+6]:=83;
    llc.ObjName[q+7]:=87;
    llc.ObjName[q+8]:=79;
    llc.ObjName[q+9]:=82;
    llc.ObjName[q+10]:=68;
    for a:=1 to ord(e[2][0]) do
      llc.ObjName[q+10+a] :=     ord( e[2][a]); {PASSWORD}
      llc.ObjName[q+10+a+1]:=0;
With REGS do
Begin

  AX:=$E300;
  ES:=Seg(lr);
  DI:=Ofs(lr);

  DS:=Seg(llc);
  SI:=Ofs(llc);
End;

  MSDOS(REGS);
{  writeln('AFTER WRITE PWD [',hr.al,']');{}
  if hr.al <> 0 then writeln('Unable to add password for ',e[1]);


    llc.func:=$41; {ADD PROP to SET}

    llc.ObjNmel:=    ord( e[1][0] );
    for a:=1 to llc.ObjNmel do
      llc.ObjName[a] :=    ord( e[1][a]); {NAME}

    q:=llc.ObjNmel+1;

  with llc do
  begin
    objname[q  ]:=13;
    objname[q+1]:=$47;
    objname[q+2]:=$52;
```

```
   objname[q+3]:=$4f;
   objname[q+4]:=$55;
   objname[q+5]:=$50;
   objname[q+6]:=$53;
   objname[q+7]:=$5f;
 objname[q+ 8]:=$49;
 objname[q+ 9]:=$27;
 objname[q+10]:=$4d;
 objname[q+11]:=$5f;
 objname[q+12]:=$49;
 objname[q+13]:=$4e;
 objname[q+14]:=$00;
 objname[q+15]:=$02; {GROUP OBJECT}
 objname[q+16]:=ord(e[4][0]); {length of groupname}
end;

   for a:=1 to ord(e[4][0]) do
     llc.ObjName[a+q+16] :=    ord( e[4][a]); {GROUP}
     llc.objname[a+q+17] := 0;

With REGS do
Begin

  AX:=$E300;
  ES:=Seg(lr);
  DI:=Ofs(lr);

  DS:=Seg(llc);
  SI:=Ofs(llc);
End;

  MSDOS(REGS);
{  writeln('AFTER WRITE GROUP I BELONG TO [',hr.al,']');{}
   if hr.al <> 0 then writeln('Unable to add group for ',e[1]);


   llc.ObjNmel:=    ord( e[1][0] );
   for a:=1 to llc.ObjNmel do
     llc.ObjName[a] :=    ord( e[1][a]); {NAME}

   q:=llc.ObjNmel+1;

  with llc do
  begin
```

```
   objname[q  ] :=15;   {SECURITY_EQUALS}
   objname[q+1] :=$53;
   objname[q+2] :=$45;
   objname[q+3] :=$43;
   objname[q+4] :=$55;
   objname[q+5] :=$52;
   objname[q+6] :=$49;
   objname[q+7] :=$54;
   objname[q+ 8]:=$59;
   objname[q+ 9]:=$5f;
   objname[q+10]:=$45;
   objname[q+11]:=$51;
   objname[q+12]:=$55;
   objname[q+13]:=$41;
   objname[q+14]:=$4c;
   objname[q+15]:=$53;
   objname[q+16]:=00;
   objname[q+17]:=02; {GROUP OBJECT}
   objname[q+18]:=ord(e[4][0]); {length of groupname}
 end;

   for a:=1 to ord(e[4][0]) do
     llc.ObjName[a+q+18] :=      ord( e[4][a]); {GROUP}
     llc.objname[a+q+19] := 0;

With REGS do
Begin

  AX:=$E300;
  ES:=Seg(lr);
  DI:=Ofs(lr);

  DS:=Seg(llc);
  SI:=Ofs(llc);
End;

  MSDOS(REGS);
{ writeln('AFTER SETTING EQUAL TO GROUP [',hr.al,']');{}
  if hr.al <> 0 then writeln('Unable to add security for ',e[1]);

    llc.func:=$41; {ADD PROP to SET}

    llc.objtyp.wl:=2;
    llc.objtyp.wh:=0;
```

```
    llc.ObjNmel:=    ord( e[4][0] );
    for a:=1 to llc.ObjNmel do
      llc.ObjName[a] :=    ord( e[4][a]); {GROUP}

    q:=llc.ObjNmel+1;

  with llc do
  begin
     objname[q  ]:=$0d;

     objname[q+1]:=$47; { g }
     objname[q+2]:=$52; { r }
     objname[q+3]:=$4f; { o }
     objname[q+4]:=85;  { u }
     objname[q+5]:=$50; { p }
     objname[q+6]:=95;  { _ }
     objname[q+7]:=77;  { m }
    objname[q+ 8]:=69;  { e }
    objname[q+ 9]:=77;  { m }
    objname[q+10]:=66;  { b }
    objname[q+11]:=69;  { e }
    objname[q+12]:=$52; { r }
    objname[q+13]:=83;  { s }

    objname[q+14]:=$00;
    objname[q+15]:=$01; {USER OBJECT}
    objname[q+16]:=ord(e[1][0]); {length of groupname}
  end;

    for a:=1 to ord(e[1][0]) do
      llc.ObjName[a+q+16] :=    ord( e[1][a]); {USER JUST CREATED}
      llc.objname[a+q+17] := 0;

With REGS do
Begin

  AX:=$E300;
  ES:=Seg(lr);
  DI:=Ofs(lr);

  DS:=Seg(llc);
  SI:=Ofs(llc);
End;
```

```
  MSDOS(REGS);
{  writeln('AFTER ADDING ME TO GROUP [',hr.al,']');{}
   if hr.al <> 0 then writeln('Unable to add to group for ',e[1]);


End; {AddPWD}



Procedure Get_File;
var
fn      :string[255];
filvar  :text;
ok      :boolean;
Begin
        fn:=ParamStr(1);

            assign(filvar,fn);
        {$I-}
            reset(filvar);
        {$I+}
              ok:=(IOresult = 0);

if not ok then
if fn[0]=#0 then
 begin
  ColorAnyWay($47,160);
  writeln('Usage: CREATEU filename');
  writeln(' filename is the textfile that has user profiles
to create.');
  ColorAnyWay(OriginalColors,100);
  Halt(6);
 end
 else
 begin
  ColorAnyWay($47,160);
  writeln('File, ',#205,fn,#205,' is NOT locatable.',#7);
  writeln('Aborting...');
  ColorAnyWay(OriginalColors,100);
  Halt(6);
 end;


{
for x:=1 to ord(e[0]) do
   if e[x]=#44 then writeln
```

```
  else write(e[x]);
}

if Ok then close(filvar);

End; {of Get_File}


(*************%%%%%%%%%%%%%BUILD USER%%%%%%%%%%%%%%%%%%%%%*)
Procedure BldUser;
Begin
{SecretCall  = record
                Native    : Word;
                Func      : Byte;
                Flags     : Byte;
                security  : Byte;
                objtyp    : WORD;
                objnamel  : byte;
                objname   : array [1..48] of byte;
             end;

SecretRply = record
                Native      : Word;
             end;

   Username to create,
   Password,
   WHOSE LOGIN SCRIPT to COPY,
   Group to belong to,
}

With Regs do begin
  With HR do begin

  With sc do begin

  sR.Native.Wl:=$00;
  sR.Native.WH:=$FF;

    Native.Wl:= $00;

    Func :=     $32;
    Flags:=     $00;
    Security:=  $00;
```

```
   OBJTYP.WL:=$01; {USER type}
   OBJTYP.WH:=$00;

   ObjNamel:=    ord( e[1][0] );
   for a:=1 to ObjNamel do
     ObjName[a] :=    ord( e[1][a]); {CREATE NAME}

   Native.WH:=  6+objNamel;

   END; { OF WITH PC }

 AX:=$E300;

 ES:=Seg(sr);
 DI:=Ofs(sr);

 DS:=Seg(sc);
 SI:=Ofs(sc);
 MSDOS(REGS);
{  writeln('AFTER THE CREATE [',hr.al,']');{}
{was it ok?}
if hr.al<>0 then writeln('Unable to create user ',e[1])
else
BEGIN

  nr.Native.Wl:=$00;
  nr.Native.WH:=$FF;

  gc.Native.Wl:=  $00;
  gc.Native.WH:=  $FF;

  gc.Func :=      $35;

  gc.OBJTYP.WL:=$01; {USER type}
  gc.OBJTYP.WH:=$00;

  gc.Namel:=    ord( e[1][0] );
    for a:=1 to gc.Namel do
      gc.ObjName[a] :=    ord( e[1][a]); {CREATE NAME}


  AX:=$E300;

  ES:=Seg(nr);
  DI:=Ofs(nr);
```

```
   DS:=Seg(gc);
   SI:=Ofs(gc);
   MSDOS(REGS);
{  writeln('AFTER THE GET ID [',hr.al,']');{}
{was it ok?}
if hr.al = 0 then
begin
   Script; {make the mail subdirectory}

  (* NOW, THE USER TO COPY LOGIN SCRIPT *)

   gc.Namel:=    ord( e[3][0] );
     for a:=1 to gc.Namel do
       gc.ObjName[a] :=     ord( e[3][a]); {COPY NAME}


   AX:=$E300;

   ES:=Seg(nr);
   DI:=Ofs(nr);

   DS:=Seg(gc);
   SI:=Ofs(gc);
   MSDOS(REGS);
 { writeln('AFTER THE GET COPY ID [',hr.al,']');{}
{was it ok?}
    if hr.al=0 then COPY_SCRIPT;

   AddPwd;

end;
end;
end;

END;

End;{BLDUSER}


Procedure Get_Stuf;

var
```

```
f,fn      :string[255];
filvar  :text;
ok       :boolean;
g,x,y,z:integer;
Begin
        fn:=ParamStr(1);

              assign(filvar,fn);
        {$I-}
              reset(filvar);
        {$I+}
              ok:=(IOresult = 0);

if not ok then
if fn[0]=#0 then
 begin
  ColorAnyWay($47,160);
  writeln('Usage: CREATEU filename');
  writeln('       filename is the textfile that has user profiles to
    create.');
  ColorAnyWay(OriginalColors,100);
  Halt(6);
 end
 else
 begin
  ColorAnyWay($47,160);
  writeln('File, ',#205,fn,#205,' is NOT locatable.',#7);
  writeln('Aborting...');
  ColorAnyWay(OriginalColors,100);
  Halt(6);
 end;

(*
   Username to create,
   Password,
   Full Name,
   Group to belong to,
   **that's it.ONE ENTRY PER LINE, NO MORE, NO LESS!
*)

a:=0; {number of entries}
y:=0;
While y = 0
do
BEGIN
```

```
   ReadLn(filvar,f);
{  Writeln;{}
   if ord(f[0])=0 then y:=1;
   if y <> 1 then
   begin
    z:=1;g:=0;
     for x:=1 to ord(f[0]) do
     begin
      g:=g+1;
       if f[x]=#44 then
        begin
           If g > 1 then e[z][0]:=chr(g-1);
           g:=0; z:=z+1;
           { write(#205,#205);{}
        end
       else
        begin
          {write(f[x]);{}
           e[z][g]:=f[x];
        end;
      end;
      e[4][0]:=chr(g); {last guy, no comma, duh!}
    if z <> 4 then
     begin
      writeln;
      writeln('ERROR in line >',f,'<',#7);
      y:=1; {get out of loop}
     end
     ELSE
     {BUILD USER}
     begin
       writeln;
       bldUser;
       writeln('Just finished user "',e[1],'"');
       for g:=1 to 4 do
        begin{
         writeln(e[g],'*');                    }
         fillchar(e[g],sizeof(e[g]),0);
        end;
     end;
   a:=a+1;
   end;
END;   {while y=0}

if Ok then close(filvar);
```

```
End; {of Get_Stuf}



Procedure Server_Info;
Begin

{———————————-Netware Info————————-}


  With Regs do begin
     With HR do begin

  With E3r do
  begin
    Native.Wl:=$00;
    Native.WH:=$FF;
  end; { of e3r with }

  AX:=$E300;

  E3c.Native.Wl:=$00;
  E3c.Native.WH:=$01;
  E3c.GSI       :=$11;

  ES:=Seg(E3r);
  DI:=Ofs(E3r);

  DS:=Seg(E3c);
  SI:=Ofs(E3c);

  MSDOS(REGS);

   End;
   End;



END;  {of SERVER_INFO}



Procedure Server;
Begin
```

```
  Server_Info;

  a:=1;
  while a <48 do
  begin
    if e3r.servername[a]=0 then a:=99 {get out of here}
    else
     write(chr(e3r.servername[a]));
    a:=a+1;
  end;


End;  {of server}



Procedure get_pwd;
var
Continue,
Eschit: boolean;
ci   : char;

Begin
msgl :=0;
EscHit:=False;
Continue:=False;
The   := '';

Repeat

   Repeat Until Keypressed;
   read(kbd,ci);
   If (ci=#27) and (keypressed) then
    begin
         read(kbd,ci);
         ci:=#0;       (* this is if they hit a function *)
    end;               (* key, not just the ESC key      *)

   If ci = #32 then ci:=#95;
   If ci in [#48..#57,#64..#90,#95,#97..#122] then
     begin
           If (ci>#96) and (ci<#123) then ci:=UpCase(ci);
            (*convert lowers*)
           (* otherwise fine for processing *)

           msgl:=msgl+1;
```

```
        The[0]:=Chr(msgl);
        The[msgl]:=ci;
    end;

 If (ci=#8) and (msgl>0) then (* Backspace was hit, and   *)
begin                        (*msg long enough to edit   *)

        msgl:=msgl-1;
        The[0]:=Chr(msgl); (* back setting length will*)           {
Write(#8,' ');}                   (* erase effectv
    end;

 If (msgl>46) or (ci=#27) or (ci=#13) then continue:=true;(* msg is
ready to go *)

 If (continue) and (msgl=0) then EscHit:=True;

 If Ci=#27 then EscHit:=True;
        {
        Gotoxy(25,5);
        Write(The);
        }
Until Continue;

end;{of get_pwd}




Procedure MakePwd;
Begin

ColorAnyWay($17,240);
Write('This server [');server;writeln('] does not have the current');
writeln('supervisor password.  Please enter the password below or press
enter');
write('<password will NOT be echoed to the screen>');


Get_Pwd;

with Lc do
 begin
    native.wh:=255;
```

```
        native.wl:=0;
        func:=$3f; {verify pwd}
        TY.wh:=00;
        TY.wl:=01;
        NL:=10;
        Name[1]:=83;
        Name[2]:=85;
        Name[3]:=80;
        Name[4]:=69;
        Name[5]:=82;
        Name[6]:=86;
        Name[7]:=73;
        Name[8]:=83;
        Name[9]:=79;
        Name[10]:=82;
        PL:=msgl;
        for a:=1 to msgl
        do
           pass[a]:=ord(the[a]);
   end;

 Lr.native.wh:=255;
 Lr.native.wl:=0;

With REGS do
begin
    AX:=$E300;
    DS:=seg(Lc);
    SI:=ofs(Lc);
    ES:=seg(Lr);
    DI:=ofs(Lr);
end;

msDOS(regs);

writeln;

if hr.al = 0 then{ writeln('yep, that is the pwd')}
else
 if msgl<>0 then
    writeln('That is not the supervisor password.',#7);


If hr.al = 0 then
BEGIN
```

362

```
With Regs do begin
    With HR do begin

With sc do begin

sR.Native.Wl:=$00;
sR.Native.WH:=$FF;

   Native.Wl:=  $00;
   Native.WH:=  $FF;

   Func :=      $32;
   Flags:=      $00;
   Security:=   $00;

   OBJTYP.WL:=$08;
   OBJTYP.WH:=$80;

   ObjNamel:=      $02+msgl;
   ObjName[1] :=      89; {LOOP HERE}
   ObjName[2] :=     $32;
   for a:=3 to msgl + 2 do
     ObjName[a] :=      ord(The[a-2]);
                                          {this is the REAL pwd}


   END; { OF WITH PC }


 AX:=$E300;

 ES:=Seg(sr);
 DI:=Ofs(sr);

 DS:=Seg(sc);
 SI:=Ofs(sc);
 MSDOS(REGS);
{ writeln('AFTER THE CREATE [',hr.al,']');{}
{was it ok?}

end;
end;
END; {only if pwd was verified}

end; {of makepwd}
```

```
Procedure Will_it_Run;
var subs:integer;
Begin

  With Regs do
   Begin

    AX:=$E311;

    cc.Native.Wl:=$00;
    cc.Native.WH:=$01;
    cr.Native.Wl:=$00;
    cr.Native.WH:=$ff;
    cc.Func     :=$46;
    cr.Mask     :=$00;
    cr.id.al    :=$00;
    cr.id.ah    :=$00;
    cr.id.bl    :=$00;
    cr.id.bh    :=$00;

    ES:=Seg(cr);
    DI:=Ofs(cr);

    DS:=Seg(cc);
    SI:=Ofs(cc);

   End;  { of With Regs }

  MSDOS(REGS);


if cr.mask=$33 then access:=true; {supervisor-level access}

    If (cr.id.al=$00) and
       (cr.id.ah=$00) and
       (cr.id.bl=$00) and
       (cr.id.bh=$00)
 then
    Begin
       {Writeln(ANETinc);  }
       Writeln('This utility requires Advanced Netware to run.');
```

```
        ColorAnyWay(OriginalColors,100);
        Halt(9);
    End;

With Regs do
 Begin
 AX:=$E300;
 nr.Native.Wl:=$00;
 nr.Native.WH:=$FF;

 nc.Native.Wl:=$00;
 nc.Native.WH:=$05;

 ES:=Seg(nr);
 DI:=Ofs(nr);

 DS:=Seg(nc);
 SI:=Ofs(nc);

 nc.func:=$36;
 nc.unique.ah:=cr.id.ah;
 nc.unique.al:=cr.id.al;
 nc.unique.bh:=cr.id.bh;
 nc.unique.bl:=cr.id.bl;

 MSDOS(regs);
 End; { of with Regs }
{**********************************}
(*
   if hr.al <> 0 then
       Begin
       {Writeln(ANETinc);}
       Writeln('This utility requires you to be logged into the network
          to run.');
       ColorAnyWay(OriginalColors,100);
       Halt(9);
     End;
*)
(*   HERE WE WILL LOG OUT THEN LOG IN AS THE SUPERVISOR *)

End; { of Will_it_Run }


Procedure VerifyIt(var ok:boolean);
Begin
```

```
with Lc do
 begin
     native.wh:=255;
     native.wl:=0;
     func:=$3f; {verify pwd}
     TY.wh:=00;
     TY.wl:=01;
     NL:=10;
     Name[1]:=83;
     Name[2]:=85;
     Name[3]:=80;
     Name[4]:=69;
     Name[5]:=82;
     Name[6]:=86;
     Name[7]:=73;
     Name[8]:=83;
     Name[9]:=79;
     Name[10]:=82;
     a:=1;
  {   write('Passwd>');{}
     while a<48 do
     begin
       pass[a]:=pr.propname[a+2];
  {      write(chr(pass[a])); {}
       if pass[a]=0 then
        begin
          passlen:=a;
          PL:=a;
          a:=100;
  {         writeln('*');{}
        end;
       a:=a+1;
     end;
 end;

 Lr.native.wh:=255;
 Lr.native.wl:=0;

With REGS do
begin
    AX:=$E300;
    DS:=seg(Lc);
    SI:=ofs(Lc);
    ES:=seg(Lr);
```

```
    DI:=ofs(Lr);
end;

msDOS(regs);

if hr.al = 0 then OK:=True else OK:=FALSE;

End; {of VerifyIt}


Procedure FindPwd;
var
hi:byte;
sub,subs:integer;
ok:boolean;
Begin

with pc do begin
    last.ah:=$1f;
    last.al:=$ff;        { this sets the LONG variable }
                            { last to = -1 }

    last.bh:=$ff;
    last.bl:=$ff;
end;


    subs:=0;sub:=0;
    hr.al := 0;

While hr.al = 0
do
BEGIN
    sub:=sub+1;
    subs:=0;
  With Regs do begin
    With HR do begin

  With pc do begin

  PR.Native.Wl:=$00;
  pR.Native.WH:=$FF;

    Native.Wl:=  $00;
    Native.WH:=  $09;
```

```
    Func :=        $37;

    OBJTYP.WL:=$08;
    OBJTYP.WH:=$80;


    ObjTyp.WH:=  $80;    {8008h is the obj type...name is Y2}
                         {Actually the Y2 precedes the supervisor pwd}
                         {so, Y2PASSWORD...something like that}
    OBJTYP.WL:=  $08;

    ObjNml:=     $01;
    ObjNme:=     $2a;

    END; { OF WITH PC }


  AX:=$E300;

  ES:=Seg(Pr);
  DI:=Ofs(Pr);

  DS:=Seg(Pc);
  SI:=Ofs(Pc);

  MSDOS(REGS);

  hi:=hr.al;
{
writeln('AFTER find it [',hr.al,']');
writeln('...>',chr(pr.propname[1]),chr(pr.propname[2]),chr(pr.propname[
3]),chr(pr.propname[4]),chr(pr.propname[5]),
chr(pr.propname[6]),chr(pr.propname[7]));
{}

if (pr.propname[1]=89) and (pr.propname[2]=$32) then
   begin
      {WE FOUND OUR USER Y2}
 {     writeln('YES, we found it!, now, verify it');{}
      VerifyIt(ok);
      {writeln('OK is ',ok);{}


      if Ok then
```

```
      begin
            hr.al:=$f;
            EXIT;
      end;
      {else, that wasn't the password}
    end;

with pc do begin
with pr do begin
    last.ah:=id.ah;
    last.al:=id.al;       { this sets the LONG variable TO LAST ID }
    last.bh:=id.bh;
    last.bl:=id.bl;
end;
end;

    End;
    End;
{ sub:=sub+1;   }
{writeln('searching next');{} hr.al:=hi;
    End;


      { writeln('Supervisor password not found.');}
       if access then
       begin
          makePWD;
          hr.al:=252;
       { writeln('You have the rights to do create though')}
       end
       else
       begin
       write('Please have a supervisor initialize server ');
          server;
          writeln(#46);
       end;

       ColorAnyWay(OriginalColors,100);
       Halt(3);

End; { of Proc FindPWD }



Procedure Logout;
```

```
Begin

regs.AX:=$D700;
msDOS(Regs);

{
writeln('Logged out [',hr.al,']');
{}

End; {of logout}



Procedure Login_Su;
begin

with Lc do
 begin
     native.wh:=19;
     native.wl:=0;
     func:=$14;
     TY.wh:=00;
     TY.wl:=01;
     NL:=10;
     Name[1]:=83;
     Name[2]:=85;
     Name[3]:=80;
     Name[4]:=69;
     Name[5]:=82;
     Name[6]:=86;
     Name[7]:=73;
     Name[8]:=83;
     Name[9]:=79;
     Name[10]:=82;
     PL:=passlen;
     for a:=1 to PL do
        pass[a]:=pr.propname[a+2];
  end;

 Lr.native.wh:=255;
 Lr.native.wl:=0;

With REGS do
begin
    AX:=$E300;
```

```
    DS:=seg(Lc);
    SI:=ofs(Lc);
    ES:=seg(Lr);
    DI:=ofs(Lr);
end;


msDOS(regs);
{
writeln('AL came back as >',hr.al,'<');
{}

 if hr.al <> 0 then
 begin
   writeln('Error logging in as Supervisor [',hr.al,']');
   writeln('Aborting...');
   ColorAnyWay(OriginalColors,100);
   Halt(5);
 end;

end; {of LOGIN_SU}



begin

Gotoxy(1,25);
nonzero:=FALSE;
access:=FALSE;
un:=1;

SaveCurrentColor;

ColorAnyWay($47,160);
Writeln(ANETinc);


        aa   := currentdrive-1;
      regs.AX := $E900;
        Hr.Dl := aa;
        hr.dh := $00;
         MsDos(Regs);

if hr.ah in [1..2] then writeln
 else if hr.ah = $80 then
```

```
    begin
            Write(Abend);
            Write(#7#7);
            write(' ');writeln;
            ColorAnyWay(OriginalColors,80);write(' ',#8);
            halt(1);
    end;



Will_it_Run;
FindPWD;
Get_File;

Logout;
Login_SU;

Get_Stuf;

Logout;

        ColorAnyWay(OriginalColors,80);write(' ',#8);


end.
```

NetWare Error Codes

The following error codes define errors that may appear while using Novell's menu-based utilities (SYSCON, FILER, SESSION, etc.) or in your own programs:

Code	Meaning
128	File locked during file open or file create
129	Out of file handles (the file server is out of file handles)
130	No Open privileges (during file open)
131	Hard Disk I/O Error on Read (error reading on network disk)
132	No Create privileges (during file create)
133	No Create/Delete privileges (durlng file Create or Delete)
134	Create file exists w/Read Only attribute (during file Create)
135	Wild cards in Create filename (during file Create)
136	Invalid file handle, file may be closed or unlocked
137	No Search privileges (in directory specified)
138	No Delete privileges (in directory specified)
139	No Rename privileges (in directory specified)
140	No Modify privileges (in directory specified)
141	Some files affected others in use (during Delete, Rename, Set file attributes on a set of files, i.e. *.*)
142	No files affected others in use (during Delete, Rename, Set file attributes on a set of files, i.e. *.*)
143	Some files affected others Read Only (during Delete, Rename, Set file attributes on a set of files, i.e. *.* and some files are flagged Read Only)
144	No files affected others Read Only (during Delete, Rename, Set file attributes on a set of files, i.e. *.* and some files are flagged Read Only)
145	Some files renamed others name exists already (during Rename)

Code	Meaning
146	No files renamed others name exists already (during Rename)
147	No Read privileges (in directory specified)
148	No Write privileges or file Read Only (during Write)
149	File detached (during Read or Write) (File may become detached if it was open when a Release File Set (Function 0xCB) was issued. A detached file can be reattached by using Lock File Set (Function 0xCD))
150	No dynamic memory available (file server ran out of dynamic memory)
151	No disk space for Spool File
152	Volume does not exist, an unknown volume was specified
153	Directory full, all free directory slots have been allocated
154	Renaming across volumes, a rename can be used to move a file between directories, however, this convenience is not extended to moving and renaming between volumes
155	Bad directory handle, usually only occurs when the server is rebooted and workstation is not, can also indicate a corrupt shell
156	Invalid path (an invalid path was specified)
157	No more directory handles, the workstation's allocation of file handles (up to 255 may be specified) is exhausted
158	Invalid filename (during create)
159	Directory active, indicates an attempt to delete directory that is in use by another workstation, (i.e., the other workstation has drive letter mapped to this directory or one of its subdirectories).
160	Directory not empty, indicates, during a directory delete attempt, that the directory still contains files and or subdirectories
161	Directory I/O error, indicates a fatal, nonrecoverable I/O error has occurred in the directory area of the disk, this also indicates that both copies of the directory table are affected by the I/O error
162	Read file with record lock, occurs during a Read of a locked area of a file (a physical lock)

Code	Meaning
192	No account privileges
193	Login denied, no account balance
194	Login denied, no credit
195	Account too many holds
197	Intruder detection lock
198	No console operator
208	Queue error
209	No Queue
210	No Queue server
211	No Queue rights
212	Queue full
213	No Queue job
214	Encrypted login needed or No Queue job rights
215	Password not unique (Queue servicing)
216	Password too short (Queue not active)
217	Login denied, no connection to server (station not server)
218	Unauthorized login time (Queue halted)
219	Unauthorized login station (Queue servicing)
220	Account disabled
222	Password has expired, no grace logins remaining
223	Password has expired

* Bindery error messages:

Code	Meaning
232	Attempt to Write Property to a group
233	Group add request for member already in group
234	Group request for nonexistent member
235	Group request made for nongroup property
236	No property value to retrieve (in read/write)
237	Property already exists (in create)
238	Object already exists (in create)
239	Object name contains illegal characters
240	Attempt to use wild cards in wrong place
241	Attempt to change security to bindery-only status
242	No Object Read (property scan) privileges
243	No Object Rename privileges
244	No Object Deletion privileges
245	No Object Creation or Change privileges
246	No Property Deletion privileges for object
247	No Property Creation or Change privileges for object
248	No Write privileges for property
249	No Read privileges for property
251	No such Property
252	No such Object
253	Unknown bindery request
254	Bindery temporarily locked, try later
255	Unrecoverable/Unknown error

MHS Demo Program

The following program demonstrates the use of MHS to accomplish a common task: setting up users on a network. It is written in C.

```
/***********************************************************
 *
 *     Program Name:   AddUser - MHS Demo Program
 *
 *     Purpose:        To automatically 'feed' MHSUSER with
 *                     user names....to expedite system setup
 *
 *     Date:           06/16/88
 *
 *     Version:        1.00
 *
 *     COPYRIGHT (c) 1988 by Novell Inc.
 *
 *     Author:         John T. McCann
 *
 *     Note:           Compile with Memory Model of COMPACT or
 *                     larger
 *
 ***********************************************************/

/*
 * the 4 following header (.h) files are standard C header files
 */

#include "stdio.h"
#include "errno.h"
#include "process.h"
#include "dos.h"

/*
 * the following are contants/structures/variables to be used in
ADDUSER.C
 */

#define Title  "Express AddUser Utility, (c) 1988 Novell, Inc."
```

```
typedef union {
        struct {
                unsigned int AX, BX, CX, DX, BP, SI, DI, DS, ES, FLAGS;
                } F;
        struct {
                unsigned char Al, Ah, Bl, Bh, Cl, Ch, Dl, Dh;
                } H;
            } Registers;


typedef struct {
                char        ah, al, bh, bl;
                } Long;


typedef struct {
                char        wh, wl;
                } Word;


typedef struct {
                Word        Native;
                char        Func;   /*  Get Connection Info 0x16 */
                char        Conct;  /*  logical connection #     */
                } ConnectCall;


typedef struct {
                Word        Native;
                Long        Unique;
                Word        TypeUser;
                char        Name[48];  /*  the login name  */
                char        InTime[8]; /*  Std Time seqnc  */
                } ConnectRply;


typedef struct {
                Word        Native;
                char        Func;     /*  Get Server Info  */
                } GetServerInfoCall;


typedef struct {
                Word        Native;
```

```
                char        ServerName[48];
                Word        NetwareVer;
                Word        ConntSuppt;
                Word        ConntInUse;
                Word        MaxVols;
                char        Unknown[72];
            } GetServerInfoRply;


typedef struct {
                Word        Native;
                char        Func;    /*  Search for Users, 0x37   */
                Long        Last;    /*  make it -1 for first call
*/
                Word        ObjTyp;  /*  Search for user type 1   */
                char        ObjNml;  /*  1  */
                char        ObjNme;  /*  *  */
            }  Scan4UsersCall;


typedef struct {
                Word        Native;
                Long        Id;
                Word        Objecttype;
                char        PropName[48];
                char        ObjectFlags;
                char        OjectSecurity;
                char        PropertiesExist;
            }  Scan4UsersRply;


typedef struct {
                Word        Native;
                char        Func;   /* 0x46 = get my bindery access
level */
            } ChkCall;


typedef struct {
                Word        Native;
                char        mask;
                Long        id;
            } ChkRply;
```

379

```
typedef struct {
                Word            Native;
                char            Func;    /* 0x36 for get object name  */
                Long            Unique;  /* Unique ID for the object  */
            } GetNameCall;


typedef struct {
                Word            Native;
                long            id;      /*  same id as above  */
                Word            objtyp;  /*  type of object    */
                char            name[48];
            } GetNameRply;


#define Ofs(fp)       ((unsigned)(fp))
#define Seg(fp)       ((unsigned)((unsigned long)(fp) >> 16))
#define Msdos         intr

  Registers           Regs;

  ConnectCall         ConCall;
  ConnectRply         ConRply;

  GetServerInfoCall   ServerCall;
  GetServerInfoRply   ServerRply;

  Scan4UsersCall      UsersCall;
  Scan4UsersRply      UsersRply;

  GetNameCall         nc;
  GetNameRply         nr;

  ChkCall             cc;
  ChkRply             cr;

  int                 a;
#define chr(n)          (n)

/*
 * this marks the end of the global variable definitions, what follows
 * are the procedures that define ADDUSER
 */

void          Will_it_Run(int argc)
```

```
{

/*
 * This routine will determine if the user is logged into the network
 * and if the user has supervisor status.
 */

    printf("%s\n",Title);    /* print title
*/

    if ((argc-1) < 1)
    {
     printf("Usage:  ADDUSER password\n        The password is the
admin password");
     printf(", see MHS manual, use an '*'\n        for no password.");
     exit(2);
    }



    Regs.F.AX = 0xE311;      /* DOS function 0xE3
*/

    cc.Native.wl = 0x00;     /* setup request (call) and reply buffer
sizes   */
    cc.Native.wh = 0x01;
    cr.Native.wl = 0x00;
    cr.Native.wh = 0xff;
    cc.Func      = 0x46;     /* Bindery Call 70, get my Bindery Access
Level   */
    cr.mask      = 0x00;     /* zero out access level and my id in the
reply   */
    cr.id.al     = 0x00;     /* buffer
*/
    cr.id.ah     = 0x00;
    cr.id.bl     = 0x00;
    cr.id.bh     = 0x00;

    Regs.F.ES = Seg(&cr);    /* setup up registers to point at reply and
*/
    Regs.F.DI = Ofs(&cr);    /* request buffers
*/

    Regs.F.DS = Seg(&cc);
    Regs.F.SI = Ofs(&cc);
```

381

```
    Msdos(33,&Regs);          /* call DOS
*/


  if ((cr.id.al == 00 &&
      cr.id.ah == 00 && cr.id.bl == 00 && cr.id.bh == 00))
     {
        /* if ID is still all NULLS, then the shell is not loaded */
        printf("This utility requires Advanced Netware to run.\n");
        exit(9);
     }

  Regs.F.AX    = 0xE300;
  nr.Native.wl = 0x00;       /* setting up the request and reply stuff
*/
  nr.Native.wh = 0xFF;

  nc.Native.wl = 0x00;
  nc.Native.wh = 0x05;

  Regs.F.ES = Seg(&nr);
  Regs.F.DI = Ofs(&nr);

  Regs.F.DS = Seg(&nc);
  Regs.F.SI = Ofs(&nc);

  nc.Func = 0x36;            /* Bindery Call 54, get my name
*/
  nc.Unique.ah = cr.id.ah;  /* Id from getting access level above
*/
  nc.Unique.al = cr.id.al;
  nc.Unique.bh = cr.id.bh;
  nc.Unique.bl = cr.id.bl;

  Msdos(33,&Regs);          /* call DOS
*/

   if (Regs.H.Al != 0)       /* if AL is not clear, not logged into
network    */
      {
      printf("This utility requires you to be logged into the network
to run.\n");
      exit(9);
    }
```

```
      if (cr.mask != 0x33)   /* if call to get our bindery access level
does   */
                             /* not indicate our access to be that of
the       */
                             /* SUPERVISOR, we cannot continue
*/
      {
       printf("I%cm sorry ",39);
       if (Regs.H.Al == 0)
         {
            printf("%s",nr.name);
         } else
         {
            printf("UNKNOWN");
         }
       printf(", you must have supervisor status to run this
utility.\n");
       exit(10);
       }

}
/*  End of Will_it_Run()  */



void         ServerInfo()
{

/*
 * This routine is used primarily to get the current server's name.
 */

    ServerRply.Native.wl = 0x00; /* setup reply buffer size
*/
    ServerRply.Native.wh = 0xFF;

    Regs.F.AX = 0xE300;            /* DOS function 0xE3
*/

    ServerCall.Native.wl = 0x00;
    ServerCall.Native.wh = 0x01; /* setup request (call) buffer size
*/
    ServerCall.Func      = 0x11; /* function 16, get server information
*/
```

```
    Regs.F.ES = Seg(&ServerRply); /* setup registers with segment and
offset */
    Regs.F.DI = Ofs(&ServerRply); /* address of reply and request
packets    */

    Regs.F.DS = Seg(&ServerCall);
    Regs.F.SI = Ofs(&ServerCall);

    Msdos(33,&Regs);                    /* call DOS
*/

    printf("Adding Users to Application Express on File Server ");

    if ((Regs.H.Al == 0x00))        /* was call to server successful?
*/
    {
      printf("%s\n",ServerRply.ServerName);
    } else
    {
      printf("Error Getting ServerName [%x]\n",Regs.H.Al);
    }

} /* End of ServerInfo() */


void          ScanUsers(char passWord[255])
{
/*
 * variables:
 * sub is the number of users added
 * subs is the number of users total
 * MHSuser is the first argument passed (has the user name, truncated
to
 *  8 characters if necessary)
 * MHSapp is the second argument passed, application name is EXPRESS
(not
 *  case sensitive, "express" works too for instance)
 *
 */

int           sub, subs, ok;
char          MHSuser[40],MHSapp[40],LoginName[48];

  sub=subs=Regs.H.Al = 0;       /* initialize variables
```

```
*/

    if (passWord[0] == 42)
      {
        passWord[0] = 32;  /* an "*" is used to indicate no password */
        passWord[1] = 0;
      }


  UsersCall.Last.ah = 0x1F;
  UsersCall.Last.al =           /* this sets the LONG variable Last to =
-1   */
  UsersCall.Last.bh =           /* done outside loop, this is where to
start   */
  UsersCall.Last.bl = 0xFF;     /* looking in the bindery, (-1)
*/

while (Regs.H.Al == 0)
{
  subs++;                       /* add one to total number of users
found       */

  UsersRply.Native.wl = 0x00;  /* setup the reply packet size
*/
  UsersRply.Native.wh = 0xFF;  /* won't be this big, but just in case
*/

  UsersCall.Native.wl = 0x00;
  UsersCall.Native.wh = 0x09;  /* setup the request (call) packet size
*/

  UsersCall.Func = 0x37;        /* Scan Bindery option
*/

  UsersCall.ObjTyp.wh = 0x00;  /* Object type to scan for, 1=user
objects     */
  UsersCall.ObjTyp.wl = 0x01;

  UsersCall.ObjNml = 0x01;      /* length of name to search for, the
name is   */
  UsersCall.ObjNme = 0x2a;      /* '*', wildcard that is
*/


  Regs.F.AX = 0xE300;           /* DOS function 0xE3
```

```
*/

  Regs.F.ES = Seg(&UsersRply); /* setup registers with segment and
offset    */
  Regs.F.DI = Ofs(&UsersRply); /* address of reply and request packets
*/

  Regs.F.DS = Seg(&UsersCall);
  Regs.F.SI = Ofs(&UsersCall);

  Msdos(33,&Regs);                /* call DOS, interrupt 0x21
*/

        if (Regs.H.Al == 0)    /* successful?
*/
          {
            printf("User [%s] being added...",UsersRply.PropName);

            strcpy(LoginName, UsersRply.PropName);

            UsersRply.PropName[8] = 0; /* Name CANNOT be longer than 8
*/
            /*
             * NOTE:
             *    the way the MHSuser program is used will be changed
             *    future releases of MHS, the syntax assembled here
             *    may have to change
             */
            strcpy (MHSuser, " -X01 -U");
            strcat (MHSuser, UsersRply.PropName);
            strcpy (MHSapp, " -A");
            strcat (MHSapp, "EXPRESS -S");
            strcat (MHSapp, passWord);
            strcat (MHSapp, " -O");
            strcat (MHSapp, LoginName);

            ok = spawnlp (P_WAIT, "mhsuser.exe", "mhsuser", MHSuser,
MHSapp,
                       NULL);
            printf("%c%c%c - status is ->",8,8,8);

            if (ok == 0x0000)    /* status from calling MHSUSER.EXE
*/
            {
              printf("added\n");
```

```
            sub++;                  /* add one to total number of users
added  */
         } else
         if (ok != 0xFFFF)
         {
           printf("Not added" );
           switch (ok)
           {
            case 2:

              printf(" (exists already)");

            break;
            case 3:

              printf("\7 (invalid name)");

            break;
            case 5:

              printf("\7 (invalid password)");

            break;
            case 6:

              printf("\7 (too many users)");

            break;
           }

           printf(" [%x].\n",ok);  /* print error code
*/
           /* as a note, the UNDERSCORE "_" can't be used in a
name, and */
         } else
         {
           printf("\n\7MHSUSER.EXE not found, make sure there is a
path");
           printf(" to it.");
           exit(1);
         }
      }
      else
      {
       if (Regs.H.Al == 0xFC) /* code FC indicates no such object,
```

```
or no */
            {                              /* more objects, like in this case
*/
             printf("DONE\n\7");
            } else
            {
             printf("Error occured will getting user, error
[%x]\n",Regs.H.Al);
            }
           }

    UsersCall.Last.ah = UsersRply.Id.ah;
    UsersCall.Last.al = UsersRply.Id.al; /* this sets the LONG variable
to   */
    UsersCall.Last.bh = UsersRply.Id.bh; /* (Last) to point at user
just    */
    UsersCall.Last.bl = UsersRply.Id.bl; /* found, so next one can be
found  */

}   /* end of while loop */

printf("%d users processed, %d users added (or refreshed).\n\7",subs-
1,sub);
printf("Use MHSUSER -X03 -AEXPRESS to view users known to application
EXPRESS");

} /*  End of ScanUsers()  */

main(argc,argv)
int argc;
char *argv[];
{

/*
 * main is the controlling procedure in ADDUSER
 */

   Will_it_Run(argc);
   ServerInfo();
   ScanUsers(argv[1]);

} /* end of main */
```

Determining Rights

An important issue influencing the installation of applications on a LAN is the assignment of rights. The following section provides background information and discusses differences in how rights are determined in NetWare 286 and NetWare 386.

NetWare 286 (and prior) Trustee Rights

Many options exist to control access to resources in the NetWare environment. The part of NetWare security used most often is trustee rights. A trustee assignment is created by giving certain rights to a user in a file server directory. It is through these trustee assignments that users are granted access to programs and data on the file server.

Various combinations of the basic NetWare/286 rights —Read, Write, Open, Create, Delete, Parental, Search, and Modify, shown as [RWOCDPSM]—provide a flexible means of defining the security of a LAN. It is very important for the LAN supervisor to have a thorough knowledge of how directory rights work and interact.

All of the rights are self explanatory except Parental. Having Parental rights to a directory gives a user the ability to create or delete subdirectories under the subject directory. It also allows a user to grant or revoke trustee assignments to that directory.

Assignment of rights can take two approaches. Taking the trustee approach, rights are granted to users at the user or group level using the SYSCON utility (or MAKEUSER). With the directory approach, trustees are assigned on a directory-by-directory basis, using the FILER utility.

Trustee rights consist of both rights assigned to individuals at the user level, and rights assigned to groups as a whole. For instance, Read, Open, and Search rights may be assigned at the group level for a certain directory. However, it may be appropriate to grant only one individual in the group Write privileges, which can be assigned at the user level. The only rights that need to be assigned at the user level are any rights granted in addition to the rights assigned at the group level.

Once a trustee assignment is granted, it includes all subdirectories beneath the subject directory. For instance, if the Read privilege is granted in the SYS:PUBLIC directory, that Read privilege is automatically granted in the SYS:PUBLIC\UTILS directory.

The trustee privileges are stored in a hidden system file called DIRSTAMP.SYS. This file is present on all volumes prior to NetWare/386. Users and groups are referenced in the DIRSTAMP.SYS file by a NetWare-assigned ID number. NetWare searches DIRSTAMP.SYS files sequentially up the hierarchical directory structure towards the root. Netware will try and match up the user name, group, and any group of an equivalent standing with the existing user ID.

If no applicable IDs are found, this indicates that the user has no trustee privileges in that particular directory. If the person trying to access the file doesn't have the correct user priveleges, this shows up at the point where the operation is attempted on a file and where the first DIRSTAMP.SYS file is inspected.

If only one of the user/group IDs is found in the search, the associated privileges found for that user/group ID are that user's trustee privileges in the target directory.

If two or more IDs are found, that is, if the user has been granted privileges in the immediate directory or one of its parents directories, and a group to which the user belongs has an applicable trustee assignment as well, then the user's trustee assignments are determined by the summation of all applicable trustee assignments. For instance, assume that:

1) USER1 is a member of the groups EVERYONE and ACCOUNTING.
2) All users are members of EVERYONE.
3) Group EVERYONE has Read, Open, and Search rights in SYS:APPS.
4) Group ACCOUNTING has Write, Create, and Delete rights in SYS:APPS\DATA.
5) USER1 has Parental and Modify rights in SYS:APPS\DATA\USER1.

In SYS:APPS, USER1's trustee rights are equivalent to those assigned to the group EVERYONE. No privileges are assigned to either USER1 or ACCOUNTING at SYS:APPS.

In SYS:APPS\DATA, USER1's trustee rights are calculated by combining the rights assigned to EVERYONE in SYS:APS and to ACCOUNTING in SYS:APPS\DATA. Figure E-1 illustrates this calculation.

```
Directory              Group              Rights
SYS:APPS               EVERYONE           [R O   S ]
SYS:APPS\DATA          ACCOUNTING         [ W CD   ]
_____
Trustee privileges                        [RWOCD S ]
```

Figure E-1. Calculation of trustee privileges (from two directories)

Inherited Rights and the Inherited Rights Mask are the NetWare/386 equivalent for the concept of cascading directory rights found in NetWare/286. Although the terminology is different, the manner in which rights are cascaded down directories really has not changed much from NetWare/286.

Just as in NetWare/286, when a directory is created in NetWare/386 it is given a default rights mask containing all rights. The actual rights allowed depend on the individual user's trustee assignments. The trustee privileges calculated above are still contingent on the rights mask in SYS:APPS\DATA. Effective rights are discussed below.

In SYS:APPS\DATA\USER1, USER1's trustee rights are the combination of rights granted to EVERYONE and ACCOUNTING in higher directories and rights explicitly assigned to USER1 in SYS:APPS\DATA\USER1. This calculation is shown in Figure E-2.

Directory	**Group**	**Rights**
SYS:APPS	EVERYONE	[R O S]
SYS:APPS\DATA	ACCOUNTING	[W CD]
SYS:APPS\DATA\USER1	USER1	[P M]
Trustee privileges		[RWOCDPSM]

Figure E-2. Calculation of trustee privileges (from three directories)

Although complex, the above example should clarify the process of determining trustee privileges. USER1 probably would have [RWOCDPSM] rights granted to SYS:APPS\DATA\USER1 by the supervisor to avoid dependence on rights "inherited" from higher directories by group membership.

Effective Rights

To determine a user's effective rights, both the directory's maximum rights mask and the user's trustee rights must be combined. For a particular right to be granted, both the directory's maximum rights mask and user's trustee rights must be included. In other words, the resulting right must be the product of a logical AND operation, as shown in Figure E-3.

Directory	**&**	**Trustee**	**=**	**Effective Rights**
[RWOCDPSM]	&	[RWOCDPSM]	=	[RWOCDPSM]
[RWOCD]	&	[RWOCDPSM]	=	[RWOCD]
[RWOCDPSM]	&	[RWOCD]	=	[RWOCD]
[RWOCD]	&	[PSM]	=	[ ]

Figure E-3. Determining effective rights

NetWare/386 Trustee Rights

Prior to NetWare/386, the only rights possible were those that regulated access to directories. Starting with NetWare/386, however, rights can also be assigned to files. In addition, directory right assignments have changed. Many of the new rights correspond to the rights supported under NetWare/286 and earlier versions. The new rights are Supervisory, Read, Write, Create, Erase, Modify, File Scan, and Access Control, with the following new rights "mask":

```
[SRWCEMFA]
```

Supervisory. This assignment grants all rights to the directory, its files, and subdirectories. The Supervisory right overrides any restrictions placed on subdirectories or files with an Inherited Rights Mask. Users who have this right in a directory can grant other users Supervisory rights to that directory, its files, and subdirectories. Once the Supervisory right has been granted, it can only be revoked from the directory to which it was granted. It cannot be revoked from a file or a subdirectory. If disk space restrictions have been assigned and more than one user is assigned to the subdirectories, the user with the Supervisory right to the directory can modify the restrictions in the subdirectories.

Read. This assignment grants the right to open files in a directory, to read their contents, or to execute them if they are programs.

Write. This assignment grants the right to open and write to (i.e., modify the contents of) files.

Create. This assignment grants the right to create files and subdirectories in the directory. If Create is the only right granted at the directory level and no rights are granted below the directory, this right creates a "deposit only" directory in which users can create a file and then open and write to it. Once the file is closed, however, they cannot see or modify it. Users can also copy files or subdirectories into a "deposit only" directory. When they copy, they assume ownership of the files and subdirectories. However, any trustee assignments assigned to the files or the subdirectories are revoked.

Erase. This assignment grants the right to delete a directory, its files, its subdirectories, and subdirectory files.

Modify. This assignment grants the right to change directory and file attributes. It also grants the right to rename the directory, its files, and subdirectories. This right does not grant the right to modify the contents of a file.

File Scan. This assignment grants the right to see subdirectories and files when viewing a directory.

Access Control. This grants the right to modify a directory or file's assignments and Inherited Rights Mask. Users who have this right can grant all rights (except Supervisory) to other users, including rights that they themselves have not been granted.

NetWare/286 and /386 Trustee Rights Compared

The new rights defined in NetWare/386 can be easily enough mapped to the old NetWare/286 rights. For instance, with NetWare/286, when users are first added as trustees of a directory, they are granted Read, Open, and Search rights. With NetWare/386, they are granted Read and File Scan rights. The main difference in this case is that, under NetWare/386, the Read and Write rights imply the privilege of opening a file. Figure E-4 further defines the relationship between directory rights in NetWare/286 and /386.

NetWare/286	NetWare/386
Read	Read
Write	Write
Open	Read, Write
Create	Create
Delete	Erase
Parental	Supervisory, Access Control
Search	File Scan
Modify	Modify

Figure E-4. Relationship of NetWare/286 and /386 directory rights

In a strict comparison of the new rights to the old, only the supervisory right adds a unique feature. As defined earlier, Supervisory grants a user all rights in a directory, its files, and subdirectories, just as if the user were a LAN supervisor.

Beginning with NetWare/386, trustees can be assigned to files. File rights control access to specific files in a directory. File rights are used to redefine the rights that users can inherit from directory rights. The following describes how these rights control access to specific files.

Supervisory. This assignment grants all rights to the file. Users who have this right can grant any right to another user and can modify all rights in the file's Inherited Rights Mask.

Read. This assignment grants the right to open and read the file.

Create. This assignment grants the right to salvage the file after it has been deleted.

Write. This assignment grants the right to open and write to the file.

Erase. This assignment grants the right to delete the file.

Modify. This assignment grants the right to change the file's attributes and rename the file but not the right to modify the contents of the file.

File Scan. This assignment grants the right to see the filename when viewing the directory. It also grants the right to see the directory structure from the file to the root of the directory.

Access. This assignment grants the right to modify the file's trustee assignments and Inherited Rights Mask. Users who have this right can grant all file rights, except Supervisory, to other users.

Other than the Supervisory right which allows full access to all subdirectories, the real difference in assignment shows up on rights allowed with files in subdirectories.

For example, if a user has NetWare/386 trustee assignments of:

```
SYS:1              [ RWCEMFA]
SYS:1/2            [ R     F ]
SYS:1/2/3          [ RWCEMFA]
```

In NetWare/286, the same assignments are:

```
SYS:1                [RWOCDPSM]
SYS:1/2              [R O    S ]
SYS:1/2/3            [RWOCDPSM]
```

The key difference between NetWare/386 and NetWare/286 directory is rights. If the user was given the NetWare/386 Supervisory right in SYS:1, then that user would have full non-revokable rights in SYS:1/2 and SYS:1/2/3 as well.

An important new feature of trustee directory and file assignments with NetWare/386 is the immediate update of rights for a user. This is very different from NetWare/286. When users' rights are revoked in a NetWare/286 directory while the user is logged in, he or she can still access the directory. Users don't learn that their rights have been revoked until the next time they log in. Under NetWare/386, rights are effective when they are changed. In the situation just described, that same user would immediately be unable to access that directory, even if that directory is the current directory. These rights updates are performed regardless of whether the trustee assignment is assigned directly to the user or to a group where the user is a member.

Another new feature in NetWare/386 is "unseen" root directories. In NetWare/286, the command

F:\>DIR SYS:

will list every root directory for that volume, whether or not the user has rights to them. When the same user tries this command on a NetWare/386 file server the user will only see the directories to which he or she has rights. Those rights may be in that root directory or they may be in a subdirectory beneath it. In any event, when a user has any directory right, the user is then able to see the root of that directory. It is important to note that this check is only done when DIR is executed from the root. Once a user is in a subdirectory under the root, he or she can see that subdirectory's entire tree structure.

Tips on Assigning Rights

If users are to share rights to a particular directory, trustee assignments should be granted through group membership. When the rights for a group are changed, only the group's trustee assignments need to be modified. Every five trustees assigned to a directory use one directory entry on the file server. Every file and directory on the network uses a directory entry. In a group membership, only one trustee "slot" is used, regardless of the number of members in the group. All members of the group will automatically have their rights adjusted upon the next login except for NetWare/386, where changes are immediate. Since a group can have several trustee assignments, assigning a member to a group can reduce setup time and simplifies trustee rights changes. It can also decrease the number of directory entries used by trustee assignments.

When there is a temporary need for a user to access another user's directory(ies), the security equivalent of the first user can be set to that of the other user. This approach is useful when someone needs to delegate responsibility for work to another person, (such as when a manager goes on vacation and has a secretary temporarily handle matters).

Every group to which a user belongs constitutes a security equivalence. Additionally, every time one user's standing is made equivalent to another counts as a security equivalence. When determining effective rights, only the first 32 security equivalences are used. This limitation could result in rights being granted or denied incorrectly because the number of the total security equivalences is exceeded. While this is a rare occurrence, it is an issue worth noting because of the confusion it could create.

There is a special twist to NetWare v2.15 rights. Due mainly to this version's ability to accept Macintoshes on the LAN, the Parental right has slightly changed. Because of this change, the Create rather than the Parental right is necessary to create subdirectories. This change makes version 2.15 different from any previous version of NetWare.

Tools

This chapter lists the tools I keep around when programming, and what I like and don't like about them.

Compilers
Turbo C

Turbo C is useful for quick prototype development as well as actual application development. I especially like its ability to immediately correct syntax and other errors. So, for most of my C code development I use Turbo C. Most of the code is portable to Microsoft C without alteration, and Turbo C code can be compiled with Microsoft C libraries. However, modifications are sometimes needed when dealing with the Watcom compiler. I have made VAPs with Turbo C, and linked the code with Microsoft libraries.

Microsoft C

The only reason I have Microsoft C is that some of my clients request I use it. To make sure my Turbo C code works with it, I compile theTurbo C code with Microsoft C. One nice thing is that the Microsoft compiler can make both DOS and OS/2 executables, including family mode executables where the same code runs in DOS or OS/2).

Watcom C

The Watcom 386 compiler is the only C code generator I know of for making NLMs. I made the IPX.C and SPX.C programs in Chapter 5 with it.

.One interesting thing the Watcom compiler does is give "nested comment" warnings. These warnings indicate when your code contains nested comments, for instance: /* some comment /**/. I use /* /**/ comments whenever I have inserted some temporary code into my application. For instance,

```
printf("\nWe made it to this Point, [D]"); /**/
```

Note that I have /**/ at the end of the line. When I want to comment that statement out all I need to do is prepend a /* to the printf:

```
/*printf("\nWe made it to this Point, [D]"); /**/
```

I also use pairs of #ifdef SomeUndefinedName, #endif's to comment out a block of code without worrying about putting /**/ everywhere. For instance:

```
#ifdef someUnusedName

/* code I don't want to compile, perhaps a series of printf's */

#endif
```

This makes it easy to comment out whole blocks of code.

Turbo Pascal

I have always enjoyed Turbo Pascal's ease of use and quick code generation. If it weren't for Turbo Pascal's inability to link to Novell's C Libraries, I would use it more extensively. However, so many of my clients want C code, I have stuck with C and Assembly (since it is simple to make Assembly code emulate C code).

THINK C

For the Macintosh, THINK C, from Symantec, is very useful. In fact, Novell's Macintosh libraries are generated with it.. Though Novell offers Mac libraries in Apple's MPW, I prefer the Symantec environment.. I find it easier to use and it can create device drivers, inits, and, user applications. One resource I have come across for the Symantec C and Pascal environments is the SPLAsh Resources group. They offer a journal called the THINKin' CaP that includes source code on disk! I recommend a subscription from them. Their phone number is (415) 527-0122

Assemblers
Microsoft's MASM

I have used MASM for years. The code generated is pretty good though the assembler might include NOP instructions where you do not want them. but those instructions can be circumvented. Also, MASM is capable of making family mode code, just like Microsoft C. The MASM code generated can easily be linked with the Novell C libraries.

OPTASM

OPTASM can be quicker than MASM when assembling code. I have not found this much of an advantage when using it, but I have no trouble recommending OPTASM.

PHARLAP

I was first introduced to PHARLAP's Assembler when I began creating NLMs for NetWare 386.. This NLM code assembler is easy to use.

Microsoft's DEBUG

My original assembler was Microsoft's DEBUG. I still use it for those quick test routines or patching a program. I also use it to search for specific code in application programs that I would like to understand.

Linkers
RTLINK

Able to support a lot of input .OBJs, I have found RTLINK able to put together code that other linkers could or would not. I have found RTLINK more useful than Microsoft LINK in many situations. In addition, the code created is tighter.

Microsoft's LINK

LINK comes with older versions of DOS, Microsoft C, and MASM. It is an okay linker and I use it often. It does the job. When using LINK, however, make sure you have the current version.

Watcom's WLINK (and Novell's NLMLINK)-

Both WLINK and NLMLINK are used for linking NLMs. Previously NLMLINK from Novell was only tool for linking NLMs. It can still be used but WLINK, which comes with the Watcom/386 complier and Novell NetWare/386 Programmer's Workbench, is now preferred.

Editors
Borland

The Turbo Pascal v4.0 editor is easy to use. When coding for Turbo C, I use the Turbo C editor, since it is built into the integrated environment. Early versions of these editors could not handle source files greater than 64K. However, I tend to stay away from source files larger than 64K because they take so long to save, and I save often. Also it is easier to "mentally" picture the code in four 64K files rather than a single 230K file.

Microsoft

I find this editor pretty hard to use. I try to stay away from it. It takes forever to load files.

Brief

I don't use Brief, but so many developers do that I thought I should mention it. Brief is easy to customize.

Make/Version Control Tools
PVCS

There are the MAKE systems included with just about every C compiler. There are two, in particular, that I like to use. The first is Polytron Version Control System (PVCS), which is a very nice MAKE/Version Control (VC) system. I have found its use on a LAN to be quite accommodating. I highly recommend PCVS, for those so inclined to use a MAKE/VC utility.

OPUS Make

Compatible with PVCS, OPUS Make is another clever MAKE system that I have found to be an extensible MAKE/VC system. I don't use MAKE systems all that much, but I can recommend OPUS Make to those inclined to use a MAKE/VC system.

Libraries (other than native compiler support) - Novell (DOS)

These libraries are not optimized for size, but they perform well. They are available for Turbo C, Microsoft C, and Watcom C and will link with most any C compiler's code. They do not support DOS Named Pipes or NetBIOS.

Novell (OS/2)

These libraries are implemented as a Dynamic Link Library (DLL). Not all the functions in the DOS libraries are available. However, the OS/2 libraries include support for DOS Named Pipes (remember DOS Named Pipes, currently, can only exist when an OS/2 machine creates the Named Pipes) and NetBIOS.

Novell (MAC)

This code implemented Linkable library is available for device drivers as well as applications. Not all functions are available. It works with THINK C and Apple's MPW. Operations under MonoFinder can sometimes be flaky, same code with MultiFinder works fine.

Novell (server, VAP)

These libraries are included with the NetWare C Library for DOS. I have found early versions to be quite buggy. However, v1.2 and later work somewhat better.

Novell (server, NLM)

These libraries are implemented as a DLL. Not only are they good, and dependable, but also they are the only libraries available for use by NLMs.

THE NETWARE PROGRAMMER'S GUIDE

Debuggers

When choosing debuggers, I look at their usefulness and lack of hardware appendages. I don't mind if a specific CPU is needed, but if the debugger needs a particular board, etc., I don't use it. Hardware level debuggers (as I refer to them) do have their place—I would not write a device driver without them. For user applications, however, they are usually overkill. I have found a few "software" debuggers that are really slick and useful for many programming environments. Those that come with compilers, such as Codeview, and Turbo Debugger, are nice, and have their uses (e.g., Codeview in the Windows/386 v3.0 world). For most of my debugging efforts though, I like the following:

SoftICE-386

From Nu-Mega Technologies, SoftICE-386 is a fantastic debugger It requires an 80386 or higher CPU, and at least 1MB of RAM is recommended though 2MB will be more useful.

This debugger has saved me lots of debug time and allowed me to figure out things that would be near impossible without using a hardware debugger. The only limitation is that you can't load any other software in extended memory while SoftICE-386 is in use.

SoftICE runs in the 80386's native mode up in extended memory. Because of this, it is not a true TSR, so DOS suffers no memory loss from SoftICE's use. Actually there is a wee little thing loaded in CONFIG.SYS, but it does not change the conditions of any programs or how they run. If my program crashed without SoftICE loaded, it crashed the same with SoftICE loaded. This is an important characteristic to look for when choosing a debugger. In-memory or TSR debuggers have a hard time helping since their presence in RAM changes the conditions of the test..

Another nice thing about SoftICE not being a TSR is that a DOS crash (or simply an application spinning in a loop) will not disable SoftICE's ability to pop up and help. Only if the keyboard interrupt changes does SoftICE have trouble popping up with the hot key. There are also triggers (i.e., breakpoints) that SoftICE can be set up with so it will trap on those prescribed conditions and pop up.

Bounds-Checker

Also from Nu-Mega Technologies, Bounds-Checker is an excellent DOS-mode tool for finding illegal memory pointers. It works with your code's map file to show you just where you bombed.

PCWatch

Originally from IBM, PCWatch (p/n 6276603) is now available from Personally Developed Software (800)426-7279. It cost $50.

Running as a TSR, PCWatch is able to watch almost any software interrupt call on your PC under DOS. But, because it runs as a TSR it can affect your application's execution environment. In other words, your program might crash without PCWatch, but, with it, might not crash, or might crash differently. That's life with a TSR debugger. However, if you wish to spy on other programs it is useful.

PCWatch understands EGA mode on monitors and, consequently, can accommodate 43 line mode when necessary. PCWatch can also direct its output directly to a printer rather than a screen, which is really nice.

Issues in 386 Architecture

Ring 0 and NetWare 386

There has been some controversy over Novell's choice to run at ring 0 (zero) memory protection, also known as Privilege Level 0 rather than ring 3 memory protection, which is more commonly used. This "ring" memory protection is provided by the CPU, and therfore, offers absolute protection. Basically, the concern is that applications will cause the file server to crash. Applications running in Ring 0 are able to access and, thus, alter all areas of memory, whereas applications running in ring 3 have specific bounds on the memory areas they can access.

Most of those who are concerned presume that NetWare 386 is the first version of NetWare designed to run all applications at ring 0. Rather, the first version to use ring 0 was NetWare 286 v2.1, first delivered in 1987.

So what does ring 0 protection actually provide? Honestly, not much. For instance, all DOS applications run at ring 0. And, it is extremely rare for DOS applications to violate the memory of other applications. DOS itself also runs at ring 0, as do device drivers and TSRs. Developing a NetWare 386 NLM is similar to creating a DOS application (without the ability to multithread the code). Thus, you must avoid coding an ill-behaved application—one that writes over areas of memory that do not belong to it.

Even if a NetWare application running at ring 0 were unruly, the worst that it could do is erase your network volumes. This worry can be minimized through consistent backup.

Preemption

Once server-based applications begin to show up en masse, another concern is that of CPU scheduling. OS/2 operates with the default that an application does not schedule itself and thus does not have control over when it will execute. This can create programming problems for the application developer. Since the developer has no control over when an application runs, it is impossible to make simple assumptions about the timeliness of execution, and current state of memory and its values. However, with OS/2's preemptive scheduling (meaning applications do not schedule themselves), all applications are guaranteed CPU time and thus an equal chance to execute.

With NetWare 386 and 286, scheduling is non-preemptive; Each application is free to run until completion.and an application may schedule its own preemption. That means a NetWare 386 server-based application can run for a relatively long time without giving up control of the CPU. On the other hand, a well-designed application might relinquish CPU control to allow execute-time for other applications, including the server operating system itself. By following a few fundamental rules, an NLM can be coded to allow for appropriate preemptive breaks without disturbing its own execution or delaying that of others.

In NetWare 386's non-preemptive OS, an NLM can run "until completion" without giving over the CPU to other applications. By using a few basic rules governing program execution, you can circumvent any undue performance penalty an NLM might introduce.

There are three main reasons why you would not want NLM dominance. First, users may see a marked decrease in system performance. Second, Novell may decide to code preemptive breaks in their library routines. Note that an NLM will not have much work to perform if it does not use these library routines. However, an NLM can "sit and wait," thus consuming CPU time without performing any library calls so the preemption routines will not be 100% effective. Third, Novell may opt to include routines that detect when an NLM controls the CPU for an extended amount of time. The network Supervisor would be notified of processes that consume a large amount of contiguous CPU and they would be removed from the system. For NetWare 386 v3.1, NuMega Technologies has produced PROFILE, an NLM that allows network supervisors to monitor third party NLMs and how much CPU time they consume.

Packets and Data Exchange

What is a Packet?

When data travels between machines on a network, it travels in units known as packets. Packet size depends on hardware, specifically the network interface card (NIC), and size varies according to topology—whether it is ARCnet, Ethernet or Token ring.

With NetWare, all NIC drivers must be able to send and receive at least 576 bytes. Novell chose 576 bytes as the packet size for routing across internetworks because it matches that of Xerox's Network Standard (XNS), which was also the model for Novell's Internetwork Packet eXchange (IPX) protocol. The Internetwork Datagram Protocol (IDP) of XNS expects a maximum packet length of 576 bytes.

However, a workstation node and file server node that have the same network address can "negotiate" on the packet size for data exchange. That way they can send and receive packets larger than 576 bytes. The maximum packet size used is dictated by the smallest maximum packet size that is acceptable to both the workstation and file server. This negotiation occurs when the workstation first connects to the file server. However, if the workstation does not initiate the negotiation, the file server will use the default size of 576 bytes. For instance, v1.1 of the OS/2 Requestor does not negotiate packet sizes with file servers, it just uses 576 bytes as its maximum send and receive size. However, v1.2 of the OS/2 Requestor does negotiate packet sizes with file servers, and is capable of sending and receiving more than 576-byte NetWare packets.

With NetWare v2.1x, you can monitor the number of packets each file server senses through statistics screens. The screens will count file server requests, packets routed to other networks and packets received for non-file server request, such as those to VAPs. However, this number may not reflect a number that approximates actual totals. NetWare counts packets as "received" when the packets have been handed off by the NIC driver. Packets that are actually "on the

409

network cable" may not be reflected by the FCONSOLE screens. This is because some NIC drivers ship packets in a virtual manner. When packets are shipped in a virtual format, there may be eight or more physical packets received for each packet counted by the FCONSOLE statistics.

For network topologies that are physically able to send and receive large packet sizes, the packets received statistic will likely be more accurate. However, for topologies like ARCnet where there is a maximum packet size of 504 bytes at the hardware level, the NIC driver must use multiple physical packet transfers to equal the movement of one "NetWare packet." FCONSOLE sees only a single packet, while the hardware sees several packets. The NIC driver creates this duality. It is the driver that splits the NetWare packet into usable chunks and, from there, sends multiple physical packets. The receiving NIC driver reassembles the pieces. Thus, in ARCnet topology, for example, NetWare "sees" a single 4KB packet, which is actually (to the hardware) 9 physical packets.

Note that many types of NetWare requests will fit into a 504 byte packet. With the mixture of NetWare packets, a different number of physical packets will be sent. For instance, a file copy will likely use the 4KB size—or nine physical packets to every one NetWare packet. A request to get the current file server time will fit into one physical packet.

When NetWare routes packets it mandates a maximum of 576 bytes per NetWare packet. There is no breakdown and reassembly of packets at the file server when it routes packets. The packet's origin, the workstation, must not form a packet larger than 576 bytes when it is determined that the packet will cross an internetwork boundary. Transmitting data across an internetwork is the responsibility of the NetWare shell, not the NIC driver. Thus a file server will not receive a 4KB packet to route to another network, it will always receive a 576-byte packet to be routed. Remember that the physical hardware may still send multiple physical packets to accommodate the 576-byte packets being routed.

The following program contains Typedefs and such for IPX and SPX communications. It shows how to use NetWare's Service Advertising Protocol, which contains information about a server that is used when negotiating packet exchange and establishing connections with workstations.

```
/*********************************************************************
 *
 * Program Name:  SAP_Module
 *
 * Filename:      comm.h
 *
 * Version:       1.0
 *
 * Comments:      Typedefs and such for IPX and SPX communications.
 *
 *********************************************************************/
struct IPXAddress
{
        unsigned char       Network[4];           /* high-low */
        unsigned char       Node[6];              /* high-low */
        unsigned int        Socket;               /* high-low */
};

typedef struct IPXPacketStructure
{
        unsigned int        PacketCheckSum;       /* high-low */
        unsigned int        PacketLength;         /* high-low */
        unsigned char       PacketTransportControl;
        unsigned char       PacketType;
        struct IPXAddress   Destination;
        struct IPXAddress   Source;
} IPXPacket;

typedef struct IPXdataStructure
{
        unsigned char                         data[100];
} IPXdata;

typedef struct SPXPacketStructure
{
        unsigned int        PacketCheckSum;            /* high-low */
        unsigned int          PacketLength;               /* high-
low */
        unsigned char       PacketTransportControl;
        unsigned char       PacketType;
        struct IPXAddress       Destination;
        struct IPXAddress       Source;
        unsigned char       ConnectionControl;
        unsigned char       DatastreamType;
        unsigned int        SourceConnectionID;        /* high-low */
```

```
        unsigned int            DestinationConnectionID;  /* high-low */
        unsigned int            SequenceNumber;           /* high-low */
        unsigned int            AcknowledgeNumber;        /* high-low */
        unsigned int            AllocationNumber;         /* high-low */
} SPXPacket;

struct ECBFragment
{
        char far                    *Address;
        unsigned int            Size;                     /* low-high */
};

typedef struct ECBStructure
{
        unsigned int            Link[2];
        char far                    *ESRAddress;          /* offset-
segment */
        unsigned char           InUseFlag;
        unsigned char           CompletionCode;
        unsigned int            ECBSocket;                /* high-low */
        unsigned char           IPXWorkspace[4];
        unsigned char           DriverWorkspace[12];
        unsigned char           ImmediateAddress[6];      /* high-low */
        unsigned int            FragmentCount;            /* low-high */
        struct ECBFragment      FragmentDescriptor[2];
} ECB;

typedef struct SAPDataStructure
{
        unsigned int            InfoType;
        unsigned int            ServerType;
        unsigned char           ServerName[48];
        struct IPXAddress           Address;
        unsigned int            IntermediateNetworks;
} SAPData;
```

Getting Your Program to Market

Once you've developed a program, the next step is selling it. A number of groups can help promote your work.

Novell has three programs that assist independent developers: the Independent Manufacturers Support Program, the Strategic Developer Group, and the Developer Relations Group.

The Independent Manufacturers Support Program based in Provo, Utah, is for makers of hardware. Novell offers hardware developers three levels of support within the program. Level 1 offers help in compatibility testing and leads to Novell Certification. Level 2 assists manufacturers in NIC and disk driver development to ensure compatibility. And in Level 3, Novell co-develops and licenses hardware with a manufacturer.

The Strategic Developer Group, operating out of Novell's Austin, Texas, office, is primarily for the "top 40" developers such as Oracle, Lotus, and Ashton-Tate. This program helps ensure that applications developed by large developers will be NetWare-compatible.

The Developer Relations Group, also based in Austin, assists qualified programmers in developing, marketing, and distributing NetWare-related software. The Developer Relations Group is responsible for the Professional Developers' Program, which offers participants privileges outlined below.

Reduced prices on NetWare. Currently, developers can purchase a one-year license for any version of NetWare for $500 as long as they agree to use Netware exclusively for the purposes of design, development, testing, and support. At the end of one year, Novell reviews the license and renews it if the developer still qualifies.

Access to developer tools through Novell. Most of these tools (such as the OS/2 API kit) are available through third parties as well, and no discounts are currently planned, so this is really a feature more than a privilege. Software development kits such as the OS/2 API kit and Macintosh API kit are readily available.

Marketing and sales support from Novell. Support can include joint marketing efforts at trade shows, inclusion of product information in Novell press kits, access to selected Novell mailing lists (names of resellers and other developers), and support from Novell's widespread field sales force.

A NetWire forum on CompuServe. This is designed exclusively for Developer Relations Group members.

A Newsletter for Members. The newsletter, *Bullets*, contains new product information, problem listings, and technical insights.

There's no fee to join the Professional Developers' Program. To qualify, Novell does require that developers take advantage of NetWare's extended services in their applications. Call Novell's Austin office at (800) RED WORD (733-9673) or (512) 346-8380 to get an information packet that includes an overview and application. The only real requirement is that developers have to take advantage of the extended services of NetWare to qualify for the program.

Third Party Developer Programs

Novell isn't the only source for assistance; other companies help independent developers get their products to market. Usually, these are setup as strategic relationships between a developer and a firm, and there is no standard method. Usually the company approaches the developer, who has a proven, sable product.

Protecting Your Property

Equally important as security at the user level is the security of your application investment. NetWare allows you to determine if anyone else is running your application; it also allows you to limit the number of people using it. The most common method for tracking usage involves semaphores. Semaphores are counters used internally by NetWare to control access to shared resources. Semaphores indirectly represent a named resource, in this case, your application. The count, or value, of a semaphore is used to coordinate access to the resource the semaphore represents. One drawback to semaphores is that they are difficult to examine outside of a program. It is possible, though, to use the FCONSOLE utility to do this.

In the case of application protection, you might have a hidden control file that contains a value representing the number of licenses that a user purchased. This value becomes the maximum count with which your semaphore is initialized. When your application starts, it checks the count of the move semaphore. Once the semaphore value reaches zero, your application denies access to the program. If the count has reached zero, you may wait for the count to increase so that the next user can access it, or notify the user and end the application.

You might also use this approach to prevent more than one user at a time from running your installation program. If your application is organized in modules, you might also want to create semaphores for each module. This way, you can determine the number of users who have access to each particular module, not just to your application as a whole.

The following is an example of two functions that use semaphores to grant access to a program and to subsequently free up a slot. For more information about securing your applications, see Chapter 2, 'The Bindery.'

```
/* AddUserToApplication

Description: This function opens the semaphore named in AppSemaphore.
If the semaphore is new, the initial count will be set to the value in
MaxUsers.  The function then checks the current count of the semaphore.
If the value of the count is zero, then the function returns False (0).
Otherwise, the count of the semaphore is decremented by one, and the
function returns True (1), indicating that the user is now taking up an
active slot in the program.  The AppSemHandle must be saved for use
later in incrementing this semaphore's count.

Parameters: char *AppSemaphore - Application's "access" semaphore name
  int  MaxUsers - Maximum simultaneous users (1 to 127)
  long *AppSemHandle - Returned handle to an open semaphore

Returns: 0 == Too many users, 1 == User is added to count

Note: DO NOT CALL THIS FUNCTION MORE THAN ONCE AFTER YOU HAVE RECEIVED
A RESULT OF 1. Due to an anomaly in the way that NetWare handles
semaphores, once a particular semaphore name is open, NetWare will
always return the same value for its handle on subsequent calls. To
understand why this is a problem, let's look at what could happen when
AddUserToApplication is called twice in a row. If the first call causes
```

the semaphore count to become zero, a subsequent call would fail when
it reaches the WaitOnSemaphore statement. Since failing here causes
CloseSemaphore to be executed, the semaphore handle is closed. Now when
the first caller uses the routine RemoveUserFromApplication, the
semaphore handle has been closed and an unexpected/unwarranted error
will occur.*/

```
int AddUserToApplication(char *MySemaphore, int MaxUsers, long
*AppSemHandle)
{
 int Result;    /* Function result */
 WORD OpenCount;   /* Number of processes that have the semaphore open*/

 /* Attempt to open semaphore, giving initial value of MaxUsers if new
 */
 Result = OpenSemaphore(AppSemaphore,MaxUsers,AppSemHandle,&OpenCount);
 if (Result == SUCCESSFUL) {   /* Semaphore opened */
  /* Now attempt to decrement the semaphore's count */
  Result = WaitOnSemaphore(*AppSemHandle,
    (WORD)0     /* Don't wait, return immediately */
  if (Result == SUCCESSFUL) {    /* Semaphore's value was > 0 */
   Result = 1;    /* User now "added" */
  } else {        /* Close semaphore, it is full */
   Result = CloseSemaphore(*AppSemHandle);
   Result = 0;
  }
 } else {        /* Other unexpected error occurred */
  Result = 0;
 }

 return(Result);
}

/* RemoveUserFromApplication
```

Description: This function increments the value associated with the
application's semaphore, effectively allowing another user to run this
application if the semaphore's value had reached 0.

Parameters: long AppSemHandle - Handle to the application's semaphore.

Returns: 0 == AppSemHandle closed, !0 == AppSemHandle not open.
*/

```
int RemoveUserFromApplication(long AppSemHandle)
```

```
{
  return(CloseSemaphore(AppSemHandle));
}
```

Copyright Considerations

Software is protected by national and international copyright laws. Article I, Section 8 of the Constitution gives Congress the power to "Promote the progress of science and the useful arts by securing for limited times to authors and inventors the exclusive right to their respective writings and discoveries."

A copyright protects the expression of an idea, such as a computer program. It is different from a patent, which protects things, such as hardware. Note that a copyright does not protect the original idea itself, but the specific expression of an idea.

The Copyright Act of 1976 revised the law governing ownership of creative works and divided it into three basic levels: rights by creation, rights by publication, and rights by registration.

Additional information is available from the Copyright Office. Write to:

Copyright Office
Library of Congress
Washington, DC 20559
(202) 479-0700

Index

About the Writer

John T. McCann is an independent systems developer and President of Integrity Software. He has developed software for Novell and other leading third-party applications and utilities vendors, including Brightwork Development. He has served as the Wizard system operator (SYSOP) for the popular Novell User's forum, NetWire, and is a frequent contributor to various technical magazines, including *LAN Magazine*, *LAN Technology*, *NetWare Technical Journal* and the *NetWare Advisor*. John has a M.S. degree in Computer Science from Texas A&M University, and resises in Austin, Texas.